THE SOCIAL SAFETY NET

Canada in Decline

The Social Safety Net

THE SOCIAL SAFETY NET

Nora Loreto

DUNDURN
PRESS

Publisher and acquiring editor: Meghan Macdonald
Cover designer: Karen Alexiou
Cover image: chair: Mr Doomits/shutterstock.com; background: kues1/Freepik.com

Library and Archives Canada Cataloguing in Publication

Title: The social safety net / Nora Loreto.
Names: Loreto, Nora, 1984- author.
Description: Series statement: Canada in decline ; book 1 | Includes bibliographical references and index.
Identifiers: Canadiana (print) 20240306082 | Canadiana (ebook) 20240306104 | ISBN 9781459753105 (softcover) | ISBN 9781459753129 (EPUB) | ISBN 9781459753112 (PDF)
Subjects: LCSH: Canada—Social policy. | LCSH: Canada—Social conditions—21st century. | LCSH: Neoliberalism—Canada.
Classification: LCC HN107 .L67 2024 | DDC 306.0971—dc23

We acknowledge the support of the Canada Council for the Arts and the Ontario Arts Council for our publishing program. We also acknowledge the financial support of the Government of Ontario, through the Ontario Book Publishing Tax Credit and Ontario Creates, and the Government of Canada.

Care has been taken to trace the ownership of copyright material used in this book. The author and the publisher welcome any information enabling them to rectify any references or credits in subsequent editions.

The publisher is not responsible for websites or their content unless they are owned by the publisher.

Printed and bound in Canada.

Dundurn Press
1382 Queen Street East
Toronto, Ontario, Canada M4L 1C9
dundurn.com, @dundurnpress

This book is dedicated to the people of Gaza, whom Canada, in its decline, has massively failed.

Contents

Introduction

St. Patrick's Day, Quebec City, 1985.

The St. Lawrence is still frozen over, though water breaks through in areas closer to the shore. The majestic river looks like winter, with big chunks of ice sticking out above its surface, calling for an ice canoe to be run across it by a team of intrepid *canotiers à glace*. We're lucky to still have this much ice cover by St. Patrick's Day today.

On top of the cliff that holds up la Haute-Ville, and on the same block as St. Patrick's High School and St. Patrick's Church, a grand chorus closes out a gala on the stage of Quebec City's largest theatre, the Grand Théâtre. They sing the classic American song "When Irish Eyes Are Smiling," in front of a wooden set of the interior of a house. Just before the curtain drops, four honoured guests slip away from their balcony, to appear onstage at the back of the set. They walk down the stairs of the theatre set to join the front row of the chorus. Performing their alliance, their collective colonial origins, Brian Mulroney and Ronald Reagan, flanked by their wives Mila and Nancy, sing along. Brian is given the pleasure of soloing the song's last line, which he warbles with confidence but little sense of tone: "Sure, they steal your heart away." The line is repeated and the quartet, alongside the rest of the performers, holds the last note. Green and white balloons fall from the rafters onto the crowd. Two Irishmen, descendants of a mass migration of people fleeing poverty, now find themselves at the top of the political world, singing in front of a fake country home. Their unified voices, singing a song of Irish diaspora pride that American politicians have belted out from Warsaw to China's Great Wall, are showing all of North America that the chill between Canada and the United States that marked the Pierre Trudeau era is a thing of the past.

This gala is the media highlight of what would be dubbed the "Shamrock Summit," and the summit marks a turning point in Canada's history. It isn't just that Canada's prime minister will enjoy a few years of warm relations with his American counterpart, or that both countries are now led by men of Irish descent. The summit lands in the middle of a decade of massive change. Behind it is a postwar period when a version of Canada in which settler Canadians took tremendous pride was built. Ahead of it are decades of undoing much of what was built in the previous forty years. Reagan has already laid out his plans to transform the United States, but Mulroney is still green; he was elected not even seven months earlier in a historic landslide, but the wheels of change have already been set in motion.

· · ·

The year 1985 is as close to the end of the Second World War as it is to the 2025 federal election. The forty years that came before 1985 and the forty years that have come after have been radically different. The social, economic, and political differences of these two eras created two separate Canadas: one that grew in the shadow of two world wars and economic depression, and another that has gradually unwound everything that was built from postwar prosperity.

I was born in 1984, in the middle of this eighty-year chunk. It was the year that Mulroney was elected and that Orwell imagined as the future in his famous novel, near the upper end of what would eventually be called the millennial generation. When I hear the sound of Brian Mulroney's voice, honestly, it soothes me, as if I'm sitting in earshot of the TV in a high chair hearing him speak during the midday news show (or watching the CBC show *Midday*). While I was raised in the shadow of the 1970s and 1980s, the only Canada I have ever known was deeply influenced by the man who brought neoliberalism to Canada. Our Margaret Thatcher, but Irish. Our Ronald Reagan, but Canadian.

The transition from the postwar welfare-state period to present-day Canada has been a decline. Under the cover of financial crises, Mulroney introduced neoliberalism to Canada through tax cuts, spending cuts, and free trade, and the slide has never stopped. Indeed, we could argue that it has actually accelerated. A decline is a continual loss of something, whether that be strength, power, numbers, quality, or as the *Canadian Oxford Dictionary* says, vigour. Deterioration. Regardless of where one sits on the political spectrum, the notion of decline shades the discussion of every issue. From housing (we used to have affordable housing and now we don't!) to education (education used to be higher quality, but now kids are being shortchanged!), from healthcare (we used to be able to rely on the public health system, but now we can't!) to whatever else (why doesn't anything work?), we talk about this moment as if we have accepted that Canada is in decline, regardless of whether or not we use that word.

But where did this decline come from? And does "decline" mask a darker truth: Was Canada ever great to begin with? Indeed, "decline" is not the perfect word to describe a settler-colonial state that has never achieved a state of justice or truth, especially about itself. But the postwar period did bring about prosperity that was used, for the first time, to create better lives for Canadians beyond the ruling class. However, the spoils of that prosperity were not shared equally, and, as the welfare state and its social safety net started to fall apart, Canada had two options. We could have expanded the net and shared even more of that prosperity, giving coverage to people who had been intentionally left out. Or, we could have snipped at the net itself, transforming not only what people could access from state services, but also what they believed they should receive from their state. This latter process was how neoliberalism came to Canada. In Chile, it came with bombs. In the U.K., it came with police violence against striking miners. In Canada, it arrived through smiling politicians singing Irish songs and through promises that actually, no, nothing would be made worse; we would all, in fact, live much better.

To understand our particular decline, we must go back to the start — right to Canada's early colonial origins — and proceed through to the evolution of the colonies into provinces united through our current federation. Many of the reasons why our decline looks the way it does can be explained by moments in our past, and not just moments from the mid-1980s. From Canada's early origins through the postwar period and the dawn of neoliberalism, the country's status quo — the character of any given moment in which Canadians find themselves — has been constantly evolving, improving especially for the elite. At the same time, it's been devolving for everyone else, especially over the past forty years.

Neoliberalism is an economic, political, and social theory that shifts power away from collectives of people and toward financial markets. It derives from liberalism, the classic notion of the free individual and laissez-faire economics that places faith in market forces to regulate themselves, and then remixes liberalism to place markets themselves at the centre of everything: our economy, our politics, and our society. Neoliberalism was a reaction to Keynesianism, the economic philosophy of John Maynard Keynes, which guided the creation of what Canadians called their welfare state. The twentieth-century French sociologist Pierre Bourdieu describes neoliberalism like this (emphasis his):

> The movement toward the neoliberal utopia of a pure and perfect market is made possible by the politics of financial deregulation. And it is achieved through the transformative and, it must be said, *destructive* action of all of the political measures ... that aim to *call into question any and all collective structures* that could serve as an obstacle to the logic of the pure market: the nation, whose space to manoeuvre continually decreases; work groups, for example through the individualization of salaries and of careers as a function of individual competences, with the consequent atomisation of workers; collectives for the defense of the rights of workers, unions, associations, cooperatives; even the family, which loses part of its control over consumption through the constitution of markets by age groups.[1]

Policies are implemented to consolidate this financial power as citizens are told directly and indirectly that the most important unit in society is a balance sheet, not a life. Under neoliberalism, anything that the elites believe stands in the way of the markets, and of their pursuit of profits, is seen as a threat that needs to be neutralized. From radical feminists to conservative church ladies, any group that organizes collective action is de facto an enemy of the neoliberal economic order. Every time a union insists that a company make work safer, or that workers should be paid more, or that corporations should pay for their workers' pensions, these groups — unions and workers — become enemies of this new economic order. And so, slowly, the economic order based on Keynes's theories has transformed from one that took collective care to one that specifically seeks to destroy our notion that community exists and that we need it.

Margaret Thatcher sought to break the miners' strike in 1984 because the union posed an existential threat to her project to convince the world that there is no such thing as society. In 1987, Thatcher said this in an interview:

> I think we have gone through a period when too many children and people have been given to understand "I have a problem, it is the Government's job to cope with it!" or "I have a problem, I will go and get a grant to cope with it!" "I am homeless, the Government must house me!" and so they are casting their problems on society and who is society? There is no such thing! There are individual men and women and there are families and no government can do anything except through people and people look to themselves first.[2]

For Thatcher, society isn't all of us together, collectively. By existing, society poses a threat, not just to government itself (even though, very technically, government is just the organized expression of any society), but also to the market. Community doesn't just make it harder for neoliberalism to operate; community poses an *existential threat to neoliberalism*. Society as democracy poses a threat, and voters must be neutralized. If democracy reins in capitalism by confronting and tempering market forces, the system must find ways to disenfranchise and confuse potential voters. When democracy is diluted from a collective force to an individual one, it ends up serving capitalism, because average people have been told that there is no such thing as society, and we don't have a community around us to confirm otherwise. There is no *us*, there is just *me*. And the useful thing about this formulation is that it is extremely difficult for *me* to take on the market or a political decision that I dislike or to stop a project that might destroy my community. Individual boycotts don't work. No single person has the power to take down a powerful corporation on their own. The only thing that has ever worked is people acting together.

To obliterate a notion as fundamental and all-encompassing as society requires a full-frontal attack on anything and everything that organizes people into groups. If you remove a person from all connections they have to others within their daily lives — whether in their neighbourhood, their workplace, their ethnic community or religious organization, their sports club or social club — you can start to convince them that they are not part of anything called society. That individual then loses critical social connections: deep friendships or acquaints, collective experiences, and common knowledge. And suddenly, the person becomes untethered from their own world. How are they able to fight against tax changes that will undercut spending to healthcare when they no longer have any networks to draw on?

Of course, it's impossible to fully isolate individuals from one another, but through things like debt, low wages, and increasing responsibilities (that members of the community might have helped with before), we each suddenly realize that maybe we are really alone in this world. Eventually, once we realize that anything that could get in the way of someone's pursuit of profit has been obliterated, we no longer have the tools to collectively fight back, or even conceive of ourselves as part of something that might be able to fight back, against a powerful force.

Neoliberalism didn't come to Canada overnight. In 1985 it would have been impossible to take away people's community supports and hope they didn't notice. It took years and years for the pieces to fit together. Sociologist William Carroll argues that neoliberalism doesn't destroy as much as it transforms. Indeed, Canadians probably would have noticed destruction. But transformation is much more difficult to pin down. Carroll writes, "Neoliberalism, then, does not involve a hollowing-out or by-passing of the state so much as a shift in the state's priorities and a reshaping of its modalities."[3] Concepts like deregulation, contracting out, downloading responsibilities from one government to the next, funding caps, wage freezes, free trade, globalization, privatization, tuition fee increases, and user fees are all part of the packet of neoliberal reforms that have become so normal, so mundane, and yet so vague that most Canadians tune them out. In the forty years since the Shamrock Summit, neoliberalism went from being a fringe idea cooked up by a bunch of right-wing businessmen and political thinkers in the shadow of the Second World War to become the dominant political theory underpinning Canada's economy, political system, and society.

The transformation of postwar society into market-centric neoliberalism isn't just the result of changes in public policy. Fiddling with public policy alone would not cause a shock strong enough to force people to assume neoliberal logic. The public policies were accompanied by a social paradigm shift that impacted people directly. Bourdieu explains it like this (emphasis his):

Without a doubt, the practical establishment of this world of struggle would not succeed so completely without the complicity of all of the *precarious arrangements* that produce insecurity and of the existence of a *reserve army of employees rendered docile by these social processes that make their situations precarious*, as well as by the permanent threat of unemployment.... The ultimate foundation of this entire economic order placed under the sign of freedom is in effect the *structural violence* of unemployment, of the insecurity of job tenure and the menace of layoff that it implies. The condition of the "harmonious" functioning of the individualist micro-economic model is a mass phenomenon, the existence of a reserve army of the unemployed.[4]

When people are targeted in their workplaces, their livelihoods become less stable. This then gives rise to worsening social conditions. Carroll writes, "As neoliberal policies take effect, social divisions and inequities tend to proliferate increasing the need for a well-armoured state."[5] People who are scrambling to make ends meet have less and less capacity to think about society as a whole. And so the state comes in to give us more "freedom." A strong state can then effectively surveil the population, whether that's poor and/or unemployed individuals, people fighting to unionize or to improve their working conditions through a union, or people engaging in anything else that the state deems to be terrorism or public disorder — anything that is a threat to neoliberalism.

The transformation of the population from members of communities to individualized, isolated individuals underpinned the neoliberal shift during the 1980s. Now neoliberalism is just about to hit middle age. The millennial generation grew up hearing about the myth of progress: that Canada is always progressing to become better; that our public services are always innovating and becoming stronger; that systemic oppressions are increasingly being identified and stamped out; and that the long arc of history in Canada bends toward justice. From our brutal colonial origins to a sophisticated society that promises no one will be left behind, the story of Canada is one of constant progress and improvement.

This is what generations of Canadians have grown up believing. As neoliberalism matures, this story sounds more like a fairy tale, impossible to believe in anymore. Our condition has declined, but our myths have yet to catch up with these changes, creating mass cognitive dissonance that leads us to question what in the hell happened.

Bourdieu was writing in 1998, but here's what his "reserve army of employees rendered docile by these social processes that make their situations precarious" looks like in Canada today: the portion of the workforce engaged in non-standard work grew from 28 percent to 34 percent between 1989 and 1994, and then stayed about at 34 percent until the 2000s.[6] "Non-standard work" is a catch-all phrase that includes everything from part-time work to gig and side employment. Between 1993 and 2016, part-time employment grew slightly across all age groups for men, and it grew significantly for women twenty to twenty-four years of age.[7] Disabled people, who already have less access to the job market than non-disabled people, are more likely to work in precarious employment.[8] These figures don't consider increasing precarity in full-time jobs, where managers have too much power, where bosses can install spyware on workers' computers to more easily build a case to fire them, and where salaries have not kept up with inflation.

Canadians are paying their living expenses by taking on massive amounts of debt. Household debt hit 184.5 percent of household disposable income in June 2023.[9] That means that for every dollar of disposable income a household has, it's borrowing $1.85. Together, Canadians collectively owe $2.32 trillion — a number higher than Canada's total gross domestic product (GDP).[10] If the labour market is a battlefield, the bosses have turned precarious work into a weapon of mass destruction, and our government's refusal to intervene in the market has turned Canadians into servants of their household debts.

These are the forces that have killed community and allowed neoliberalism free rein to transform Canada. These are the forces that have caused the decline. People's lives have become oriented to servicing their debts and paying for a standard of living they're told they should have, one that is impossible to attain with their current income. Debt frightens individuals away from taking financial risks. Debt chains workers to jobs they hate, jobs that are dangerous, or multiple jobs. Debt creates mental health and physical health crises. And for what? So that some individuals can get stinking rich while the vast majority loses sleep over the next interest rate hike?

We are considered walking financial objects, not human beings, whether we are paying through the nose for the luxury of internet and cellphone access, or we're paying through the gut because of high food prices, or we're paying to keep a roof over our heads by working our asses off. The social decline in Canada is brutal and isolating, felt even more by marginalized people. For the ones who profit off of this violence, the status quo of neoliberalism suits them very well.

Underpinning the decline is the condition of Canada's welfare state. The welfare state is the sum total of public services that help keeps society together, and it has been demonized, undermined, cut, hacked, and slashed. Services are labelled as frivolous handouts, users are attacked for being lazy, and public sector workers are called spoiled.

Everything about Canada's decline goes back to the moment when colonizers imposed a system that made an artificial distinction between commerce and society, dividing what we today call social services from the rest of our lives. Canada's social services grew out of traditions that were imported here by French and English colonizers. The foundations of our social safety net — our education, healthcare, and social services — are therefore rooted in colonial societies. In chapter 1, I outline how these colonial practices and attitudes led to the evolution of certain models of care and, importantly, demonstrate how these services were used to impose and entrench white supremacy in Canada. From the beginning of colonial history until the start of the First World War, these services were coordinated by private groups, benevolent societies, public boards of health, or, in the case of French Canada, the Catholic Church. That all changed during the war, when the federal government had to figure out what to do about the tens of thousands of returning soldiers. The end of that war started a new era of centrally coordinated social programs that would form the basis for Canada's welfare state.

In chapter 2, I explore how Canada built its welfare state following the First World War up to the end of the Second World War, when the first widespread report into the social services necessary to help people avoid poverty was published. The Marsh Report was popular among Canadians because of the progressive social reforms it proposed but was hated by politicians. Leonard Marsh's recommendations would not be adopted, but because radical left-wing politics were growing in popularity, politicians started to adopt new universal programs, fuelled by postwar prosperity and the desire to build Canada into a white Christian nation that could hold its own on the world stage. While politicians were still focused on strengthening the markets, they did agree that there needed to be basic supports for people who were unemployed or had families.

But the heyday of social program creation wouldn't last. As the 1970s turned into the 1980s, economic crises were used to weaken welfare-state reforms so as to be friendlier to capitalism, at the expense of helping people.

This is where Brian Mulroney enters the story. Chapter 3 explains how his tenure was marked by discussions surrounding free trade, getting rid of a manufacturers' sales tax, and replacing it with a lower, "simpler" tax called the goods and services tax (GST). His reforms reduced the amount of money that the provinces received from the federal government to pay for social services but also the amount of revenue his own government received through taxes. He popularized deficit reduction as a primary goal of government, even though he never achieved the balanced budget that he owed so much of his political career to. Mulroney left Ottawa's books in the red, giving cover for Paul Martin Jr. and Jean Chrétien to impose the biggest cuts to the Canadian state in the history of the country. Chapter 4 picks up here, examining how deep those cuts went and how their impact has echoed across decades in subsequent budgets for all levels of government.

In chapter 5, I look to the provinces and examine the interaction between the neoliberal federal government and neoliberal provincial governments. The provinces act in opposition to the federal government, either because they can gain political favour by so doing or because their decisions are constrained by decisions made in Ottawa. Yet the provinces adopt the same neoliberal rationale as does the federal government. While provincial governments cry poor and call for Ottawa to increase their funding, many still cut taxes, undercutting their own revenue base. Alberta and British Columbia were early adopters of neoliberal doctrine, but eventually even the Parti Québécois (PQ), Canada's most successful social democratic party, turned to Mulroney's deficit-reduction platform as a political priority. Canadians are being hit on all sides by neoliberal policy, and the decline that was set in motion in the 1980s and solidified in the 1990s is now undeniably reaching them in hundreds of different ways.

All of the transformations made in the 1980s and 1990s create the conditions for Canada's current social services crisis. In chapter 6, I summarize how neoliberal policies have impacted our personal finances, our community health, and our ability to push back against these forces. Market ideology, when imposed on public services, strains them beyond their limits. Management becomes more powerful, while staff burn out due to inhumane working conditions. Canadians rely more on the charitable and not-for-profit sector, which takes on the services that either were offered by the state in the past or are now needed thanks to new problems faced by individuals. I look specifically at healthcare, examining how politicians have played with it over the years and how delivery has changed under the pressure of funding cuts from all levels of government.

Finally, in chapter 7, I argue for a way forward. We can stop this decline, but we need to be organized and clear about what it will take to turn things around. Fundamentally, Canadians must fight to force our government to give up land and pay reparations to Indigenous Nations. Since many of our current difficulties flow from colonial structures imposed centuries ago, we cannot fix the most fundamental issues without first addressing the land and resources stolen by Canada. Land Back and reparations have to be the basis for moving forward, regardless of how we seek to disrupt the status quo. As the adage goes, until everyone is free, no one is free, and history shows that when policy excludes and marginalizes people, there are always negative repercussions for the majority.

There are before us two options: we can chase reforms, or we can chase radical change. Both have benefits and disadvantages, and while I favour one over the other, we need to understand the differences between the two. But most importantly, regardless of the kinds of changes we fight for, we need to change the way we talk about the social and financial structures that have been normalized by neoliberal politics. Changing what has been sold to us as "common sense," when it is anything but, is the first step to stopping this decline.

This is the first book in a series called Canada in Decline, and there is so much more to come. Discussions about corporate power and the failures of Canadian democracy will have their own volumes. By starting with the social safety net, I am starting with what impacts us all directly on a physical, emotional, and financial level: the daily failures of our system, the indignities of social programs left to fall into disrepair, the twenty-hour hospital shifts, the bodies and minds that break under the pressure of this system. By starting here, we see who is responsible for this state of decline and what we must do to turn things around, not only to restore some of the services that helped previous generations of Canadians to live better, but also to correct the failures of those past eras. While the welfare state was never meant to help everyone — indeed, it intentionally left out many Canadians — its transformation to serve the market first and foremost has made things worse for all of us.

Who could have known this is where we would be, thanks to events like the Shamrock Summit, held mere blocks from where I write these words? The joyful, carefree singing of "When Irish Eyes Are Smiling" in a city that still rushes out to celebrate St. Patrick's Day, despite the fact that only ten men in the entire city were born in Ireland[11] (and I know 20 percent of them personally), reminds us that telling people *a* truth can be far more powerful than telling people *the* truth. *A* truth would be that our friendship with the United States is mutually beneficial to both countries. *A* truth would be that Mulroney could not pay endless amounts of money on social programs. But *the* truth? *The* truth is much different. While we can wrap ourselves in truths that aren't actually borne out in our daily lives, the people in power know very well that *a* truth, regardless of how untrue it might be, can be a powerful political tool. They just need to find the right formula to turn *a* truth into *the* truth. And they have done it — they have convinced us that neoliberalism is our only way forward.

Back in 2004, culture critic Henry Giroux warned that neoliberalism in the United States was already producing deadly and scary consequences. Neoliberalism fostered the conditions to create and legitimize "the central tendencies of proto-fascism," wrote Giroux. Carroll explained that these conditions "range across the corporatization of civil society, the mobilization of a fearful nationalism, the rise of an Orwellian Newspeak that impairs the capacity of the American public to think critically, the broad militarization of culture and, tellingly, the reduction of the state to its repressive functions."[12] Carroll and Giroux were writing at the turn of the 21st century, more than two decades into the neoliberal experiment. Militarized police, increasing secrecy from within government, and ever greater use of force against poor communities all herald a rising fascism that has been easy for some to ignore. But some of us saw it long before the rise in violence against transgender people, before the trucker convoy took over downtown Ottawa, before the United We Roll campaign, before the pledge to create a barbaric cultural practices hotline — before any of these things reared their heads in the mainstream. And it is here that the need to stop this decline is so obvious, and so imperative.

During the Shamrock Summit, a journalist asked Ronald Reagan if he had had a chance to sample some "Canadian salmon." Mulroney jumped in to answer: "At lunch. Smoked salmon." He paused. "Small, small portions, because we have a serious financial problem to deal with," Mulroney added, his Irish eyes smiling. He held back a chuckle, then turned and shared it with Reagan.[13] The Pacific Salmon Treaty came into force that same day, so salmon was an obvious pick. (Though was it Pacific salmon or Atlantic salmon? Rhetorically, it didn't matter.) Mulroney, indulgent but not too indulgent, was broadcasting for the cameras make-believe thrift over a lunch that he didn't pay for, to an audience of Canadians who did pay for their lunches and would catch this clip on the evening news. Mulroney's lighthearted comment about the need for thrift would be echoed by politicians of all political stripes, at all levels of government, and in all regions of Canada, over and over. This false allyship, this "we're all in it together" approach, would become the dominant way in which politicians talk about public policy, finances, and markets: folksy, lighthearted, but serious, too. Mulroney's "serious financial problem" was the excuse to set in motion the beginning of the neoliberal transformation of Canadian politics and the country's economy and society. And it has proceeded slowly enough that, while some have noticed, most Canadians only feel the effects of a policy years after it's been introduced. Just like those of us who live along the St. Lawrence notice less and less ice covering the mighty river each year.

CHAPTER 1

From Before Confederation to 1945

I n my favourite series of children's books, Captain Underpants, author Dav Pilkey always tells a story within a story. Usually before chapter 3, the following line appears: "But before I can tell you that story, I have to tell you *this* story." Likewise, before I can tell you about Canada's decline, I have to back up — not just a few decades, but a few centuries — and anchor the discussion of Canada's welfare state and social safety net in our origins as a colonial nation. Colonialism and our social safety net have gone hand in hand since the very beginning of European presence in Canada. To say Canada is in decline requires us to believe that, at some point, Canada was great, and that it's getting worse. But that's not really our story. In the past, social programs were implemented to help a majority of people while causing tremendous harm to a minority, so yes, there is decline, but the story is more complicated than that.

Canada's social safety net grew alongside the colonial nation state during a period of nation building to create what we understand as Canada today. Everything from poverty-reduction measures to healthcare, from pensions to education, was built to bolster a white Christian nation that might someday be able to leave the basement bedroom of Mother England. Social services grew as a result of colonial expansion and the interests of a growing European community as it massacred the inhabitants of the land and stole their territory. Charity was not only key to the functioning colony but also the cover under which Canada was colonized. As Canada aspired to become its own country, services became the engine of population growth and health. Over time, they grew too important to be left to the ad hoc nature of health boards or local communities, and government took on more and more responsibilities, laying the foundation for the welfare state of the post–Second World War boom. The boom created social conditions that made socialism and socialist policies increasingly popular, and liberal politicians reacted by absorbing or co-opting these ideas into social policy. Thanks to this pressure, politicians created the first universal social programs, forming the foundation for what many Canadians recognize as our present-day social safety net.

Colonial Nation Building

As long as there has been a colonial presence in Canada, there have been health and social services that look familiar to what we have today. And yet, before colonial nations made landfall, Indigenous Nations that have lived on this land since time immemorial coordinated complex social systems that kept people healthy and secure (for example, providing access to good food and sophisticated food management to ensure that food was both diverse for dietary needs and plentiful). Nations throughout what is now British Columbia respected traditional laws that protected people from food-borne illness by promoting hygiene. Health, education, and social services were not distinct from the rest of everyday life. Through ceremony, spiritual practices and know-how, active lifestyles, and community care, such services were integrated into the lives of all people. There were no institutional schools that separated children from their communities for six hours every day. Children were raised by extended family members and learned from aunts, uncles, cousins, and other relations through doing, alongside siblings and cousins. The idea that social services should be separated from the daily life of a community is a European concept. How those services were delivered to the community — either through benevolent societies or dictated by one's obedience to god — depended on the colonizers: English or French.

Social services don't exist where there is no society. The goal to expand and sustain the colonies necessitated new services to care for the colonial settlers. The first significant nation-expanding project in New France began when 727 *filles du roi* were imported from France to populate this new white colony. These women produced thousands of offspring whose descendants today reach past twenty million, including 9 percent of Quebec's current population.[1]

While Indigenous Nations had embedded education, welfare, and social supports in the rhythm of daily life, colonization broke this relationship. Colonialists coordinated these services mainly through groups driven by faith. Colonial structures with colonial goals were developed to coordinate health and social services to make the territory habitable for white Europeans, funnel resources back to England or France, protect the motherland's stake in the ground, and promote the empire's interests. Colonial governance wasn't democratic, even as Enlightenment-inspired structures worked their way into society. Over just two hundred years, the holistic, integrated social systems that had operated for millennia on this land we call Canada were violently attacked and supplanted by colonial practices that ensure there will always be poor people.

Poverty was an outgrowth of these colonial practices, and there were important differences in how the French and the British managed poverty.[2] In Lower Canada, the responsibility was out-sourced entirely to the Catholic Church, which then provided services through their network of hospitals, schools, and other institutions. The first hospital, called Hôtel-Dieu, opened in 1638, and the Bureau des pauvres was created in 1685, both operating out of Quebec City. Rooted in French traditions, social welfare in New France was seen as an issue that required solidarity rather than as an individualized problem. Services were funded by individual and parish donations and by subsidies from the French Crown.[3]

Between 1763 and 1786, United Empire Loyalists who had fled the United States and settled in Nova Scotia and New Brunswick brought with them a version of England's Act for the Relief of the Poor 1601, which established that responsibility to care for poor citizens lay with the parish.[4] Because Quebec had been operating its own social service system for more than a century by then, even when Quebec fell to the British, the 1601 law didn't apply in Quebec the way it was applied in the Maritimes. This law evolved to become the Poor Law of 1843, which University of Toronto professor Stuart Jaffary characterized a century later as "one of the most hated pieces of legislation in British history."[5] The Poor Law mandated that government bodies collect funds to pay for institutions and to support the poor, but it was never applied to Upper Canada. There, during the mid-1800s, poor relief was shifted from the state to become the responsibility of individuals, families, or private philanthropy.

The relief wasn't substantial or fundamental; for example, the colonies would pay money only if there was a disaster that needed immediate relief, such as an epidemic or a fire. Municipalities contracted out caring for the poor, often to the lowest bidder, which created horrific conditions for poor residents of the colony. The poorest people were placed on an auction block, where they'd be bid on. The cost of their room, board, and other expenses would be set, and the winning bidder would purchase them and own their labour. From the *Saint John Daily Sun* in 1884: "Paupers will be let to the lowest approved bidder for a period of time on Wednesday the 31st December instant at the Railway Station at 2 o'clock P.M."[6] The auctions ended when it became clear that they were a more expensive way to deal with the poor than to simply house them in poorhouses.

In the Maritimes, local parishes and municipalities operated poor auctions and outsourced service coordination for the so-called deserving poor to welfare societies. The "undeserving poor" rarely got help.[7] In Halifax in the 1830s, more than half of the "inmates" living in poorhouses were children. Fishermen in St. John's found themselves "idle and destitute for seven months of twelve,"[8] which meant that the city had "a larger proportion of poor than in other British settlements." Social commentators, politicians, and benevolent societies alike insisted that any non-disabled person who could physically work must do so. Their aid should therefore be tied to a day's wages. Aid to the non-disabled poor was seen as a win-win; it stopped people from becoming beggars, and society gained a worker. However, the work was often concocted rather than integrated — people made up jobs for the poor to do, rather than having them fill an empty role. Projects pushed in local newspapers included clearing rocks from town squares in Saint John and building road works in Newfoundland. In 1842, in reference to the women who lived at the almshouse, the grand jury of Saint John argued that "even nursing mothers should be required when in health to earn their living."[9]

With the classification of people experiencing poverty as deserving or undeserving, poverty was moralized as either something the community had the responsibility to help address or solely the individual's responsibility to correct. This conception underpinned the promotion of white supremacy, as Black, Indigenous, and other marginalized people were more often than not forced into poverty.

It normalized who Canadians accepted as being poor, and, in most cases, laid the blame for their poverty at the feet of the poor themselves, allowing the broader systems that create poverty to remain invisible to many.

In Upper Canada, the local justice of the peace was responsible for the poor. He delegated his responsibility to voluntary poor-relief boards, which then funded programming for individuals who could not work, usually because of disability. The boards were independent, and they funded hospitals, orphanages, and workhouses. Poverty was seen as a moral failure rather than a systemic failure.[10] But, as people refused to morally unfail themselves out of poverty, the need to spend money on poverty outstripped others' perceptions of the poor, and gradually charitable organizations were funded by the state. Charities and agencies that were affiliated with religious organizations, ethnic groups, and special interests became vehicles to boost a person's social status.[11]

In Quebec, the church reached into every aspect of people's lives and tightened its grip on society even more by creating elite associations, social movements, and mass media outlets.[12] Guided by a collective approach espoused by the Catholic Church, Quebec had supports for both the so-called deserving and undeserving poor. The presence of the Catholic Church is a key reason why Quebec's modern welfare state, formed when most services previously overseen by the church were nationalized, remains more robust than in the rest of Canada.

In the rest of the country, benevolent and welfare societies didn't just provide some charitable relief for the poor; they were important tools for class formation. A group of Halifax-based "business and professional men" founded the Halifax Poor Man's Friend Society on February 17, 1820. Members would visit poor people to offer them assistance in the form of money, food, or employment. The society sought to "relieve the wants of the numerous poor, and destroy the system of public begging."[13] At the time of their first annual report, society members were all esquires and Right Honourables — men who came from society's upper crust. The society made an impassioned plea to those who could afford to give money, quoting Psalm 41: "Let him remember that the enjoyment of health and strength *to day*, is no security against the shafts of disease and sickness *to-morrow*; and while he is pondering upon this, let him recollect that the language of inspiration is 'Blessed is he that considereth the poor: the Lord will deliver him in the time of trouble. — The Lord will preserve him and keep him alive, and he shall be blessed upon the earth; and thou wilt not deliver him unto the will of his enemies.'"[14]

The Halifax Poor Man's Friend Society, and indeed many charities that gave money to the poor, had their critics: people who didn't believe that charity was an appropriate response to poverty. Services intended for the poor, especially the non-disabled poor, were seen as actually enhancing poverty among some segments of society. To that, the society rooted their arguments again in religion and insisted that there remained a need to help people:

> To an objection, however, frequently made against charitable institutions, that they have a tendency to encrease [*sic*] pauperism, your Committee would ... make the following reply. — "There is a line of distinction which both reason and religion point out. — When charitable aid encourages indolence, and diminishes or destroys responsibility to be industrious and frugal, its tendency is obviously pernicious; but where it only relieves the distresses of the inform and impotent who are unable to resort to labour, or provides the means of being industrious, to those who are

constitutionally able to support themselves by cor-
poral exertion, they cannot see that it offers any
incitement to idleness and vice."[15]

Aid and religion went hand in hand in all of the colonies that
would become Canada. In Toronto at the turn of the century,
Christmas Day was an especially significant time for groups like the
St. George's Society and the Irish Protestant Benevolent Society to
give to the poor. The latter group's charity was "confined exclusively
to the deserving and respectable poor, and the greatest pains [were]
taken to examine into the genuineness of each individual case."[16]
Benevolent societies were fractured along the lines of ethnicity and
religion. This made it difficult to coordinate relief work. Some activists fought hard to create aid systems that were non-partisan and
would help people regardless of their ethnicity or religion. Such
divisions mirrored divisions within society, especially related to the
fact that in Saint John, for example, Catholics far outnumbered
Protestants among people who were impoverished.[17]

Forcing people to work in order to receive much-needed aid created a pool of cheap labour. The Newfoundland legislative council
released a report in 1849 that suggested that the St. John's poor com-
missioner's office should also act as a labour bureau. Artisans and
labourers, the report reasoned, could be paid less than the ordinary
rate of wages. In Saint John, the editor of the *Morning News* suggested
that public works should be reserved for the period that seasonal
workers were out of work so that a pool of cheap labour was available
to take on low-paid work. Stone breaking and paving roads became
favoured relief jobs for several decades in Halifax, Saint John, and St.
John's. Cheap labour was also used to build public buildings, lay rail
for railway expansion, and build telecommunications infrastructure.[18]

The belief that a job is a path out of poverty has guided all government poverty-reduction reforms to help poor people, right up to the

recent Covid-19 benefit packages that gave money only to people who were working when lockdown was instituted. People didn't receive aid in 1840 simply because they were poor, just like they didn't receive aid in 2020 simply because they were poor. Those who received aid were eligible because they had demonstrated that they had worked for salary in the past year, and to keep that aid during the Covid-19 pandemic, they had to promise they were actively looking for work.

Charity and colonization run through English Canada and French Canada alike, and while each had different approaches and different goals for social services, they shared the same basic idea: help the colony above all else. Unlike today, the basis of both the English and French models was collectivism — though that collectivism had a limit. In English Canada, the collective existed to support a colonial project that maintained a strict wealth- and race-based hierarchy. In French Canada, the collective existed to support itself, to reinforce the ranks of the faithful who wouldn't be too bothered by English Canada's control.

These origins of Canada — from how the elites treated the poor to how service was provisioned along moral lines — are the foundations of our modern society. Both the origins of the welfare state and the ideology that drives neoliberalism can be found within. A welfare state is critical if a country aspires to create a cohesive society, building what Quebecers call *un projet de société*, where the state is funded by the people to create services that the people can use. But the individualized approach to poverty — the notion that it should be exploited for cheap labour and that poverty is the fault of someone who simply doesn't work enough — finds expression in neoliberalism as well. At the dawn of the 20th century, decades before the current political system was built in Canada, the societal project to turn the colonies into one white Christian nation was firing on all cylinders. And charity was at the heart of how the new country helped its citizens.

Creating a White Collective Identity

In the earliest days of colonization, the primary reason that so-cial services existed — in Quebec in particular — was to convert Indigenous people to Catholicism, and later, to push non-practising or lapsed Catholics back into the pews.[19] But the Catholic Church went well beyond the borders of Quebec in its colonial project to conquer Indigenous Peoples through proselytizing. In the late 1800s, Catholic institutions expanded west and religious orders es-tablished hospitals and schools. And because they were established during aggressive colonial expansion across Canada, as waves of immigrants arrived seeking free and available land, these religious organizations coordinated Canada's genocide.

Similar to the ways that neoliberalism sees collective action as a threat, to colonial Canada, Indigenous Peoples and Nations were seen as a threat, and thus their spiritual practices, languages, cultures, commerce, and economies needed to be eliminated. Secwépemc political leader Arthur Manuel pinpoints the fundamen-tal reason why Indigenous Peoples have been forced into widespread poverty: "The Canadian settlers stole our land under the British North America Act and, when they did this, they instantly became rich and we became poor. Indian reserves measure approximate-ly 0.2% of the country (in BC it is 0.36%), and that means that Canada has seized 99.8% of our territory. That is the reason we are so dependent on the government. They stole our wealth and left us without enough on which to survive on our own land."[20] By separ-ating Indigenous Peoples from the land, Canada not only tried to crush culture, language, economy, and health, but it also separated Indigenous Peoples from the possibility of participating in the colo-nial economy as equals to whites.

In 2021, I was walking around Wascana Lake, out front of Regina's legislative assembly, and I came across the statue *Called to Serve*, also known as the Sisters Legacy Statue. It features two nuns, one representing a teacher and the other representing a nurse. As noted on the Wascana Centre website, the bronze statue, designed by Jack Jensen, calls to mind "the courage and commitment of religious women across Saskatchewan who established needed health services and education to their local communities, laying the foundation for modern day education and healthcare delivery in Saskatchewan." Written on the statue are the names of sixty religious orders, honouring 5,500 sisters who worked across the province starting in 1860. Even though I hoped that this was a relic of many decades gone by, I could tell by the lettering on the plaque that the statue was new. It was installed in 2015 and has been vandalized several times, once right after 751 unmarked graves were found at the former site of the Marieval Indian Residential School at Cowessess First Nation. Marieval was operated first by the Sisters of Notre-Dame-des-Missions de Lyon and later by the Sisters of Saint-Joseph de Saint-Hyacinthe. French names, both for the orders and the sisters themselves, dominate stories of abuse at residential schools dotted across western Canada. Catherine Larochelle from *Histoire engagée* argues that residential school history in western Canada is both a story of Canadian genocide and a story of how Quebecers played unique and specific roles. Oftentimes, religious orders weren't entirely funded by the government or even by the church or the different orders. The money to pay for salaries, buildings, food, and clothing came directly from French Canadian parishes. The Catholic Church became the handmaiden of genocide, funded by white Catholic Quebecers operating alongside the seemingly benevolent world of mainstream health and education services.

As the bronzed religious sister who was a nurse tells passersby, healthcare was an important element in Canada's genocidal project. The federal government established Indian hospitals, segregated institutions that often worked closely with residential schools that ran experiments on children. In addition to the Catholic, Anglican, and

Methodist churches, new religious sects grew and used violence to force people into their religious folds, usually with the blessing of the federal government.[21] Two hospitals in particular, Fort Qu'Appelle Indian Hospital in Saskatchewan and Dynevor Indian Hospital in Manitoba, showed the government that Indian hospitals could be run at half the cost of mainstream hospitals. Cost cutting has never been benign.

Just as heath institutions facilitated genocide, so too did schools. Residential schools were conceived of at the same time that the foundation of Canada's mainstream public school system was being built. A key figure in the creation of both was Egerton Ryerson, who thought that education was as important and necessary to people "as air and water." He believed deeply in universal access to education; through education, the colony could reduce poverty and social problems. He was appointed chief superintendent of common schools in Canada West (Ontario) in 1844, at a time when there were about 2,500 elementary schools, and parents paid local property taxes as well as tuition fees. Eventually, Ryerson pushed for schools to be free, and three streams developed: primary, secondary, and collegiate.[22]

Ryerson was a social reformer. He wanted to improve the colony, not disrupt it, and he believed deeply in the need for racially segregated schools. In southern Ontario, Black families were encouraged to set up their own schools so their kids didn't need to go to white schools. Some courts denied Black children access to white schools. But the recommendation that led to the birth of residential schools was found in the Bagot Commission Report from 1844. It argued that the best way to destroy Indigenous culture and to anglicize Indigenous people was to separate children from their families and place them in boarding schools. Ryerson concurred, believing that religious mass education rooted in preparing students for work was fundamental to achieving this goal. His recommendations as superintendent played an important role in how schools were established during this period.[23] Schools operated in the service of a white Christian Canada. For white people, a religious education helped them become the ideal Canadians, ready to work if they were men, or ready to sew, clean, and push out babies if they weren't. For Black or Indigenous people, schools were a powerful location of social exclusion and genocide.

The impact of using social services for racist social construction continued well into the 20th century. As one report from the *Philanthropy Journal* explains, "It would be fair to say that the collective role of the voluntary sector in Canada's assimilation project not only included but extended well beyond residential schools to the 'Sixties Scoop,' and continues to this day in the provision of health, education, and social services."[24] At the start of the 1900s, movements that sought to extend suffrage to women, clean up urban centres, and develop public health and recreation services all flowed from racist and colonial rationales that sought to improve the colony for white people only, similar to the attitude that guided Ryerson. Operating alongside the nation-building projects of health, education, and social service development and delivery, and as governments either assumed responsibility of them for the first time or took on more responsibility for certain programs, these tools of genocide became more complex. Modern Canada stands on the shoulders of this; everything, right down to the embedded racial hierarchy that still rules in this country, can be traced back to these decisions. It is important to understand the racism and genocide embedded in the social services that Canadians have come to identify with and cherish, with all the warts, injustices, and problems that come with them.

A Modern Social Services Sector Takes Form

At about the same time as early anti-poverty measures like poor auctions and poorhouses were operating, colonial governments set up the first institutions that would lay the foundation for modern social services, like boards of health. During the 1830s, cholera spread quickly in the colonies, killing 10 percent of the population of Quebec City and nearly 15 percent of the population of Montreal in just three months. Nova Scotia, New Brunswick, and Newfoundland established boards of health and tried to control epidemics by creating public health legislation for quarantines. In Upper Canada, public health legislation was less a priority, but local boards of health were still created to respond to the threat of an epidemic. In western Canada, this role was taken up by the Hudson's Bay Company because they were already managing people and territories, infectious diseases included. In the late 1800s, Montreal had the highest mortality rate of any city in British North America. During the smallpox epidemic of 1885, Ontario's relatively new board of health actually extended its service to Montreal, as the province of Quebec had nothing similar. Ontario's board of health managed Montreal's public health campaign against smallpox, and by 1887 Quebec had established its own provincial board of health.[25]

As the population grew and Canada matured, demands on health and social services increased and became more complex. Governments, sometimes begrudgingly, started to provide some of these services. But where white settlers could rely on colonial governments to create boards of public health to manage a cholera outbreak, the same systems were being used to clear western Canada of the peoples who had lived there forever and to force assimilation of the ones who survived the combined catastrophes of violence, forced removal, forced starvation, and disease. Starvation coordinated by the federal government led to unimaginable death rates among Indigenous people. For example, from 1881 to 1886, the mortality rate from tuberculosis alone rose from 40 deaths per 1,000 to 127 deaths per 1,000, significantly higher than among adjacent settler communities. In fact, historian James Daschuk argues that the further away an Indigenous community was from federal government assistance, the healthier its members were. Proximity to government assistance was a deciding factor in the level of health of a given community.[26]

The early 1900s were an important time of expansion for Canada, not only for its social services, but also for the Confederation itself. At the turn of the century, Canada was composed of the four founding provinces, plus Manitoba (which joined in 1870), British Columbia (1871), and PEI (1873). The Northwest Territories were transferred to Canada in 1870, and Yukon became a territory in 1898. When Saskatchewan became a province in 1905 — the same year as Alberta — it enacted the most advanced piece of public health legislation in the country up to that point. In using an act of government to create public health legislation, Saskatchewan was ahead of other provinces, where public health boards were less able to handle comprehensive responses to pressures like epidemics, unclean water, or lack of sanitation. For health, and especially public health, the state played various roles of coordination, sometimes funding agencies, boards, or departments to operate. The legislation passed in Saskatchewan, on the other hand, uploaded this responsibility to the provincial government, which had the administrative structures in place to handle these pressures more systematically.

But from the first systems of social aid established in colonies in eastern Canada up until the First World War, Canadian governments mostly stayed out of the provision of other social services.[27] The federal government did, however, see industrial expansion as an opportunity for Canada to create its own industries. And that meant Crown corporations. The Ontario government established

Ontario Hydro in 1906. The federal Liberals created the Canadian National Railway in 1919. Once these large systems had been created to provide services for citizens, it became more and more apparent that similarly large systems could be created for health and social services.

As with public health legislation, the first laws related to universal social programs were passed by the provinces. In 1914, Ontario passed the Workmen's Compensation Act, Canada's first social insurance law that made financial contributions by employers compulsory. In Manitoba in 1916, the first mothers' allowance was instituted. At the federal level, conscription triggered major reforms in social services. The First World War ballooned the federal government's budget from $185 million just before the war to a peak of $740 million during. Government debt exploded, reaching $1.2 billion (equivalent to approximately $24.6 billion in 2023 dollars, according to the Bank of Canada's inflation calculator). Income tax did not exist yet, and before the war 85 percent of federal government revenues had come from "customs duties, postal rates, and tariffs on imported goods." The explosion in spending necessitated new revenue streams. With pressure coming from unions, religious organizations, farmers, and other groups demanding that the wealthy pay their share for Canada's war effort, the political moment was ripe for Canada to introduce taxes on businesses' profits (in 1916) and personal income (in 1917).[28]

At the same time, left-wing forces were regrouping, trying to figure out how to use their growing power to resist wartime policies that would harm working people. The Trades and Labour Congress debated whether or not they should call a general strike in 1917 to oppose conscription, by then already law. Instead, members decided to form a labour party and fight for their vision of Canada through elections. The Canadian Labour Party ran candidates in dozens of ridings, mostly in Ontario and Winnipeg. In western

Canada, care was taken to not challenge Socialist Party candidates in some ridings, and in others, rather than run under the Labour banner, Labour candidates ran as independents. While the best results for the Labour candidates were in Hamilton and Temiskaming, reaching 30 and 40 percent of the vote, in the twenty-seven other ridings where a Labour candidate ran, they didn't poll higher than 20 percent. However, conscription had a big impact on left-wing organizing, and labour and agriculture radicals continued to organize for working people to receive more of the profits that had been made off the war industries.[29]

With conscription, tens of thousands of Canadians had a loved one fighting abroad, so there was little question of the political popularity of equipping soldiers. Income tax became the key fundraiser, taking money directly from Canadians to fund the war effort. As a spoonful of honey to help the medicine go down, the government passed the War Charities Act at the same time it created income tax, which allowed people to reduce their taxable income by donating as much money as they wanted to war charities that the government had specifically identified, like the YMCA or the Red Cross. Once the war was over and the wartime legislation had been repealed, the government maintained a 10 percent tax deduction for donations to the charitable sector. But the definition of what constituted a charitable organization remained narrow until 1930, when the federal government amended the Income War Tax Act to allow tax deductions for donations to any charitable organization as defined by British common law.[30] The First World War didn't just create a need for Canada's federal government to start collecting taxes. It entrenched in law the financial demands of government and offset those against the ideology of charitable giving, but only for government-directed reasons.

The balance of political forces also shifted during the First World War. In 1917, voting rights were extended to all servicemen and all women who had a direct connection to a serviceman: mothers, sisters, wives, and widows. At the same time, the government disenfranchised about fifty thousand Canadian residents, all of them immigrants from nations that Canada considered enemies. Foreign (enemy)-language publications were outlawed, too. The government also took aim directly at working-age men who were not employed. In 1918, it passed the "anti-loafing" law, which outlawed any adult male from not being regularly employed. The penalty was $100 (approximately $1,670 in 2023 dollars) or six months in jail if they didn't pay the fine. The law was used to punish union leaders and organizers.[31] Repression, under the guise of the war effort, shaped how Canadians pushed for changes and against government policy, which was extremely difficult while the government was wholly focused on the war.

But once the war was over, there was a spike in radical organizing. The return of tens of thousands of veterans, many of whom had been disabled during the war, triggered movements that demanded the creation of programs to care for them. Soldiers had been promised that their jobs would be waiting for them, but when they got home, many found that their jobs were gone. Unemployment was high, and Canada — like the rest of the Western world — was in the grips of an influenza epidemic. In Winnipeg in particular, some veterans were unimpressed to discover immigrants from central and eastern Europe working in jobs they thought should be theirs. There, in early 1919, what began as a riot against businesses either owned or staffed by immigrants ultimately developed into the Winnipeg General Strike, and veterans found themselves on both sides — both fighting against immigrants and fighting alongside them for expanded services. Returning soldiers needed help from government to integrate back into the new peacetime economy, and earlier social programs were wholly inadequate.

The year 1919 was a time of important change, and soldiers mobilized alongside labour leaders to try to get more support from government. Their first attempt — a $2,000 (about $33,000 in 2023 terms) subsidy for years of lost wages when they were at war — was rejected by the government, but a new era had arrived. People expected more from government than they had in the past.[32] On September 1, 1920, the Returned Soldiers' Insurance Act came into force. It gave up to $5,000 to each veteran or widow of a veteran and, if a veteran could demonstrate that they were injured in the line of duty — proof that required a doctor's exam and evaluation from the Board of Pension Commissioners — they could receive a pension that was tied to how much their injury affected their ability to work. It was a century after the era of the Halifax Poor Man's Friend Society, and still government support to stave off poverty was closely tied to one's ability to work. The board was not to take into account compassionate reasons such as the accomplishments of an individual soldier or the details of their particular sacrifice; all decisions were based purely on how physically disabled someone was and the prognosis for future work.[33] Soldiers who suffered psychological effects or internal injuries caused by poison gas, for example, had a much harder time convincing the board that they deserved a pension.

Veterans' groups, farmers, and workers had been experimenting for years with different ways to organize themselves and fight for more access to services and resources. The rise of socialism and the shock of the First World War demonstrated the need for collective organizing like never before in Canada. This resulted in a period of impressive growth of labour unions and, subsequently, radical action. Trade union membership grew from about 50,000 in 1900 to more than 175,000 in 1913. Membership then dipped to 166,000 in 1914 and down to 143,000 at the end of 1915, partly due to union members enlisting. But the number of workers on strike rose steadily, too: from 50,000 workers taking strike action in 1917 up to 148,915 workers by 1919, bolstered by returning servicemen.

Membership in unions grew to nearly 380,000 in 1919 — more than a sevenfold increase over 1900's 50,000.[34] This increase in unionization and worker organization created the coherence among the population necessary to demand more from their governments and their bosses.

One year after he was elected member of Parliament (MP), William Lyon Mackenzie King was appointed to be Canada's first-ever labour minister. He had cut his teeth in industrial relations early in his life and therefore had experience with the relationship between work and poverty. But he also felt threatened by rising worker radicalism. He strongly believed that the only way to maintain peace between labour and capital and their competing interests was to create a firm system of corporate control that oversaw industrial relations in a fair and humane manner. It wasn't too far away ideologically from the perspective that pushed Otto von Bismarck to create Germany's first public pension system in 1889. In the late 1880s, Bismarck's oppressive tactics against the socialists (banning the socialist party, cracking down on striking workers with violence) weren't working, so he co-opted their ideas, including creating universal health insurance, paid for by employers and employees and managed by the state. It was the first program of its kind in the world and expanded to include accident insurance in 1884, disability in 1889, and unemployment in 1927, the same year that Canada got its first pension plan.[35]

Mackenzie King had promised to create a system of public pensions during the 1919 election, when he was opposition leader, but it was actually made law thanks to two members of the Labour Party — James S. Woodsworth and Abraham Heaps — who gave Mackenzie King a majority government in 1925. In exchange for their support, they insisted that Mackenzie King implement an old age pension plan, which happened two years later.[36] The first general public pension legislation offered $240 per year (just over $4,000 in 2023 dollars) to all British subjects — by default excluding all Indigenous people, as well as anyone whose heritage was not tied to the British Isles — who were seventy or over and who had lived in Canada for more than twenty years.

Personal donations had been key to funding government services during the war, and revenue generation had been especially successful with wildly popular war bonds. But this extra money dried up in the 1930s as many people became unemployed and destitute during the Great Depression. There were not enough public agencies to help people who needed help, and there was no way that charities could fund the needs triggered by the Depression. Lots of Canadians couldn't afford mortgage payments and ended up living in their cars or in tent cities (sound familiar?). People sought help from municipal agencies but, as most of the municipalities' money came from property taxes and that income was now extremely limited, the provinces were forced to step in. The provinces were overextended, too, so they turned to the federal government. Growing unrest, especially among radical socialist and communist groups, pushed the federal government to create the first national welfare program in 1935: the Employment and Social Insurance Act.[37] The act set a national minimum wage and federal labour standards, mandated unemployment insurance, and called for many other welfare reforms. With the government having already experimented with a national universal pension program following the First World War, it was a logical next step to create an employment insurance program. However, as the 1935 act infringed too much on provincial responsibilities as defined by the British North America Act, it was doomed; it was declared unconstitutional and never put into force.

It took until 1940 to develop an act that could pass, and Canada's first unemployment system took effect on January 27, 1942. Enrollment in the program was mandatory for most industries, except for professionals such as doctors, government services, seasonal workers, and anyone who made more than $2,000 per year. In its first year, the system covered about 42 percent of Canada's workforce. The government paid to administer the program and contributed 20 percent of the combined employer and employee contributions. To be eligible, workers had to demonstrate that they were available and able to work. They had to have left their previous job for just cause and paid into the system for 180 days over a two-year period. Anyone involved in a labour dispute was ineligible for the program. Governments made minor changes to benefits and eligibility requirements between the 1940s and 1970 but, for the most part, the program remained unchanged until 1971, when near universal coverage was implemented and new features were added like maternity, sickness, and retirement benefits.[38]

Nation building had produced the first elements that would form Canada's social safety net. To build a prosperous Canada, independent from Britain, it was necessary to replace colonial structures that invested all authority in colonial representatives with federal and provincial ones. Colonization ensured that the white settler population grew too large for ad hoc services to be sufficient, and thanks to the prosperity that came with the wartime economies in the early 20th century, Canada could afford to create these new systems and had the sophistication to coordinate them. But nation building wasn't devoid of political priorities. There was always a tug-of-war between the Liberals and the Conservatives, whose slightly different vision of Canada was still very restrained. Just as it was necessary for Labour MPs to help Mackenzie King create old age pensions, the pressure of left-wing parties played a key role in expanding the welfare state and showing Canadians an option that put people over corporate profits.

The End of the Two-Party Era

As Canada matured beyond its British and French colonial roots, this era also saw a maturing of Canada's left. Bolshevism in Europe, radical organizing related to the First World War, and the success of left-wing politicians gaining office all impacted left-wing participation in politics. A coalescence of left-wing forces sought to create a political alternative through a national party. The Co-operative Commonwealth Federation (CCF) was founded in 1932, just seven years after Labour representatives led by Woodsworth and Heaps forced Mackenzie King's government to create old age pensions. The CCF and other socialists at the time saw the markets emerging as critical forces in Canadian society and were worried that, if markets were left unregulated, the kind of strife that marked the Great Depression would become normal.

Underpinning the political program and vision of Canada espoused by the CCF was a document called the Regina Manifesto, released in 1933. The manifesto starts like this: "We aim to replace the present capitalist system, with its inherent injustice and inhumanity, by a social order from which the domination and exploitation of one class by another will be eliminated, in which economic planning will supersede unregulated private enterprise and competition, and in which genuine democratic self-government, based upon economic equality will be possible." It continues, "Power has become more and more concentrated into the hands of a small irresponsible minority of financiers and industrialists and to their predatory interests the majority are habitually sacrificed. When private profit is the main stimulus to economic effort, our society oscillates between periods of feverish prosperity in which the main benefits go to speculators and profiteers, and of catastrophic depression, in which the common man's normal state of insecurity and hardship is accentuated."[39]

The manifesto was inspired by socialism. It called for workers to own the means of production, for changes to the tax system to weed out income inequality, for the economy to be centrally coordinated by the government, for the creation "of a commission of psychiatrists, psychologists, socially minded jurists and social workers" to deal with crime and punishment "in order to humanize the law," and for the abolishment of the Senate because it had "developed into a bulwark of capitalist interests." The manifesto was a radical document that galvanized Canadian politics and changed the course of social discourse for years to come. Ten years after it was issued, halfway into the Second World War, the CCF's popularity surged in Canada, making all other parties nervous and convincing them to adopt their own policies to undercut the popularity of this socialist political movement.[40]

Canadian politicians weren't benevolent, hoping to build societies of full employment and with measures that would protect everyone from market fluctuations. And as the leader of the Liberal Party from 1919 to 1948, including almost twenty-two years that he spent as prime minister, few politicians left as important a mark on Canada's social safety net as Mackenzie King. During the period from the end of the First World War until almost the midcentury, Mackenzie King led Canada through industrialization and maturity as the colony grew into a nation more independent from Britain. He was a corporatist who preferred an industrial relations model, in which owners, management, labour, and the community co-operated on labour standards. "Co-operating" is a bit of a stretch, since he also believed that managers had the superior intellect and workers were inferior, so this four-way "co-operation" was never balanced. Mackenzie King also had no use for independent unions; his own history managing industrial relations demonstrated his preference for dealing with industrial councils, also known as company unions, rather than autonomous labour bodies.[41] He never really trusted workers to self-organize, and he advocated for unions to be externally controlled, like company unions, which radically reduced the unions' capacity to agitate. He and others warned that adopting John Maynard Keynes's ideas too quickly, or expanding the state too much, would lead to economic disaster, socialism, or both. Professor Alvin Finkel, in his book *Social Policy and Practice in Canada: A History*, writes, "Having experienced the anguish and militancy of Canadian workers during the Depression, the cautious prime minister reasoned that a postwar return to Depression conditions could precipitate chaos and perhaps revolution. However, as a cautious man, King remained reluctant to commit his government to expensive social programs for which he would then have to impose taxes."[42] In building modern Canada, Liberals and Conservatives alike were pulled by the popularity of radical politics, but they also pushed against socialist ideas and activists. They picked off their most popular policy proposals and softened them to such an extent that no corporation would suffer from their reforms.

From the Depression and into the Second World War, discussions about how to manage the economy and create services to support a growing workforce were fuelled by the economic theories of John Maynard Keynes. Keynes's theories deeply influenced how politicians in Western countries understood the process of nation building and offered a roadmap to protect people from the ravages of capitalism that so many experienced during the Great Depression. Keynesian economic policies assumed that market failures would happen unless government intervened to limit negative consequences for citizens. Understanding that the free market on its own could cause tremendous harm to individuals, Keynesian economic policies sought to balance market forces with democratic power and decisions. In 1930, Keynes wrote an essay called "Economic Possibilities for Our Grandchildren," which imagined that, one day, the need to work could be eliminated, thanks to scientific advances and better organization of the economy. He wrote, "I would predict that the standard of life in progressive countries one hundred years hence will be between four and eight times as high as it is to-day. There would be nothing surprising in this even in the light of our present knowledge. It would not be foolish to contemplate the possibility of a far greater progress still." Keynes, writing in the shadow of the biggest economic crash in history, believed that governments could create social supports that could reduce suffering and the reliance on work for all people, by 2030. Rapid mechanization and growing industrialization could conceivably create a world where people were free from the bonds of working and from poverty. The only problem, Keynes mused, was that a leisure-related malaise might become endemic because there would no longer be anything to do: "Three-hour shifts or a fifteen-hour week may put off the problem for a great while," he suggested. Notably absent from this ideal is class struggle. Social advances and setbacks are linked to classes of people struggling against each other for more access to labour or resources or money. Also missing is the fact that people are the producers of profits. Machines on their own cannot create wealth. The 1929 market crash exposed how vulnerable average people were to market shocks, and Keynes argued that economies and governments had the tools they needed to better regulate these shocks and insulate people from them; they just needed to use them. But Keynes was no socialist. Where his ideas were dominant among Liberals and Conservatives, socialist agitation pushed politicians to think beyond market regulation and toward full democratic control of the markets.

Inspired by Keynes, and with the threat posed by the CCF, the Liberals and Conservatives had a political roadmap to build a Canada that was fairer and more just. This was happening during another world war, in which more than 1 million Canadians (from a population of 11.5 million) signed up to fight in Europe. But it was a difficult time for radical politics. Mackenzie King invoked the War Measures Act and made it illegal for anyone to criticize the war. Censorship was made legal and citizens could be detained without charge. In 1940, Mackenzie King called an election and won a sizable majority government. Japanese, Jews, Italians, and other "enemies of the state" were interned all over Canada while Mackenzie King steered Canada through the war. Mackenzie King was careful to avoid mandating conscription, knowing how deeply it had scarred English-French relations during the First World War, but in 1944, when it was clear that his power was at a stake, he agreed to it, and thirteen thousand people were forced into the military. Farmers and organized labour opposed conscription.

When soldiers returned to Canada, and after Mackenzie King won re-election again in 1945, his government created the Veterans Charter, which gave benefits to veterans, and introduced the baby bonus; both programs provided money to a significant portion of the population. The postwar baby boom and economic prosperity were both just about to start significantly changing Canada. A new middle class was emerging, and it became the idealized notion of what Canada is: a notion that became part myth, part reality for some Canadians, and an era against which our current moment is constantly being compared.

· · ·

The economic boom that followed the Second World War created the foundation for modern Canada — the nation and the idea — that would endure far beyond the many social programs. Canada, the nation, would understand itself as a peacekeeping, peaceful haven, unlike countries that experienced endless war or strife. Canadians were lucky simply by birthright, and politicians of all stripes expanded limited protections to individuals based on identity, like the first piece of rights-based legislation, the

Canadian Bill of Rights, passed by Conservative John Diefenbaker in 1960. The idea of Canada was entwined with the vision of a white Christian heteropatriarchy where women were called Mrs. Husband's Name, services for the poor centred around religious or community organizations, and WASP-iness (characteristics and priorities of the white Anglo-Saxon Protestant communities) would sometimes clash with French Canada, which was growing ever smaller beyond the borders of Quebec itself.

However, Canada at this time was miles away from understanding itself as a nation built on genocide. Indeed, residential schools continued to run at full capacity, organized by religious societies at first, but then transferred to the federal government in 1969. The genocide was, for most Canadians, out of sight, out of mind, even though Indigenous communities and parents made Herculean efforts to bring attention to the horrors and abuses within these institutions — efforts that ranged from legal challenges to lobbying, from protests to hiding children away from Indian agents to protect them from being taken to residential schools.

This era — one where an estimated 150,000 Inuit, First Nations, and Métis children were forced to attend residential schools, and an estimated 30,000 children were stolen from their parents and placed for adoption in white families in Canada and all over the world — was also the era where the crown jewel of Canadian identity, our welfare state, was born.

We don't often hear about how white supremacy cohabitated with welfare-state expansions. Unemployment insurance legislation came into force in July 1941, three months after the same government mandated that all individuals with Japanese heritage living in Canada had to register with the government, which set the stage for twenty-one thousand people to have their homes and possessions seized and for many of them to be pressured into being deported. That year, as Canada was actively colonizing the Arctic, Inuit were given numbers instead of names, which they were expected to wear, embossed on a disk and attached to a necklace.

By the middle of the 20th century, white supremacy was the standard framework within which social services — veterans' pensions, universal pensions, and employment insurance — benefitted white Christian Canadians while rejecting all other peoples in the country. Its strong sense of self was based on white collective identity, an identity that would be exposed for its prejudice and violence decades later, as marginalized communities became better positioned to assert their rights, call for inquiries into the violence perpetrated against them, and demand restitution for past wrongs. The welfare state had grown to protect and care for Canada's white majority. As it was stretched beyond this demographic, it started to tear, and rather than putting in the resources necessary to expand state services to all, governments started to cut it back completely.

From the earliest days of white settlement in Canada, social services have been hived off from the day-to-day lives of average people. Individualistic notions of charity and deservingness and the puritan notion that the best medicine for poverty is hard work have never left Canadian consciousness. And as these services became the primary vehicle to force violent settler expansion westward, Canada's health and social services infrastructure grew more sophisticated at the same time it was reinforcing structures that coordinated genocide. To say that this reality has warped how Canadians understand and experience their modern social services is an understatement.

Mackenzie King's government, and many thereafter, implemented some recognizably Keynesian social reforms under pressure from the increasingly radical ideas of Canadian socialists. But Canada was only a few decades away from the creation of universal health insurance, borne out of a historic showdown between one province, one premier, and doctors in an attempt to create a universal public healthcare system. Behind all the political jousting were average people; the system was working well enough for some and destroying the lives of others. Both groups would achieve some modest improvements in social services in the economic boom that followed the Second World War.

CHAPTER 2

Postwar Boom to 1970s Bust

As the 20th century hit its midpoint, a new world had emerged, completely changed by rapid modernization and global events. We got a taste of what this was like during Covid-19. In an instant, our lives changed. One day, as my partner was submerging a bag of brown sugar in a grocery bath he had drawn to wash Covid-19 from the packaging (before we knew anything about the virus, and before he knew the bag had a hole in it), I sat a few feet away, listening to the radio and thinking that at least I had this radio to tell me what to do. Unlike my great-grandfather's first wife, who was killed by the Spanish flu.

But Covid-19 was just one event. Canadians lived through several colossal events in the first half of the 20th century, and each had important impacts on politics and Canadian identity. Writing in 1943 in the *Canadian Journal of Economics and Political Science*, Stuart Jaffary argued that "the distress of these dark decades had driven home the necessity for decent social insurances and assistance services." That, plus the war effort that England, Canada, and the United States had been engaged in meant that governments had to consider what to do with an economy that had been completely restructured to prioritize wartime needs but would inevitably have to change again for what would come once war was over.

By the start of the Second World War, Canada was engaged in its first sweeping debate on social services. What kind of services should Canadians expect of their government? What level of poverty was unacceptable? How responsible was Canada for the well-being of its citizens? These were not simply questions about providing social services. They were wrapped up in the project of nation building and rights of citizenship. The Second World War showed Canada that it could take a place beside the great nations of the world, and many Canadians were asking "Well, what kind of nation should we be? What kind of services should be considered a right of citizenship or residence?"

These questions guided the Marsh Report, the first comprehensive review of social services and the standard of living. The Marsh Report showed Canadians that it was possible to design government programs, funded through collective revenue like taxes, to reduce misery and suffering. If Canada had a Donald Trump and his slogan were "Make Canada Great Again," it would have been this period where it fit best, with politicians implementing new nation-building programs that underpinned the boom of the postwar period, and with mostly white fathers making enough money for mostly white mothers to stay home and support capitalism through billions of dollars in unpaid domestic work. As marginalized people left out of this arrangement started to fight for more access, and as governments pulled back their support for these social programs, the welfare state started to unwind, kicking off the decline that Canadians experience today in all corners of their lives.

From Keynesianism to the Marsh Report

As reluctant as Prime Minister Mackenzie King and his acolytes were to create social programs, popular pressure was mobilizing, drawing on people's personal experiences in paying for the necessities of life. Debt related to healthcare, while still very much part of daily life in Canada at the time, soon became the target of activists who wanted a fairer society. In her 2008 book *Payback*, written as part of the Massey Lectures series, Margaret Atwood wrote about how her mother could not leave the hospital with Margaret's newborn brother before the hospital bill was paid: "My mother was still in the hospital, because my father hadn't received his monthly paycheque and thus couldn't pay the bill and bail her out, hospitals at that time [1937, in Montreal] having a lot in common with debtors' prisons. My father was finally able to spring my mother, but paying the hospital bill — ninety-nine dollars, as I found from looking in my mother's account book — used up all of the paycheque." Hospital debt would slowly be seen as backward and wrong, even immoral. In countries where Keynesian reforms were adopted and where there were higher union density rates and strong social democratic political parties, more people had access to medical insurance than ever before.[1]

In 1942, about 2.6 million workers in Canada were covered by unemployment insurance, but another one million workers were not. In 1943, the government rushed to create a study into social security, overseen by a recently appointed government researcher named Leonard Marsh. Marsh had been a student of William Beveridge, the author of a similar report in England that inspired Canada to move quickly to write its own. Marsh was active in the League for Social Reconstruction, a group that developed a kind of Canadian socialism that was reformist and constitutionalist. He was concerned with class segmentation and how it was creating inequality. In 1940, before the Beveridge Report came out, Marsh had written an analysis of class in Canada, saying, "Many Canadians are reluctant to admit that their country has a class structure.... But this does not dismiss the other evidence of the class division of the population which exists in terms of inequalities of wealth, opportunity, and social recognition. These barriers are not the horizontal ones of geographic regions or distinctive ethnic cultures but the vertical ones of a socio-economic hierarchy."[2] Class was not as deeply entrenched in Canada as it was in the United Kingdom, but there was undeniably a class structure. Poverty was still a fundamental feature of the system, and colonial patronage and wealthy capitalists still formed the upper class. Little has changed to this day. Canada's class structure is uniquely Canadian, forged on our own pauper auction blocks, in paid access to higher education, in patronage appointments, and in enforced segregation to protect whiteness.

Over two months in 1943, Marsh and a handful of staff prepared a document about how social programs could end extreme poverty across the country. Indeed, rather than leaving poverty reduction to benevolent or other private societies, Marsh argued that eliminating poverty should be the job of the state. Writing in 2004 for *Policy Options*, Antonia Maioni wrote, "Marsh believed that governments should be responsible for constructing a postwar social order in which the responsibility of physical security would give way to an essential role in the provision of social security."

Writing the same year the Marsh Report came out, academic Stuart Jaffary noted that the report tried to establish what a minimum standard of living should look like in Canada: "For two centuries, our thinking has been dominated by the misconception of laissez-faire economics that the family income of the wage-earner should be limited to wages," Jaffary wrote. "For two centuries wages have been the source of inadequate family incomes for a large part of our wage-earners; vast human distress and misery have resulted."[3] Marsh had tried to establish what we would today call a living wage. He itemized how much money people living in Toronto in 1939 had to spend to survive:

- $25 per month to rent a house with five rooms (that's about $514.47 in 2023 dollars — sorry, folks);
- $0.75 per week for transit;
- $3.57 for insurance, medical and dental costs, and savings; and
- $1.39 for recreation (alcohol, tobacco, and vacations excluded).

He determined that a reasonable monthly wage for a couple was $69.29 and for a family of five was $122.85 (approximately $2,343.14 in 2023 dollars) and that half of urban families and three-quarters of rural families were earning less than what he considered the absolute minimum to live decently. Marsh also recommended that income supplements should work together: a family might draw from an income supplement to get to the level that Marsh clocked to be the desirable minimum, but a universal children's allowance and maybe also unemployment insurance could also help if the family was eligible. All these would be paid for through tax revenue and coordinated by the federal government.[4]

One of the biggest problems Marsh identified in his report was housing. "Canada, of all industrial nations, has paid least attention to public housing and still lacks any national housing policy. Subsidized public housing is a post-war imperative," he argued. And Marsh decried the lack of natural resource development: "The protection and utilization of soil, water, and forests requires both active imagination and large expenditures." Marsh proposed universal medical insurance (including sick and maternity benefits), universal funeral benefits, and the extension of disability pensions to anyone who might be working (at the time, they were limited to survivors of industrial accidents or war). Marsh concluded: "It has yet to be proved that any democracy which underwrites the social minimum for its citizens is any the weaker or less wealthy for doing so."[5]

The Marsh Report received mixed responses. Politicians were embarrassed by it. Businessmen were outraged by it. Media spent a great deal of time writing about it, and it triggered an uptick in popular support for left-wing politics.[6] Many Canadians loved it, and thought it was ready-made legislation that simply needed to be tabled in the House of Commons. The government didn't commit to implementing any of Marsh's recommendations.

Marsh estimated that the cost for all of these programs would come to about $900 million (approximately $17 billion in 2023 dollars). The Tories' response to his report was written by feminist and social welfare campaigner Charlotte Whitton, who argued that Marsh's reforms would be "debilitating to the national moral fibre,"[7] demonstrating yet again how intrinsically moral value and the economics of living were intertwined. There were already hostile articles written about what Beveridge recommended when Marsh developed his report. In response to the Marsh Report, a comment in the magazine *Canadian Forum* asked whether or not parts of the social security recommendations contained therein were "the price that Liberalism [may be] willing to pay in order to avoid socialism."[8] The CCF was supportive of Marsh's proposals — unsurprising, since in addition to being a social reformer, Marsh played an important role in the leadership of the CCF.[9] It called for the proposals to be implemented but also noted that, without restructuring the economy, the Marsh Report reforms wouldn't get at the root problems that drive poverty.[10]

The Marsh Report was the first time that the Canadian welfare state was articulated so broadly. This federal report laid out the possibilities for achieving the values of the welfare state: social security, full employment, and minimum standards like a minimum wage. Even though it was never acted upon, it was very influential. After it was released and Canada had transitioned back to a peacetime economy, the next era saw the creation and expansion of social programs that formed the bedrock of Canada's social safety net before it started to collapse under the weight of neoliberalism.[11]

History professor Michael Horn argues that the Marsh Report was simply too radical for the times and too incompatible with capitalism to have been adopted wholesale. A.E. Grauer, economics professor and author of other social security papers for the federal government around the same time as the Marsh Report, dismissed most of Marsh's suggested reforms. Grauer didn't think Marsh had identified the right answers; instead, he said, groups of experts in every field should come together to hash out the best way forward, a typical bureaucratic response. Again the old refrain came up: universal insurance programs could encourage sloth. Universal child allowances wouldn't be as effective as whatever teachers, child psychologists, and administrators might be able to create. Nursery schools that took care of children's health and nutrition could do a much better job than simply handing money to parents, Grauer argued.[12] White Christian morality was never far away from the criticisms of Marsh's report.

The same year that the Marsh Report was released, another important report proposed the future of public health insurance. Called the Heagerty Report, it was presented by Ian Mackenzie, minister of pensions and national health, and chaired by J.J. Heagerty, director of public health services in the Department of Pensions and National Health. Where Marsh had only a few months to produce his report, Heagerty and Mackenzie had a year to produce theirs and then another two years to circulate it among various groups to drum up support for their proposals. Heagerty met with representatives from the Canadian Medical Association and labour, farmers', and women's groups. He proposed that Canadians pay twenty-six dollars per year for basic coverage as part of a massively expanded, better integrated, nationally coordinated insurance plan that would cover everything: specialists, nursing, hospitalization, and prescription drugs.

The Heagerty Report forced a discussion about federal versus provincial funding. While Marsh recommended that the federal government be responsible for all of his suggested program, Heagerty recommended much more provincial involvement in managing healthcare. Marsh imagined there would be complementary provincial and federal legislation to oversee a healthcare system, whereas Heagerty recommended that the responsibility be left with the provinces, with direct federal funding for medical care and for public health. But to avoid the lengthy process of a constitutional amendment, the federal funding should establish national standards, and provincial legislation would be drawn up to help the provinces create their side of the program. Heagerty wanted to see provinces enact legislation that ensured the "efficient use" of federal money for health insurance before they were given anything. Grauer, whose own work argued that the provinces' uneven capacity to administer social programs made downloading services to them a bad idea, felt that these two proposals "raise[d] the whole question of Dominion-Provincial financial relations."[13] This question of the economic relations between the provinces and the federal government still dominates provincial-federal debates to this day.

Despite the goal of a fairer society for all citizens that was at the heart of these postwar reforms, Canada was still a white supremacist nation. White men were the biggest beneficiaries of these reforms, and it showed. Reforms that sought to reach full employment didn't extend to women, nor did they usually extend to racialized men. Some women and racialized people managed to make their way into this booming postwar economy, but mostly their participation was in low-wage, precarious work like domestic work or jobs with unsteady, atypical hours. There was a hierarchy of "deserving" Canadians, and white working men, at the top, were given a social contract that promised social services and benefits that could encourage workers to join unions and Canada to reach full employment, an attractive proposition for a cohort that had recently experienced the deprivations of the Great Depression.[14] As if women and racialized individuals had not also suffered.

The road to reform was full of political struggle between federal politicians and activists. It took sustained, ongoing activist agitation to mainstream the belief that the state should play a stronger role in managing the economy and society. Just as it was when soldiers struggled for veterans' pensions or when left-wing politicians fought for old age pensions, a strong left-wing flank ensured that at least some of Keynes's ideas took root.

The birth of healthcare as a universal social program bore this out most clearly. Despite popular support for healthcare, there was intense opposition to it as well. In 1944, after nearly two years of consultations, Mackenzie King presented the revised health plan to the provinces. With the growing threat of the CCF and the election of Tommy Douglas in Saskatchewan, Mackenzie King's Cabinet was more concerned about fighting off political opposition from the left than in developing a full welfare-state program. They just happened to coincide. The proposed health insurance legislation pitted farmers' groups and organized labour against doctors and medical professional groups, the former wanting a national universal system and the latter preferring the fee-for-service model. Public opinion was strongly on the side of the farmers and labour leadership. But the patchwork approaches to healthcare among the provinces restricted political opportunities to push a more universal system into place. In 1945, BC, Ontario, and Quebec refused to give up their power of taxation in order for the federal government to partially fund health services. Douglas's Saskatchewan was well into creating its own system, and Manitoba was just passing its own act. By 1948, urged by his new minister of national health and welfare, Paul Martin Sr. — father of future finance minister and prime minister Paul Martin Jr. — Mackenzie King untied provincial health grants from the proposed new health insurance plan to avoid constitutional problems. It passed. But it still wasn't a universal program.

The CCF, and specifically the Saskatchewan CCF under Tommy Douglas, can certainly claim victory for having pushed Canada to adopt a universal system of healthcare. In 1944, they were elected on a platform that promised universal pensions, healthcare, children's allowances, unemployment insurance, and workers' compensation. They had never held power before, and their victory in Saskatchewan began twenty years of progressive rule. The year they were elected, they passed radical legislation that gave workers important rights, rights that no one else in North America had access to, such as the mandate that if a company violated workers' rights too many times, the government had the right to appoint a custodian to run the company.[15]

During the 1949 election, all federal parties supported national health insurance. But in the 1950s, as a new Red Scare took over, particularly with the sensational McCarthy hearings in the U.S., universal programs including healthcare were disparaged as socialist plots more and more often, hurting their popularity. Liberals and Conservatives alike saw how popular social supports were but remixed these programs to help maintain capitalism, an approach that completely undermined the priorities of the CCF and other socialist and communist activists.

Writing in 1976, Horn argued that few people in Canadian history have had as much impact on the creation of the welfare state as Marsh had, even if his ideas were mostly rejected when he released his report. Social welfare by the mid-1970s was a patchwork; it didn't include important services like dental care, for example. The money it gave people wasn't enough, and Canada spent much less, as a percentage of GDP, on social security than most countries in western and northern Europe. Politicians' support of capitalism, and of capitalists, ensured that the redistributive powers of the economic system were limited. While some wealth from higher income earners would be shared with poor people, enough wealth to ensure that no one lived in poverty would never be redistributed.[16] Poverty was therefore normalized, something to be seen as part of the natural rhythm of any society and not something manufactured by the economic system itself. When an economic system creates poverty and reinforces it through reforms that keep people in poverty, it's easy to conclude that poverty is a human failing, something as natural as greed or hunger. This normalization made it even easier for politicians to brush off their role in creating poverty and instead blame poverty on the individuals who were impoverished, as they always had always been blamed, going back more than one hundred years.

Canadian Keynesianism: The Interregnum?

Within just a few decades, social programs progressed from being popular ideas to real-life programs to something in which Canadians took tremendous pride. Healthcare wasn't just something people accessed when they needed it; it became a part of Canadian identity. But the programs remained exclusionary, coupled with official government policies that elevated the positions of white Canadians while oppressing and marginalizing non-white Canadians. For example, Canada's immigration policies limited the number of non-white immigrants to Canada. Before reforms in the 1960s, immigration policy decisions permitted certain races to be denied access because they were considered "unsuitable" for the Canadian climate. This severely limited the arrival of racialized, especially Black, immigrants, while white non-anglophone immigrants were permitted to enter with few restrictions. From 1945 until 1951, about 157,000 people displaced by the Second World War settled in Canada, including many Holocaust survivors and others from eastern Europe. Most were from Ukraine and Poland. This was the single biggest wave of immigration to Canada during the 1900s. These immigrants were more educated than those in previous waves but were sent to distant regions of the country to do low-income work.[17] West Indians were mostly denied entry, though some who had work lined up as a domestic or a railway worker or had a contract to work in a mine were accepted.[18] Professor Nicole Bernhardt warns, "Many authors glorify the welfare state without paying attention to the limitations of the market-based rationales that underpinned policy choices within that era and the implications for racialized Canadians in particular."

Canada's immigration policies didn't change much until 1967, when the federal government introduced a points system. The higher the number of points a person got in nine categories, the more likely they were to be admitted. Five of the categories were explicitly related to the labour market, tying immigration decisions primarily to labour. People could also come to Canada to work, without being able to access citizenship. In 1966, just before the points system was unveiled, the federal government created the Seasonal Agricultural Worker Program, forcing international workers in agriculture to work without any path to permanent residency, thus creating a subclass of migrant workers. In 1973, the Temporary Foreign Worker Program was created to expand the kind of work that migrant workers could do, but it still locked them out of permanent residency. The first year of the program saw 264 men arrive from Jamaica. Today, there are about 40,000 temporary foreign workers in Canada each year, and the United Nations has said that the program facilitates slavery-like conditions.[19]

The Temporary Foreign Worker Program binds a worker to their employer. Because wages are so low, temporary foreign worker positions drive down wages for similar work.[20] But as temporary workers are, more often than not, racialized, the program also feeds into racist tropes about what a racialized worker deserves to be paid and where racialized workers fit into Canada's economy. The impact of increased immigration and reliance on temporary foreign workers meant that people needed to access welfare programs, but because those programs were geared toward white men with steady jobs and stable incomes, racialized temporary workers weren't eligible. They needed support from a system that was not built to help them.

In implementing what I call "Goldilocks Keynesianism" (not too hot, not too cold), Canada entrenched certain root causes that have continued to make things worse for some Canadians, and various gaps have never been filled. The measures that politicians implemented placed Canada in the middle of Sweden at one extreme, with its 66 percent union density and strong social democratic parties, and the United States on the other, with union density that never scratched 15 percent and no social democratic party option.[21] Bernhardt describes it like this: "Accepting a moderate version of Keynesianism, Canadian policy makers sought to ensure market-based economic stability through limited interventions. These interventions were never intended to challenge the hierarchies produced by the capitalist system, but merely to ensure that the inequalities introduced and maintained by the market did not reach levels that invited public wrath." Or, as R.M. Campbell put it in a report for the Economic Council of Canada in 1991, "While some countries adopted a fairly statist, interventionist variant of Keynesianism, Canada adopted what turned out to be the 'mainstream' version of Keynesianism — at what appeared to be the midpoint in the trade-off between planning and the market."[22]

The market was emerging as a defining political instrument. While the postwar period was one of state expansion and growth, many Canadians mistook this boom for progress toward what a modern Canada should look like: fair, safe, and economically prosperous. Rather than turning out to be the new world order, however, it took only a few decades for the postwar period to look more like a blip. William Carroll argues, quoting Gary Teeple, that "the era of social democratic reform, from World War II until the 1970s, constituted an 'interregnum between the age of competing imperial powers and the coming of the global economy.'"[23] An interregnum, as in a moment of temporary break as one era dies away and another rises in its place.

While Keynesianism itself was good for political debates, Canada's version of the Keynesian welfare state wasn't particularly controversial. Politicians of all stripes contributed to expanding it throughout the postwar period. In many provinces, it was conservatives who built public education, healthcare, and social services. Prime Minister Lester B. Pearson created the Canada Assistance Plan, the Canada Pension Plan, and medicare — all, interestingly, during five years of a minority government.[24] The political balance was flexible enough that parties could more or less do what they wanted to without breaking with Keynesian system, at least until the latter half of the 1970s.[25] Governments created Crown corporations and maintained an adequate tax base to ensure that revenues were available to pay for the social programs that Canadians had come to rely on. These programs, writes University of Waterloo Ph.D. student Jessica Gill, were "designed to support families and communities by fostering higher wages, decent working conditions, stable employment, and social benefits such as pension plans, unemployment insurance, welfare, and disability benefits." Gill lists key programs that underpinned Canada's welfare state: unemployment insurance, family allowances, the Canada Pension Plan, the Medical Care Act, and the Canada Assistance Plan. There was also a boom in social housing construction; from 1964 to 1978, 205,000 units of public housing were built.[26]

Keynesian reforms did not stop income inequality from existing, but they did stop income inequality from significantly increasing. Wages for lower-income workers grew at about the same percentage rate as salaries for higher-income workers. A survey of income inequality produced by the Canadian Centre for Policy Alternatives that tracks income inequality from the postwar period to the present day reasons that while wealth inequality persisted, people at all levels of income had rates of increase in their incomes. Lars Osberg argues "that [wage] stability was an implicit social contract in which capitalists got growing markets, increasing dividends and continued political dominance while workers got jobs, rising wages and a taste of economic security through an expanding welfare state." While the reforms were not radical, they did push the governing Manitoba New Democratic Party (NDP) and the federal Liberal governments to pilot a guaranteed minimum income program from 1974 to 1979 in two communities, Winnipeg and Dauphin. The results showed that the impacts of poverty reduction were wide reaching: domestic violence in Dauphin went down, workplace injuries went down, farm and vehicle accidents went down, and mental illness improved when compared to surrounding areas. For example, hospitalization rates dropped 8.5 percent.[27] The pilot ended when both governments lost power in 1979 and incoming parties thought that the program was too expensive to operate.[28]

Moderate Keynesianism served Canada well in a number of ways. Gone were the days of extreme unemployment seen during the Great Depression. Union density was growing and wages were stable. Canada's GDP per capita grew more rapidly from 1946 to 1980 than it did from 1981 to 2019, meaning that the economy was growing and offering more prosperity to more people. Where it grew on average by $640 per year in the earlier period, this slowed to $596 per year by the end of the later one.[29] It was also rhetorically a critical time; a kind, gentle nation grew to assert itself on the world stage, proud of its universal social programs. And for those who wanted to entrench Canada's racial and gender hierarchy, Canada's welfare reforms reinforced racial capitalism by creating the invisible though intentional forces that ensured that, through economic policy and political interventions, power within mainstream Canadian society remained white and male.

An Untenable Situation: Keynesian Collapse

Despite the welfare state mitigating some of the worst ravages of the market for the average white male, the markets were already growing too strong to be held in check by modest state-coordinated programs. Economist Jim Stanford writes, "This expansionary postwar 'golden age' eventually ran up against its own internal limits and contradictions. As in other advanced capitalist countries, the happy recipe of strong profits and business investment, rising living standards, and Keynesian welfare-state fine-tuning began to disintegrate." He cites Polish economist Michal Kalecki, who could see that the tensions between Keynesianism and capitalism would eventually become untenable. The push to get workers into jobs that were secure and gave them income security, along with programs that fostered both, expanded people's expectations, "sparking increasing conflict with the interests of capitalist employers in maintaining a compliant, disciplined, low-cost workforce." As always, workers were demanding more — better wages, more secure jobs, social services — and this posed a direct threat to market capitalism, which needed a desperate and income-insecure workforce to easily exploit. Critically, the business investment that drove postwar expansion had slowed.[30] Where productivity, as measured by output per worker, was about 3 percent during the 1950s and 1960s, that dropped to 1 percent in the 1980s and 1990s.[31]

There wasn't just a slowdown in productivity. Inflation was high and governments were gathering larger and larger deficits. To manage the collision of these three economic problems, politicians had two diverging options. They could follow the trajectory of the previous three decades, invest in people and expand the welfare state to better support people who had been excluded and close the income inequality gap. They could be more involved in the economy, build new industries and help to give productivity a shot in the arm. They could aim for full employment, especially among racialized and otherwise marginalized workers. Or, they could go in the opposite direction.

Welfare-state expansion in the postwar period had given people just enough and had marginalized enough individuals that mainstream popular sentiment never coalesced around demanding more government interventions in the market or, god forbid, actual socialism. As more people found their way into work, there was increased pressure on the welfare state, which had originally been set up for a significantly smaller population. By the 1970s women were less likely to stay at home and do the unpaid work necessary to liberate husbands to work in manufacturing. Racialized people were demanding more of their rights and access to the same levels of support that white people had. Indigenous movements were organizing around civil and territorial rights, and Indigenous Peoples were demanding control over their own social services after decades of abuse at the hands of non-Indigenous groups like the Catholic Church and the federal government. These movements were adding stress on the welfare state that politicians refused to address directly, making the system even weaker than it already was.[32] Paul Pierson writes about how "new social risks" — risks related to shifting trends that de-emphasized white male dominance in the workforce as women and racialized peoples' participation grew — had an impact on fundamentally transforming the welfare state. Pierson argues that social policy was unable to tackle problems caused by "deindustrialization, heightened wage inequality, increased family instability and increased female labour-market participation as factors not adequately addressed by 'industrial social policies' targeted primarily on male breadwinners."[33] Welfare policies could not, in their current forms, address the problems that were associated with these social and economic changes. Bernhardt argues that "significant degrees of precariousness, marginality, and exclusion were accepted as norms of the Canadian workforce," and it was racialized workers and women who found themselves working in these positions more often than not.

With the proliferation of low-waged work in which racialized workers were overrepresented, the private sector drove their industries and set their own wages, standards, and expectations around workplace conditions. Canada's "economic apartheid," a term coined by academic Grace-Edward Galabuzi, became entrenched. Wages were connected to race, with average wages for white workers outpacing average wages for Black and Indigenous workers. And yet, even though racialized workers were often excluded from welfare-state reforms, the reforms still created a floor that brought up all workers. As these reforms were steadily eroded, their disintegration was felt even more acutely by racialized workers because the inequality baked into the system grew far worse. In 1982, a Black man working in Toronto could expect to make roughly as much as a white worker. By 2015, a racialized worker in Toronto was making 52 cents on the dollar compared to a white worker.[34]

Bernhardt argues that Canada, unlike social democratic countries in Europe, never tried to better equalize wages, nor did Canadian politicians institutionalize collective bargaining. Nordic countries like Sweden distributed more wealth, but because Canada's welfare policies were not tied to industrial relations, like collective bargaining, the welfare state in Canada was far more vulnerable to pro-market reforms. Indeed, it was much weaker than most Canadians realized. And worse, it meant that people who were systemically excluded from many of the protections of the welfare state found themselves in even more precarious situations as the welfare state was hacked to bits in the coming decades.

• • •

If the three decades that followed the Second World War were dominated by Keynesian-inspired policies, the decades that followed them were marked by the gradual erosion of everything that postwar prosperity built. As pressure was required to ensure that politicians enacted even modest social reforms, politicians were always looking to erode government involvement in market regulation. Rather than there being a backlash to Canada's Keynesian interregnum, the natural rhythm of politics in Canada was to slowly, though intentionally, move away from government involvement in the economy and society, and a new political ideology born immediately after the Second World War was the perfect thing to take Keynesianism's place. Neoliberalism combined elements of neoconservative ideals with liberal notions of freedom — individual freedom and freedom from the state — to create a political force that Keynesian social economics could not resist. And due to the number of people the welfare state left behind, it also created new class entrenchment that upheld white supremacy. Where governments saw market failures such as the crash of 1929 as inevitable events to be managed, or at least to partially protect citizens from, neoliberalism instead focused on government failure. Government involvement in and of itself was positioned as a negative force in the markets, and problems, whether social or economic, were coded as government failures and not market failures.[35] Rather than seeing a program like Unemployment Insurance (UI) as an important support for someone who is out of work, UI became seen as *the reason* why people were out of work: If they were given financial assistance while unemployed, what incentive did they have to go back to work?

Economic and social policy went from assuming that government should play a role in managing markets to believing that markets need far less control. The market, free of regulation or control by government, was given carte blanche to transform the economy and society. With the memory of 30 percent unemployment and men being shipped off to the wilderness to work in relief camps fading in the face of the postwar boom, neoliberalism's rationale captured the minds of politicians of all parties and gave them the justification to restructure the economy to give market forces the power to define economic policies. If government had a debt crisis, for example, the solution wasn't to increase revenues through corporate taxes. It was to cut back programs. At the same time, while the postwar period was an era of shoring up resources using nationally coordinated economic policies, neoliberalism drove politicians to chase strategies that would make Canada's economy competitive in the global economy. And this outward-facing approach tied Canadian economic growth to international markets, which became so powerful that they could dictate how economic policy should be managed.[36]

Neoliberal economic policy seeks to privatize all that was previously public — Crown corporations, public lands, public agencies, utilities, and social programs — all with the goal of reducing how much the state spends both on the programs themselves and on the bureaucracy needed to administer these programs, though oftentimes, new, even more complex bureaucracies must be built to manage outsourced social programs. The idea that people need to be freed from the shackles of their own government permeates neoliberal ideology and was summed up best when Ronald Reagan, during his inaugural address in 1981, famously said, "In this present crisis, government is not the solution to our problem; government *is* the problem." He argued that the system that had been set up to protect citizens from market forces had instead been stymieing their economic success. Frustrated by sky-rocketing inflation and lack of support from government services, it was easy to place the blame at the foot of government itself, and not on the miserable market forces that rewarded greed, profiteering, and dangerous and unacceptable working conditions. In his speech, Reagan said, "It is no coincidence that our present troubles parallel and are proportionate to the intervention and intrusion in our lives that result from unnecessary and excessive growth of government," as if a more obvious statement had never been said. With these words, Reagan encapsulated what the prevailing approach would be for the next four decades. And it became the greatest sleight of hand of late-20th-century politics.

In 1984, when Margaret Thatcher said that she wanted to not just break the miners' strike, she wanted to obliterate their notions of community, she was telegraphing the most fundamental shift of all, from understanding welfare reforms as a collective approach to confront and mitigate collective problems, to understanding the state as being a corporate entity in the service of millions of individual clients. We were no longer to conceive of ourselves as being part of a community that benefitted from collective services. We were on our own, and how much government might support us relied on individually specific information: where we lived; how much money our bosses decided to pay us; our race, gender, or other personal characteristics; and how close our bodies functioned to what was considered "normal." The further away we drifted from any of the ideals in these categories, the less likely social services would be able to help us. Division and difference forced individualism into the mainstream and buried community and collective action behind the wall of market forces and political incentives.

For a reformist, Keynes sounds almost revolutionary in his essay "Economic Possibilities for Our Grandchildren." His dream was utopic: that in the year 2030, "assuming no important wars and no important increase in population," what he termed "the economic problem" would sort itself out and humanity would be able to live in leisure as the economy ran itself. Two years after he penned this 1930 pamphlet, Keynes admitted that everything had changed due to a "world financial panic." He described how resisting economic downtowns was a priority of every country, and his description sounds eerily like what Thatcherism, Reaganism, and neoliberalism would look like as free trade took hold in the 1980s:

> Each nation, in an effort to improve its relative position, takes measures injurious to the absolute prosperity of its neighbors; and, since its example is not confined to itself, it suffers more from similar action by its neighbors than it gains by such action itself.... Competitive wage reductions, competitive tariffs, competitive liquidation of foreign assets, competitive currency deflations, competitive economy campaigns — all are of this beggar-my-neighbor description. For one man's expenditure is another man's income. Thus, while we undoubtedly increase our own margin, we diminish that of someone else; and if the practice is universally followed everyone will be worse off.[37]

But forces, whether market forces, political forces, or social forces, don't shift all by themselves. What Keynes didn't mention is that the markets' drive for profit could not be overcome with

good reasoning and logic alone. It takes struggle. And struggle —
the fight between organized working people and the political class,
or between marginalized workers and less marginalized workers, or
between a generation who has just given everything up for war and
has come home demanding that their government provide them
with services and the government that doesn't want to afford it —
these are the forces that shaped Canada's social safety net. In his
memoir, published in two volumes in 1983 and 1986, Paul Martin
Sr. was keen to rewrite the history of health insurance to make it
clear that it had nothing at all to do with socialism. He saw this
popular program as a way for Mackenzie King to leave an important legacy for Canada, and he was an early supporter of a national
system. Take this anecdote he included in his memoirs. During
the 1957 election campaign, an executive member of the insurance
company Great West Life challenged Martin for being too soft on
socialism because he was so focused on creating a national public
healthcare program. Martin replied,

> Hospital insurance is not socialism; nor is it a so-
> cialistic device or concept; nor does it have any
> essential relationship with the socialist philoso-
> phy. Such programs as hospital insurance are just
> as much an integral part of a humanitarian, cap-
> italist, democratic philosophy as anything else. As
> you will see ... it is not correct to assume ... that
> I dislike pamphleteering against socialism. What
> I dislike is pamphleteering against other perfectly
> respectable programs and endeavouring to bring
> them into disrepute through "guilt by association"
> tactics — that is to say, by linking them with so-
> cialism when in actual fact there is no real or basic
> connection whatsoever.[38]

Never mind that the program was only brought to life thanks to the socialist-inspired CCF, or that so many of the welfare-state expansions were undertaken specifically in the hopes of undercutting socialism's popularity. If this is what Paul Martin Sr. needed to tell an insurance company executive, it demonstrates just how high the stakes were for the Liberals to refuse socialist politics. No wonder they picked Keynesianism light.

This race to the bottom would have profound impacts on Canadians, which started in the mid-1980s but really took off in the 1990s. By 1980, neoliberalism was already alive, already being implemented in its earliest forms in some parts of the country, and waiting for the moment that it could dominate. It would find its time and its methods soon enough to become Canada's new world order. And we can point to one man — and his transborder bromance — who first decided to make this shift in a significant way: Brian Mulroney.

CHAPTER 3

The Paradigm Shift

As Keynesianism started to collapse, a new economic world order was ready to take its place. Liberal and Conservative politicians alike argued that Canada's social services system was too big and too unwieldy and what was needed now was restraint. The new political order had been bubbling in the minds of right-wing ideologues across the English-speaking world for decades, waiting for a moment or a crisis or *something* to justify its approach, and political trends in the 1980s gave politicians their chance. Neoliberalism wasn't imposed on Canada in one fell swoop. It would take decades for it to really take hold, but its early days were undoubtedly the early 1980s. Canadian neoliberalism was a mix of neoconservative and liberal ideology, with the more conservative elements of the ideology "Canadianized" to be made more palatable for voters.

Fast forward to 1993. I hit my head on a bench playing dodgeball in grade 3. I remember navigating my grandparents, who were in town visiting, to the Georgetown Hospital — a place I had never really been, though I knew to follow the aitches. I don't know how long I was in the waiting room, but I do remember getting the rest of the day off from school and having enough time after being stitched up to go to the mall, where the local police force was giving out full-sized Crunchie bars. I was home with a bandaged head and a stomach full of chocolate and toffee before my parents came home from a day of teaching.

Did Canadians know how good we had it then? To imagine such a quick trip to the emergency department with my own children is laughable. Today, Georgetown, Ontario, has doubled in size, but the Georgetown Hospital is about as big as it was when I was a kid. Plus, because there isn't enough hospital access in nearby Brampton, people often drive to the boonies to try their luck in seeing a doctor there. From 1991 to 1994, hospital expenditures in Canada fell by 2.4 percent and hospital capacity was 4.1 staffed beds per 1,000 people — a number that had fallen from 6.6 staffed beds in 1986.[1] Today, the rate of staffed hospital beds per 1,000 people is 2 percent.[2] There I was, in 1993, bleeding from the head because someone hadn't moved a bench in our gym, receiving the most supported care I'd ever receive for the rest of my life. These trends didn't start then, though. They started earlier, and they were imposed by stealth.

Looking back, it's easy to feel nostalgic, but Canadians were growing frustrated with how things were. The business world was concerned with the welfare state, too. They had to pay taxes to sustain it, which ate into their profits. Many business leaders opposed the social safety net on ideological grounds; the state should not provide such broad-reaching services. The late-1970s recession put even more strain on the welfare state, and politicians had two choices to make: Do we help corporations or do we help citizens? You know which one they chose.

When it was adopted, Canadian politicians oriented neoliberalism toward three principles: social responsibility, fiscal responsibility, and fiscal flexibility. Despite how reasonable these principles sound, when operationalized, they meant less money for state services, more responsibilities downloaded onto provinces and municipalities, and lower taxes for the wealthy.

But everyone knows that Canadians don't like sudden, revolutionary change. So Mulroney bided his time, making small changes here and there, setting up the pins so that regardless of who was elected next, they'd be ready to come crashing down from the first bowling ball lobbed their way.

Enter: Canadian Neoliberalism

At first, the push to undo Keynesianism welfare reforms came not from neoliberal but from neoconservative ideology. Neoconservatism supports free market capitalism and opposes large and involved governments. Neoliberalism marries neoconservatism and liberalism together, placing the markets at the centre of decision-making at the expense of communities. But the two ideologies aren't the same. Neoconservatives see the welfare state as both an assault on the family and on the individual. Liberalism is far more concerned with unfettered access to the markets than with protecting the nuclear family. And so neoconservatives waged war against welfare-state reforms — war that wasn't rooted just in market ideology, but also in opposition to non-religious concepts of community, self, and, ironically enough, collective responsibility.

But neoconservatives' anti-statism ended at the state's coercive functions. While they didn't believe that the state should play any role in family affairs, they did believe that police, military, and other security forces were essential responsibilities of the state. Whereas health and education could be slashed and privatized, there would always be the need to pour more money into military and police forces. Today, we see this rationale on full display: across Canada, regardless of budgetary pressures, regardless of political leanings, police budgets increase at any cost, despite the specific crises that rage within a particular community. Neoconservative ideology has successfully confused enough people to accept a bolstered police and military force while also accepting cuts to the social services that render the need for these forces obsolete.

Neoconservatism is also morally conservative, tied closely to religious institutions and their networks of community organizations and political connections. In the 1970s, these ideologies found favour among some political parties and movements, but they weren't exactly mainstream. As people grew more accepting of ideas that conflicted with religious doctrine, neoconservatives had a difficult time popularizing their ideologies. This necessitated a version of neoconservatism that places the market at the centre of all decision-making but doesn't demand that people also adopt morally conservative positions. It is there that the marriage between neoconservatism and liberalism is so powerful: liberalism ignores neoconservatism's moral arguments while drawing on the individualistic sense of personal responsibility and freedom. Neoliberalism advocates for the same anti-state, pro–free market reforms that neoconservatism pushes, but it is "a more nuanced and less obviously harsh approach," argue researchers with Alberta's Parkland Institute.[3] It had to jibe with Canada's widespread Red Tory tradition, a kinder form of conservatism that understands that people in a community have a role in caring for one another if the colony is going to survive.

Neoliberalism is obsessed with the most basic manifestation of a society's collectivity: taxes. Neoliberal partisans advocated for radical reforms that reduced taxes, especially for corporations, and instead promoted consumption taxes and the role of the state as a tool to help people grow their private capital accumulation. Where neoconservatism is principally concerned with diminishing the role of the state, neoliberalism asks "How can the state be in the service of capital accumulation?" Neoliberalism doesn't see social services as the enemy to the nuclear family; social services are simply a new avenue by which to make money.[4] When organized effectively, social services can also help strengthen capitalism, as Paul Martin Sr. asserted. Gradually, the logic of Keynesian welfare-state reforms, where the primary role of the state was to protect individuals from the free market, was rejected. Now, governments were here to protect the free market from citizens demanding that they cough up their profits to fund social services.

The United States was ahead of Canada in its pursuit of this new world order. While Canadians were settling into the 1980s led by Pierre Trudeau, a prime minister from ages past, Ronald Reagan was advocating this new political ideology. In his inaugural address on January 20, 1981, Reagan talked about the scourge of inflation, blaming the tax system for penalizing people for being successful and bemoaning the fact that "idle industries have cast workers into unemployment, human misery, and personal indignity." He took aim at the deficit, as it was "mortgaging our future and our children's future for the temporary convenience of the present. To continue this long trend is to guarantee tremendous social, cultural, political, and economic upheavals." His speech not only laid the foundation for how he would govern, but it became the model for how governments of all parties would govern. Reagan argued that the size of the U.S. government was the greatest barrier to prosperity for ordinary Americans. Seven months after this address, he passed the Economic Recovery Tax Act of 1981, reducing the top marginal income tax rate from 70 percent to 50 percent and reducing other marginal income tax rates by 23 percent. It also lowered corporate income taxes.[5] In 1986, he cut taxes even further, giving the U.S. the lowest personal and corporate income tax rates of any industrialized nation in the world.[6]

These ideas would come to Canada, but it would take an intense campaign led by business leaders and sympathetic politicians to find favour for them among Canadian voters. A year before Reagan took office, Trudeau was elected for the last of his four terms as prime minister. It was a surprise election. Trudeau had just been trounced by Joe Clark and the Progressive Conservatives in May 1979. But Clark's government couldn't pass its first budget. They had presented an austerity budget that included increased prices for energy, higher taxes on transportation fuels, and higher contributions to unemployment insurance even though they had campaigned on cutting income tax by $1.7 billion. They lost the budget vote by 133 to 139. A snap election was called, and on February 18, 1980, Trudeau, who had already resigned as Liberal leader when the election was called, was back in the saddle.

His government's 1980 Throne Speech could not have been more different than Reagan's inaugural address, even though the two were given less than a year apart. Where Reagan rebuked the notion of government intervention with his comment "Government is the problem," Trudeau's speech framed the role of government in a fundamentally different way: "My Ministers believe that Canadians want more effective government, not necessarily less government." It promised to expand Old Age Security pensions by thirty-five dollars per month. Understanding that "energy policy is as important for Canada in the 1980s as railway policy was in the 1880s," the speech promised to create Canadian prices for oil, leading to the creation of his National Energy Policy. It promised to expand Petro-Canada "as an instrument of public policy" and increase its budget. It promised to set Canada on track so that at least 50 percent of the petroleum industry would be Canadian-owned by 1990.

Trudeau was a relic of an older era, one in which government's role was to intervene in the economy when economic forces threatened Canadians, just as Keynes had envisioned. Trudeau's tenure as prime minister was marked by regional divisions, not the least of which was the first of two referenda in Quebec for sovereignty. Less than six weeks after the Throne Speech was delivered, of the 85.6 percent of Quebecers who voted, 59.56 percent voted to stay in Canada, handing Trudeau a renewed lease on Canadian federalism that would give him the political confidence to repatriate the Canadian constitution, create a constitutional amending formula, and pass the Canadian Charter of Rights and Freedoms in 1982. But the Liberals wouldn't hold on to power for long.

Despite Trudeau's focus on oil, gas, and governance, Canadians were living through difficult economic times, and the quick ousting of Clark for Trudeau represented how volatile the population's political allegiances were. Deindustrialization had begun, and inflation was severely cutting into people's spending capabilities. In 1978, meat prices rose by 70 percent and gas prices rose by 45.5 percent. By 1981, the consumer price index was 12.9 percent, the highest it had ever been.[7] The welfare state was not able to absorb the pressure these economic forces placed on the economy after years of entrenchment. The economy was in recession for periods in both 1980 and 1981, and the average wage for a family fell by 1.5 percent during that time.[8]

Economist Jim Stanford argues that the first radical move to a new neoliberal order didn't come from government itself, but from the unelected bureaucrats that ran Canada's central bank: "The cannon shot that truly heralded the advent of neoliberalism in Canada was the interest rate shock that occurred here in the early 1980s, overseen by the Bank of Canada's then-governor Gerald Bouey," a shock that was similar to decisions made in the U.S. and the U.K. a few years prior. The Bank of Canada used interest rates to stop people from borrowing to try to rein in inflation; it jacked the prime interest rate to a historic high of 22.75 percent in the summer of 1981, which of course caused a recession. Tens of thousands of people lost their homes, and unemployment soared. This decision caused deliberate harm in order to change the expectations and behaviour of the market: "Mass unemployment was to become a deliberate, permanent feature of the economy," writes Stanford. The Bank of Canada signalled to Canadians that some level of unemployment was a natural feature of the economy, and the government acted, abandoning any hope of achieving full employment. After all, unemployment is more than just a normal part of the capitalist economy; it is also useful. It can be used to threaten workers and keep them in line, so they ask for less and are more affordable to corporations.

This economic and political volatility created conditions that swept Trudeau out of power only three years later, by Brian Mulroney's landslide victory. Mulroney had never been elected to office before, was thirty years younger than the outgoing Trudeau, and won a record 211 seats on September 4, 1984. CBC reported that Mulroney promised to "pump up the economy" and create closer ties with the United States. After years of an antagonistic relationship between Trudeau and U.S. leadership, Mulroney found a kindred spirit in Reagan, and the transformation Reagan had announced on January 20, 1981, was about to find its way up north.[9]

Enter: Mulroney

Mulroney was a corporate prime minister first and foremost. Maude Barlow of the Council of Canadians and Bruce Campbell of the Canadian Centre for Policy Alternatives explain: "The corporate sector found in the government of Brian Mulroney the clearest and most committed expression of its interests of any Canadian government in history."[10] While Barlow and Campbell may exaggerate a bit (more than the era of railway barons and the financial support they received from government?), there is truth in their observation. Mulroney overhauled how the government interacted with the economy. He broke from the prevailing status quo by creating the conditions necessary for Canadians to believe that deficits were as important as poverty, that corporations were as needy as average people, and that collective success relied on corporate success, sounding eerily similar to Reagan's trickle-down economics idea.

Mulroney's policies wouldn't completely unravel the welfare state. Jessica Gill argues, "The induction of neoliberalism into Canada was driven by particular interests; a calculated move on behalf of the corporate elite to reassert control over the elements of political and economic life that was lost during the post-war Keynesian era of social intervention." Instead, these interests would transform political life and give the economy (and the business leaders who controlled the economy) tremendous political power. This process happened slowly enough that, rather than feeling a sudden shock, the water was brought slowly to a boil, resulting in fewer hospital beds, fewer doctors, bigger class sizes, and fewer municipal services.

The Throne Speech for Mulroney's first government was given on November 5, 1984. While my father was celebrating his first birthday as a father in a small town in northwestern Ontario, Mulroney's government promised Canadians that his election signalled the dawn of a new day: "Let it be also the beginning of a new era of national reconciliation, economic renewal and social justice." (Note that "reconciliation" then meant national unity among provinces and regions, not reconciliation with Indigenous Peoples.) The speech promised that the tax system would be made "simpler and fairer and more accountable to the people's representatives in Parliament. The rights of taxpayers must be protected." And it announced three priorities to renew the economy: to reduce the deficit and control public debt; to make market interventions through market-driven training opportunities and increased investments in research and to "improve the efficiency and flexibility of our capital markets"; and to "enhance risk taking, innovation and reward among entrepreneurs." As a part of this third promise, the government encouraged both domestic and foreign investment; international trade was foundational. Mulroney promised to eliminate barriers to trade, deepen the trade relationship with the United States, and "pursue with vigor and imagination new opportunities" in regions like the Pacific Rim.

Mulroney was clever. He knew that if he went too hard cutting social services, Canadians would oppose him. So he made some modest welfare-state reforms and promises, too. Another spoonful of honey with the medicine. Mulroney promised to examine the possibility of a national childcare strategy, strengthen the social security system, and oversee a comprehensive overhaul of pensions. The rhetoric sounded great. Sure, a childcare strategy would not materialize for another several decades, but it didn't matter; anyone who worried about Mulroney's plans for Canada's social safety net could relax a bit. He wasn't going to make deep cuts. He was going to rationalize the system. This was just a first budget, and Mulroney was smart enough to take it slow.

Pension reform is a good example of how he used rhetoric to allay concerns while also making changes to public policy that would actually threaten people's pensions. In 1990, Mulroney encouraged Canadians to save for their own retirement by doubling the Registered Retirement Savings Plan (RRSP) deductions Canadians could claim at tax time each year. It was a perfect neoliberal reform: give individuals the agency to save over the course of their own working lives to ensure that they can one day retire, easing the pressure on the federal government to have to pay too much in public pension funds. More and more, RRSPs became an acceptable way for individuals to save for retirement, making the need for company-administered pension plans less necessary and taking the pressure off public pensions. But there was a catch: a person needed to make at least $86,000 per year (approximately

$162,036.59 in 2023 dollars) to be able to make the maximum RRSP contribution, effectively creating an incentive for the wealthy to save for their retirements through private investments.[11]

The 1984 Throne Speech marked a turning point in Canadian politics. Most Canadians would find themselves worse off as a result, even though reforms were marketed to represent significant increases to their personal wealth. Jessica Gill argues that there were three principles at the heart of the neoliberal reforms that guided Mulroney: social responsibility, fiscal responsibility, and fiscal flexibility. Each of these would underpin not just Mulroney's social and economic policies but also policies from other political parties, as neoliberalism quickly took hold as Canada's governing status quo.

Social Responsibility

Key to understanding the principle of social responsibility is to start by assuming that resources are scarce, a straightforward fear tactic. In a world with scarce resources, programs that provide services to people who do not *appear* to need them are considered wasteful or inefficient. If a doctor is not already seeing a line of patients, the system is considered inefficient. Thus, the principal of social responsibility clashes with a fundamental tenet of the welfare state: universal programs.

Neoliberals reason that universality is bad because it isn't targeted enough. It therefore needs to be reformed to ensure that only the people who actually need support get it. Barlow and Campbell illustrate this using family allowances as an example:

> The corporate argument for taxing back universal family allowances was that they should only go to those who need it. "Why," it asked, "should a bank president earning $500,000 a year get the family allowance?" This clever piece of rhetoric

> side-stepped the important question, which is not
> how the $400 family allowance should be taxed
> but rather how the other $499,600 of the presi-
> dent's income should be taxed.
>
> The scandal is that the bank president's salary is
> taxed at the same rate of that of a school teacher."[12]

It's the same kind of thing that Bob Rae told students in the mid-2000s when he was hired to host a consultation the Liberals could hide behind to jack up Ontario's tuition fees. It's the same rationale that right-wing think tanks trot out to support privatizing health-care, and it has since become the status quo: exquisitely designed social programs are accessible only to the "deserving" poor, even if the bureaucracy to oversee such complex programs often becomes a new source of waste and glut.

The family allowance, along with pensions, was fundamentally changed in the 1980s, making it less and less available. The federal government limited access through taxation, clawing it all back from families who made $56,500 annually. As for pensions, individuals who had an income of $50,000 started to lose their public pension to taxes. Those whose income was $76,000 had their public pension virtually eliminated through a tax claw back. When Finance Minister Michael Wilson tried to bring in these measures in 1985, he limited inflationary increases to three points less than inflation. That set off massive public outrage, which caused the government to reverse its decision, but still, it started the process of defunding both social programs four years later. By 1989, neoliberalism had succeeded in delinking these two programs from inflationary increases, so as the cost of living rose, money went less far.[13] Mulroney also started to transform social housing spending, paving the way for Chrétien to stop Canada from building social housing altogether. Using the logic of targeted spending, they shifted social housing spending from mixed-income projects to programs that targeted lower-income people specifically. The mixed-income projects had enough money to sustain their buildings for things like maintenance. Lower-income housing struggled to pay for similar costs because the rental base was uniformly low — on average, too low to actually pay for these costs.[14]

Shifting from universal to targeted programs has had a fundamental impact on how Canadians understand why we even have social programs. A universal program benefits everyone: whether you're poor or rich, you are able to access a benefit by virtue of your status in Canada. Because these programs are available to everyone, everyone has skin in the game to ensure that they are high quality. This is partly why healthcare and education have stayed universal; it's easier to see how education benefits an entire society than how a universal family allowance impacts a guy with no children. When a society is full of people who've attended its public schools or have received care in one of its public hospitals, the equalizing force of universality is obvious. We all benefit when someone can become a doctor, a dentist, an electrician, or a grocer, and stratifying society by limiting access based on a person's income diminishes this benefit. Similarly, we all benefit by being able to walk into an emergency room. We especially benefit if the services are available for everyone, because we won't be pushed down a list if we can't pay to jump the queue and we can feel pretty confident that the care we receive is of the same quality as that received by a lawyer, a doctor, or our bosses. Barlow and Campbell explain the importance of universality like this:

> A program targeted to the poor becomes a poor program because the rest of us don't have a stake in maintaining its quality, and the poor don't have enough political clout to ensure that they are well served.

> Targeted programs divide the rich from the poor and from the somewhat poor. Universal social programs encourage a sense of solidarity, of community within our society.[15]

Back in 1991, Barlow and Campbell saw what was coming. They saw how society would change as universality was replaced by targeted programs, which sound good but really just make things harder for everyone by limiting access.

Replacing universality with targeted programs also creates those famous cracks in the system that swallow up so many people. Either they make too much or make too little to be able to access a certain program, or they have to wait until their income reaches a certain level, or they have to wait for an assessor to determine whether or not they're "deserving." Targeted programs necessitate a system of coordination that a universal program does not require. They *create bureaucracy*, which is ironic considering that many of the proponents of these programs claim they'll reduce bureaucracy and eliminate red tape. Individuals regularly find themselves trapped in a bureaucratic nightmare as they try to access this or that program because of the complicated and confounding desire to police every single person who walks through the door. The programs create more problems than they claim to solve, all while promising the average person that no money will be wasted and only those who deserve these programs will receive help. The principle of social responsibility actually removes responsibility from government by restricting programs to a very small number of people with increasingly specific and exclusionary needs.

Fiscal Responsibility

The second principle of neoliberalism is the principle of fiscal responsibility. This principle is rooted in the idea that all citizens must take responsibility to care for themselves and their families through work. By working hard, citizens should earn a good wage to cover the costs of housing, transportation, food, and other essentials. Just as they did in the 1800s, politicians believe that the best poverty-reduction strategy is a job and no government program can offer income security as effectively. Therefore, governments spend money on training and job opportunities to encourage people to work. But in the late 1980s, this principle clashed with a changing labour market; thanks to deindustrialization, the jobs that had underpinned the Keynesian era were vanishing. Rather than full-time, well-paying manufacturing jobs, jobs grew more precarious and less permanent, and they paid less.

The principle of fiscal responsibility guided government in how it managed two programs in particular: UI and job training and skills development. UI had been a key part of the welfare state since it was implemented after the Second World War. It was intended to even out employment gaps from region to region, especially with cyclical employment related to weather or natural patterns, like fisheries. UI gave people enough money to bridge the gap between jobs, minimizing the impacts of precarious employment. The program was funded through a combination of worker and government contributions. When unemployment rose above 4 percent, the government would kick in extra funds. It was such an important program that, during the 1982 recession, almost a third of all Canadians benefitted from UI payments. Indeed, the rationale of using jobs as the main income source falls apart during a recession, when there just aren't enough jobs to keep everyone afloat.

Barlow and Campbell argue that politicians and business people disliked UI because it gave workers too much power. They could quit one job to find another one if they wanted to because UI gave them a softer landing than if they had no backup financial supports. It also gave workers protection if they were fired: they didn't rely on a job to survive after being fired in the same way that a worker who had no social benefit did. This allowed workers to take risks. They could stand up to the boss and risk being fired because they'd get UI while looking for another job, or they could quit if they didn't want to deal with a particular boss or a particular job, and so on.

UI was also seen as a trade barrier. Along with other benefits like taxation and workers' compensation, UI was seen by some as being an unfair advantage in a competitive international market. Just after the first free trade agreement between Canada and the United States was signed, and just before job losses really picked up in the 1990s as a result, the federal government pulled $3 billion out the program, fully defunding the government portion of UI. This was more an ideological move than a move to simply save money; the government was, for the first time in two generations, out of the business of paying for any sort of unemployment insurance. The program was now fully covered by employees. Mulroney had been re-elected just five months earlier, and this radical change meant that Canada was the only industrialized nation in the world except the U.S. to have no government-subsidized unemployment insurance program. Workers in the most precarious and lowest-income jobs were hit hardest. Now they would be financially penalized for moving from job to job, which many had to do. Workers had to work an extra six weeks before they qualified for UI. The cutbacks meant that many people who would have been saved by federal help now had to turn to their province for social assistance and welfare, putting even more strain on these programs. Where UI had covered four out of every five unemployed people, fewer than one in three unemployed workers qualified after these changes. The government also froze the amount that social assistance transfer payments for Ontario, British Columbia, and Alberta could rise annually and kept the freeze in place until 1995.[16]

The flip side of the UI coin was job training and market-oriented education. The rationale went like this: if a worker is out of work, rather than helping them out with a subsidy to pay for rent, food, and transportation, they should be given the opportunity to train for a better job. Mulroney signalled his intention to tie education and training together when he appointed a young Bernard Valcourt to spearhead a new national education initiative. Valcourt was already minister of employment and so, argue Barlow and Campbell, his appointment was "a signal that the education initiative [was] part of the government's prosperity and competitiveness agenda."[17] The 1991 Throne Speech promised to quadruple spending for employers to coordinate private education and for private sector educational organizations to access money intended for literacy and job training.[18] Literacy wasn't simply something that allowed someone to enjoy reading, participate in society, or write as a hobby; it was a doorway into a job. And if a person went through that door, government expected they would be off the dole.

All of this happened while universities were also starting to be defunded, a trend that continues to this day. With more pressure on university and college budgets, plus the push to get people to change careers with the help of newer and newer credentials, the ball was set in motion for runaway tuition fees; the low-cost system of higher education that emerged as an equalizer in the postwar period was transformed in one where crushing student debt is the only way to get your foot into the door of a career. Gradually, tuition fees grew to fund record-high portions of institutional operating budgets, fuelling a debt crisis that then triggered a mental health crisis that, today, is one of the deepest and most vicious crises out there.

Fiscal responsibility divested government responsibility into the private sector, whether to bosses, to workers themselves, or to a combination of both. Workers were expected to fix their own unemployment troubles rather than have access to a program that would bridge the gap between jobs. Education became market-oriented, opening Canada up to private career colleges, educational consultants, and a training industry that pretended it could fix the decline in manufacturing just by retraining people. And the overall impact was clear: workers had less security and fewer supports and were on shakier ground. What boss is going to say no to having more power over increasingly desperate workers?

Fiscal Flexibility

The final principle of Canada's transformative neoliberal reforms was fiscal flexibility. This principle guided the federal government to take direct aim at spending with the goal of curbing the deficit. All of a sudden, the deficit became a thing that people were supposed to care about. The deficit, the result of a fiscal imbalance between state revenues and state expenses, became as important, if not more important, than things that actually mattered and were real, like whether or not someone could afford groceries or access surgery. While we've been living for decades in a reality where deficits are important political objects, turning the deficit into something that average people cared about was a difficult task in the 1980s. How did they manage to convince average Canadians that they should care as much about the federal government's accounting as they do about their own? To do this, they needed to turn the deficit into a thing that people kind of understood and that they could worry about. Political rhetoric considered the nation's finances in the same way that a voter might think of their own pocketbook. If debt or deficits were going to unbalance the budget, then it was critical to rein them in to be able to have money to spend on the services and programs that mattered.

There were lots of options on the table for cuts to balance the books, and many of them happened simply by de-indexing programs like the family allowance or pensions or by defunding UI. But the biggest chunk of money the government had to play with was social transfer payments, the money the federal government collected in taxes and then remitted to the provinces to help equalize access to and quality of public services like health and education from region to region. For their first budget, Mulroney's government changed the transfer payment formula. They first made small cuts to the amount by which the transfer grew year over year, and then they increased those cuts. Between 1985 and 1994, about $22 billion was cut from healthcare transfers as a result of their formula adjustment.[19]

The way they did this was highly technical and flew over the heads of most Canadians who were not watching fiscal policy with eagle eyes. In the early 1980s, transfer payments were composed of two parts. The first was money from direct transfer payments to the provinces that the federal government had collected from various revenue streams, especially income tax. The second was money gathered through a tax point calculation negotiated in 1977, which gave the provinces more leeway to collect income and corporate taxes. The idea was that if the provinces could raise their own taxes, they'd be encouraged to collect and spend their own taxes to fund healthcare. This second pot of money was considered part of the federal transfer even though it was collected in the province. Each side of the transfer grew at a different rate: the mass cash transfer was indexed to inflation, so the federally funded transfer increased at the same percentage as inflation. The other side grew as well, depending on wages and other economic forces that resulted in people paying higher taxes year over year.

To cut the transfer, the Tories didn't reduce the amount the provinces received. That would have raised public ire and could have forced them to back down. Instead, they took a very clever approach to slowly defund the transfer. They de-indexed the annual transfer increase from the rate of gross national product (GNP) growth and instead pegged it to two percentage points lower than GNP growth (GNP minus 2). Where GDP measures the sum of economic activity within Canada by Canadian- and foreign-owned companies, the GNP measures the total output of all Canadian-owned businesses, whether they operate inside Canada or abroad. If citizens paid more taxes in a given year, either because they made more money or because the government increased taxes, the planned transfer increase would be adjusted yet again. With only half of the transfer subject to the GNP minus 2 calculation, if the other half increased above that rate, the federal government wouldn't add extra money to the transfer at all.[20] In 1990, they further reduced the contribution to GNP minus 3 and froze transfer payments at the 1990 rate until 1994. In 1990 alone, $1.1 billion was cut from healthcare (in 2023, that would be $2 billion).

Unlike family allowances and pensions, medicare remained a universal program. With a gap growing between what the feds sent to the provinces and what services actually cost, provinces had to find more money to pay for social programs. One of the benefits of a strong national spending regime was that the federal government could give more money to regions in which healthcare was more expensive, reducing a significant financial burden on provincial coffers. For example, Newfoundland and Labrador spent double what Alberta spent to maintain a similar level of healthcare. The reduction in the federal transfer left less money to smooth out these regional differences. We know now how this turned out: a decades-long reduction in resources both to fund public healthcare and to enforce the Canada Health Act has created the crisis that plagues hospitals, health clinics, and health delivery in every corner of the country today. Monique Bégin, former Liberal minister of health under Pierre Trudeau, warned, "Medicare is a fragile institution vulnerable … to slow, quiet, behind-the-scenes erosion."[21] What was true in the early 1980s remains true to this day, though today, at least a lot of folks have found ways to make money off this invented crisis.

The fiscal flexibility principle wasn't actually about saving money or making anything more efficient; it was just about changing who controls which pockets of money, who calls which shots, and who turns on or off the taps of profits. Over the next decades, private healthcare flourished, rushing to fill the manufactured gaps that inevitably emerged and to draw profit for already wealthy individuals, hedgefunds, and pensions. Governments cut their responsibilities to increase profits — sorry, to "maximize fiscal flexibility" — with tactics like aggressively contracting out government programs to private sector agencies. This was such a new concept in 1991 that Barlow and Campbell slapped quotes around the words "contracting out," in case readers weren't familiar with what the term meant. They would be though, soon.

Each of these principles — social responsibility, fiscal responsibility, and fiscal flexibility — was driven by rationales that had built-in defences against popular pushback. Communities that resisted these changes not only had to battle the policies themselves, but they also had to tackle the supposed logic that underpinned them. There was also a paradigm shift that grew increasingly successful because, in addition to unity among decision-makers and corporate leaders, the rationale sounded like it made sense. It certainly helped that at the end of the 1980s, the CBC's *Journalistic Policy Handbook* was revised to include the word "balance" — another paradigm shift. Many journalists worried that this meant they needed to give both sides of an issue equal airtime, regardless of how unbalanced this would make a story. This subtle censorship influenced coverage, which guests to feature, and what they would soon be permitted to say.[22] The transformation of the state didn't happen just thanks to the collusion of business and government; media played a critical role as well (more on this in a future book in this series).

Imagine writing these explanations or the calculations or the federal-provincial fiscal arrangements on a placard or banner and protesting to the minister of finance. That was fundamental to the strategy: do these things but in a way that is complicated, so that people won't be able to articulate their options clearly enough to stop you.

So Who Benefitted?

The transformation of the social safety net could have gone in one of two ways. The federal government could have expanded the welfare state to include the people it had excluded decades earlier. Mulroney chose the opposite path: rather than retrenching the welfare system, he started its radical transformation. And as he did, Canadians slowly began to lose access to services. But some people finished the 1980s in a better place than where they started. There was tremendous wealth generated, not in the least thanks to free trade. Writing about Mulroney's legacy for *Policy Options* in mid-2003, retired professor Kim Richard Nossal argued that free trade in particular led to a net benefit for Canadians: "While some Canadians suffered as a result of the unemployment and dislocation that occurred as firms rationalized their operations, in the aggregate Canadians would be much better off as a consequence of the massive increases in trade." Nossal doesn't lay out who specifically was better off, though. Indeed, despite all the changes to social policy ushered in by Mulroney, his work to liberate trade from the bounds of government intervention would be his greatest achievement. Free trade promised to boost Canada's economy, create jobs for Canadians, and reduce the costs of merchandise. It was also an excuse to erode collective programs even further, like cutting the lifeblood of social services: federal tax revenue.

For example, to align Canada closer to the United States, the highest federal personal income tax bracket was lowered from 34 to 29 percent in 1987. This led to a loss of $2 billion for public coffers but was a boon for the folks in the highest income tax brackets.[23] In

1988, the average tax bill for poor working Canadians increased by 44 percent, while it decreased by 6 percent for the wealthiest ones. Since there are more working-class Canadians than wealthy ones, this tax increase helped to sow intense anti-tax sentiment among working-class voters, something that Conservatives and Liberals alike would seize upon. In 1989, the wealthiest 1 percent (who, in 1991, earned more than $114,000 a year) paid an average of $1,500 less than they'd paid in 1984. And, in 1989, 118,000 profitable companies who made a collective $25 billion in profit paid no tax on those profits at all. Of the total "share of federal revenue from taxes," corporations went from paying 17 percent to less than 9 percent. Barlow and Campbell estimate that if corporate taxes had grown at the same rate as sales and individual taxes, there would have been an extra $9 billion in federal revenues by 1990.

There were also a lot of tax cuts, loopholes, and rebates introduced that added complexity to the system but enabled anyone with higher-than-average income, and a good accountant, to reduce their own tax burden. In 1985, the federal budget introduced a $500,000 lifetime capital gains exemption, at a cost of $1.7 billion each year ($4.2 billion in 2023). This meant that someone could sell properties that generated $500,000 in profit and not pay any tax on it at all. While one-half of this benefit went to Canadians in the wealthiest 1 percent, it also set in motion the housing crisis that plagued the 2010s and beyond; half of capital gains in Canada were the result of real estate speculation. And, just because there can be no decadence without excess, the Conservatives continued something called the entertainment tax deduction. This allowed companies to deduct expenses for parties or events from their corporate income taxes, such as the cost of tickets for box seats at the SkyDome, at a cost of $1 billion per year. The result of these tax cuts, spending cuts, and tax loopholes, along with everything else, was that the Tories justified reducing federal spending as a portion of the entire economy by 3 percent: from 19 percent to 16 percent. Their goal was to get it down to 14 percent.[24] Because hey, if you're not bringing in enough revenue, the fiscal imbalance needs to be addressed with fiscal restraint!

Perhaps proof that all of this wasn't working as intended was that by 1993 Mulroney had failed to reduce the federal deficit, even though his government had produced surpluses. As Nossal explains, "But the Mulroney Conservatives proved no more capable than the [Pierre] Trudeau Liberals at grappling with government expenditures: by 1993, there had been no serious assault on the budget deficit, even though Ottawa was by then in an operating surplus taking in more in taxes than it spent on programs." With so many measures that saved a minority of people money imposed alongside the spending reduction measures, it's perhaps not a surprise that the deficit continued to rise. And as it rose, another round of justifications for austerity was made.

Mulroney understood that service disruption must be kept at a minimum if the government was going to be able to reduce its spending on social programs as much as possible without people rebelling against it. One way was to valorize the volunteer sector and encourage it to be more involved in delivering and implementing social programs. The shift in the economy from one in which women stayed home, raised children, and managed households for free to one in which more and more women worked full-time meant that the welfare state lost a critical source of unpaid labour. But if Canadians were encouraged to volunteer more, a similar level of unpaid labour would come back to help keep struggling Canadians afloat, all under the banner of volunteerism. Another way was to valorize contracting out, with groups bidding on service delivery at the lowest cost to the state. This had been part of how the Atlantic colonies, for example, coordinated their benevolent society contracts to help the deserving poor before the 1900s.[25] The rise in reliance on the voluntary sector, the slow decline in social service supports, the undercutting of the government's ability to raise revenues, and the opening up of the country to free trade set the stage for the biggest cuts ever made in a federal budget: the Chrétien-Martin budget of 1995.

. . .

If the 1980s started with an electroshock to monetary policy through interest rates, the 1990s firmly set monetary policy to be Canada's new normal. The Bank of Canada triggered another recession in the early 1990s through another interest rate adjustment, and a new paradigm in which inflation was targeted by interest rates was born. The Bank of Canada, unelected and therefore free from the chains of accountability, can increase or decrease interest rates to target high inflation without a care about the economic or social impacts it might have on average people or small businesses. In fact, Stanford argues that this role of the Bank of Canada "is now virtually sacrosanct in Canadian political economy."

The issue of democracy in all of this is important but hidden. Through neoliberal monetary policy, cuts to social spending, and fiscal policy in all of its defunding, privatizing, and back-dooring glory, democratic principles were slowly eroded along with the welfare state. Every time a private operator took on a new service, whether it was Air Canada or job training or Petro-Canada or saving for retirement, Canadians lost more of their democratic control over things that were supposed to be democratically designed, delivered, and controlled.

It's this piece that I think gets lost in the debate about what is going wrong with the economy and society today, and is the reason there is such widespread disengagement: our right of citizenship, to actually have a say over the programs that are there to help make our lives easier, has become weaker and weaker. In some cases, democracy has been completely eliminated, such as when an entity is sold off to the private sector, like the Canadian Wheat Board. In some cases, it's so severely weakened that we wonder what is the point of even voting. Nothing we say matters anyway. Forty years after this all started in the 1980s, we are still interacting with programs that we have little to no democratic control over. And we wonder why we can't seem to fix anything.

Looking back from 2001, Linda McQuaig wrote that it was interesting to see just how far things had changed from the postwar period, "when governments were expected to protect something called the 'public good'" to where she was, at the dawn of the new century, "with its deregulation, privatization and the reduction in government redistribution — the market has been given virtual pre-eminence." It's even more amazing to see the impact today, twenty years beyond McQuaig's reflections, when things that were scandalous three decades ago are now considered normal parts of society, driven by normal kinds of human behaviour: "contracting out," "fee for service," "limited intervention," "freedom." McQuaig chalked the shift up to, in part, a public message that had been sold to average people through corporate actors, who knew what they stood to win if they could capture the hearts and minds of average people: "All this has been aggressively encouraged by a network of business-funded think-tanks arguing that such policies are inevitable, given human nature, even though they are almost unique in human history."[26] And, preciously unaware of that human history, we accept the rationale but then wonder why we can't seem to change anything.

CHAPTER 4

Neoliberal Retrenchment

Nineteen-ninety. The Berlin Wall had just fallen, and the U.S.S.R. would disintegrate in a year. Abortion had been decriminalized two years earlier and Canada's women's movement was about to collapse. Cars that had mostly been angular would soon be mostly rounded. The move from the 1980s into the 1990s was accompanied by rapidly accelerating technological changes that heralded not just a new decade, but a new era — a point of no return to the time before we ever heard the grainy, piercing sound of an internet dial-up connection. While the 1980s had started to radically change the Canadian state, those changes had not yet trickled down to average people. It was a sweet moment for politicians and businessmen who wanted to continue down the neoliberal path of destruction before too many people noticed that something was up.

Up until now, I've told this story chronologically. The evolution of the Canadian state is easiest to tell chronologically when going issue by issue feels like too much of a slog. When people asked me how I planned to talk about a topic as big as the decline of Canada's social safety net, I always started by saying "It isn't a history book." But then I would explain how I was starting from the beginning and moving from decade to decade. A chronology would read a lot like history, I thought as I crawled my way forward through the years. I had to find a way to break out of history.

Lucky for my storytelling, history does two contrary things in the 1990s: it starts to slow and it rapidly accelerates. At some point in that decade, Canada became unstuck in time. Decisions made in this decade would have profound impacts on every aspect of every federal and provincial public policy decision for the next thirty years.

At the start of the 1990s, fewer issues loomed so large over Canadians as did free trade. Free trade discussions and negotiations dominated public discourse. Once the North American Free Trade Agreement (NAFTA) was signed into law, those discussions and debates were replaced by transformation. Despite activists' warnings, free trade would not be the end of Canada. But it would spell the end of Canada as it had been known in the postwar period. Free trade created a context where market logic could be applied to all aspects of the economy: not just goods that were bought and sold, but also services. In orienting services toward generating profit (or, in public sector speak, "savings"), education, healthcare, and social services would be radically transformed, even if they were largely untouched by free trade. Forces that had started many years earlier, like deindustrialization, decimated families and industrial cities and towns alike. Canada had always had international trade. Free trade transformed trading relationships that had already existed for decades, and in so doing, it changed how Canadians understood the role of markets within Canadian society.

Free Trade

In 1944, international leaders gathered at a meeting at Bretton Woods, New Hampshire, to plan what would become the new world financial order. They hammered out what a global economy might look like in the aftermath of the Second World War. From this conference emerged the International Monetary Fund and the World Bank. Leaders were deeply influenced by Keynesianism, and so, while they wanted to open up international markets to generate wealth, they were sensitive to the need to create systems that ensured some measure of democratic control. Linda McQuaig writes that the leaders were "anxious to ensure that democratic governments would have policy autonomy in the post-war global economy."[1] Democracy was still an ideal, especially in the face of a recent world war fought against fascist tyranny.

Three years later, discussions between the same nations who were at Bretton Woods coalesced into a global trade pact. The United States and the United Kingdom both felt that protectionist policies from the interwar period harmed European economies and believed that opening trade was one way to avoid this happening again. On January 1, 1948, the General Agreement on Tariffs and Trade (GATT) came into force on a provisional basis, and the stage was set for international trade to take off.[2] With the Second World War at their backs, many nations were eager to engage in global trade, and it grew steadily. Canada was particularly keen, as it relied on trade more than most other industrialized nations. In the 1960s, exports accounted for about 20 percent of Canada's national income. That rose to 25 percent in the 1970s and to nearly 30 percent in the 1980s. About three-quarters of Canadian trade was with the U.S.[3] Despite the emergence of free trade, Canada hovered around that 30 percent mark, with trade rising to 44 percent of GDP in 2000 but then falling back down to 30 percent by 2021.[4] The proliferation of free trade agreements hasn't inched trade much higher today than where it was three decades ago.

Free trade wasn't solely about increasing the amount of trade. It was used as a cover for radical neoliberal shifts in how Canada oriented itself to international capital. The biggest public argument in support of free trade was that it would give tariff-free access to foreign markets. This would help stimulate economic growth for Canadian companies and the Canadian economy as a whole. But the reality was that 80 percent of trade between Canada and the U.S. was tariff free already, and the average rate of tariffs on other exports was just 5 percent. Free trade was an important rhetorical tool — tariffs and fees are bad, just like taxes — and Canadians were primed through the discussions about free trade to accept these arguments.

There are two ways that one can look at money that is brought into state coffers through trade: either Canada raises money to pay for social services through tariffs and fees from trade, or Canada eliminates these tariffs and fees to reduce the cost of doing business, which stimulates more economic activity that should trickle down to average people through cost savings, new jobs, and new local investments. The first argument understands that a democratically elected government needs to raise money to create social programs demanded by the electorate. The second argument believes that economic activity alone creates its own benefits for average people, no pesky government required. This logic flies in the face of what the 1929 crash and the Great Depression showed Canadians, but memories are short.

For people in power, trade was mostly positive, but Canada's economy had a critical weakness: it shipped off raw materials rather than processing them at home and fostering innovation (and securing the necessary jobs and expertise) domestically. In her book *The Question of Separatism*, incorporating her 1979 Massey Lectures, Jane Jacobs states, "In relation to the United States, Canada has a colonial economy. It sells the United States, its chief trading partner, raw and semiprocessed materials, and in return buys chiefly manufactured goods." She compares Canada's approach to the country's interactions with Norway. Canada would export nickel ore to Norway and then buy back "nickel anodes, cathodes, ingots and rods, more than $100 million worth in 1979." Free trade enabled Canada to purchase what it needed from international sellers with ultra-low or no tariffs, and in exchange, its trade partners were eager to buy Canada's timber, precious metals, heavy metals, and oil and tar. With free trade, Canada had even less of a reason to develop its own processing industries (and the jobs and community benefits created as a result), cementing our role as a country that mines and exports, rather than one that develops and innovates.

But there was always a limit to trading goods. Even if Canada developed an innovation industry that started producing things like never before, there would only ever be so many things to trade. And so free trade agreements started to include services as well. During the 1980s, corporate agitators wanted more access to global markets to include services like banking, accounting, telecommunications, insurance, advertising, and culture and health services. In the 1970s, attempts by an American group to add services to the agenda at GATT meetings failed, as many countries were wary of letting massive U.S. firms into their domestic economies.[5] Because the group, chaired by the chairman of American Express, knew that it needed to take a more creative path to succeed in adding services to international trade agreements, it cooked up a plan to negotiate bilateral agreements for something called "free trade."

In 1984, a first free trade proposal was submitted to legislators in the U.S. With an ideological ally of free trade in the White House, Canada and Israel were chosen. Negotiations for the Canada-U.S. Free Trade Agreement started in 1986. The agreement eliminated tariffs, drastically reduced non-tariff barriers, and included trade in services. As industrialization was starting to slow in Canada, services were growing to become a more significant part of Canada's economy. Allowing services to be captured by free trade gave new international access to industries that had never before been subject to trade policies. More than 80 percent of new jobs created during the 1980s were in the service sector. Now, services could be conceptualized in the same way that one might think of a desk or copper. If services could be captured by free trade, that meant that they could be bought and sold for the lowest price. This scared a lot of Canadians, who were worried that it would be the end of our health and education systems, as the Canadian market would be crowded out by U.S. services. But far more insidious was that services were reconceptualized as something that could be offered for profit, like any other commodity. That logic seeped into all service delivery, whether or not the services were still delivered in a public or not-for-profit setting.

Despite the cheerleading from the business sector, free trade was enormously unpopular, and politicians and business leaders had to work hard to make Canadians feel it was actually good for them. Activists understood that Canada would be controlled more and more by international forces and that politicians could use their lack of power as an excuse for bad public policy or inaction. Groups like the Action Canada Network organized to fight free trade. Murray Dobbin calls the Action Canada Network "amazingly successful, winning the battle for hearts and minds on the [free trade agreement], but ultimately losing the war in the 1988 election."[6] Indeed, the electoral system gave people an outlet to express their political opinions but also ensured that fake majorities were doled out to undeserving governments through the first-past-the-post system. And so, as McQuaig writes, through the free trade agreement, "Washington got the boilerplate of its dreams."[7] For the first time anywhere in the world, services were now fair game for international competition, at a time when state divestment of public services created gaps that corporations were eager to rush into.[8] Everything from education to telecommunications was finally open to American markets, subject to a free trade pact that allowed companies to move more easily across the Canada-U.S. border. No doubt looked upon by four very smiling, perhaps even laughing, Irish eyes.

On January 1, 1989, the first Canada-U.S. free trade agreement came into force, heralding a new era of neoliberal supremacy. The GST came into effect shortly thereafter, reducing how much money the federal government would receive in business taxes. The GST replaced a 13.5 percent manufacturers' tax that had been built into the cost of goods with an added-on goods and sales tax of just 7 percent.[9] By the end of 1991, unemployment reached 10.3 percent, though that number didn't count those who had given up looking for work or had begrudgingly accepted part-time work. In a 1992 article called "The Lunacy of Free Trade," researcher Marjorie Griffin Cohen writes that unemployment was probably closer to 16 percent. Free trade changed everything about the Canadian economy, and, importantly, it came of age alongside a shift in how business leaders were oriented toward the United States. Whereas capitalists had originally favoured bolstering the Canadian domestic market, the corporate world was more or less in support of new free trade deals with the U.S. and eventually with Mexico.[10] Free trade laid the foundation to kick resource extraction into even higher gear; exporting unprocessed resources became an economic strategy at a time when manufacturing was taking a dive. Cohen argues, "What Canada needed was an economic policy which focused on processing resources within the country" but "free trade ... has accentuated the structural problems of the economy and has greatly weakened the ability of future governments to pursue more integrative and stimulative economic policies."[11]

And indeed, that was a likely goal of these agreements. From being the first agreement in the world to include services, to leveraging the unique trading relationship between the U.S. and Canada, to dropping into the world a new kind of trade regime, the impacts of free trade went way beyond whether or not a Canadian company like Rogers would be elbowed out of the way by an American company like Verizon. In fact, if free trade had worked according to the way its proponents sold it, our telecommunications market would probably be much more competitive, rather than leaving Canadians with some of the highest cellphone bills in the world. But back in the early 1990s, this reality was impossible to guess. A page had been turned and a new era had begun.

Many people who had warned that free trade agreements would open the market to for-profit American providers were proven right, to a certain extent. Canada wasn't sold off wholesale, the way critics worried it would be. After all, Canadian corporations wanted free trade as badly as anyone else, though not at the expense of their own market shares. But what those critics didn't fully see was that the threat to Canadians wasn't foreign; it was domestic. As politicians hacked away at the social safety net and shifted the labour market toward a lower-paid, low-job-security, service-centred economy, free trade was both an ideological frame that politicians could grind into Canadians' brains and a garden of fertile opportunities for businesses. Businesses could fill service holes left by austerity measures, further eroding the social safety net. Even better, they could make good money while doing it. The downward spiral meant that every single cut to provincial budgets, social services, or personal supports created a business opportunity not just for Canadian businesses, but for American businesses, too.

The collusion between free trade and austerity drove many Canadians into poverty. Where the poorest 20 percent of households had increased their share of income in the 1980s, in the 1990s income fell sharply for low- and medium-income households. In Nova Scotia, the wealthiest 20 percent did better after free trade, while the remaining 80 percent were worse off. Was this because of free trade specifically? It would be impossible to assert this without a doubt, but no studies have been able to clearly demonstrate that middle- and low-income Canadians benefitted from free trade. Instead, what is clear is that, between recessions and job losses, and with an increase in atypical and low-waged work, there were tremendous impacts on the overall wealth of the working class. This, combined with defunding social programs, created the perfect storm for poverty to rise and people to find themselves in increasingly precarious positions.

Brian Mulroney may have set the transformation of Canada in motion, but he certainly didn't succeed in reining in the government's debt. In 1995, the debt stood at $546 billion, and 46 percent of it was held by foreign creditors.[12] In 1996, household debt approached 100 percent of household income and then blew past that amount as Canadians more frequently relied on loans to pay for their daily expenses.[13] Household debt was rising steadily throughout the early 1990s, and in the middle of that decade a nuclear bomb would be dropped that would entrench this trend, accomplished with such stealth that there was barely even opposition to it.

The Conservatives set this stage, but it wasn't Conservative politicians who made free trade Canada's status quo. The arc of Mulroney's political tenure was coming down from the record high of his win in 1984 to his party's similarly record-breaking loss in 1993. It was the Liberals, and their charismatic, career-politician leader, Jean Chrétien, who won an election promising to end free trade and then entrenched the new status quo.

The Chrétien-Martin Years

On April 7, 2023, Sébastien Houle, a journalist with Trois-Rivières' newspaper *Le Nouvelliste*, sat down with Jean Chrétien to look back at his sixty-year political career. A month away from his ninetieth birthday, the former prime minister reflected on his life in politics. Chrétien, the eighteenth child of nineteen from Belgoville, near Shawinigan, had run in and won twelve elections. He was first elected in 1963, and his ascent to the Prime Minister's Office started in 1990, when he beat Paul Martin Jr. to become leader of the Liberal Party. Ultimately, as prime minister, Chrétien did not mimic the politics that had characterized the last Liberal mandate (that of Trudeau *père*), but instead continued along the path that had been forged by Brian Mulroney.

The central moment for Jean Chrétien's tenure as PM was his 1995 budget. Printed in greyscale with a fancy-for-clip-art image of a maple leaf on its cover (it had shadows that made the leaf look 3-D!), it was replete with typed marginalia that read like a meandering Marshall McLuhan book quoting James Joyce: "We are acting on a new vision of the role of government ... smaller government ... smarter government." Minister of Finance Paul Martin Jr. delivered the speech on February 27, 1995. While Chrétien and Mulroney both came from modest families and small Quebec towns that had economies rooted in natural resource development, Martin's father owned Canada Steamship Lines and had been a member of the federal Cabinet. Martin *fils* was the perfect pick to deliver this historic budget, which protected the wealthy and turned the screws on the poor. Two years after he lost the leadership election to Chrétien, he was holding the bag — 20 percent cut from Canada's federal spending — in the most transformative budget in the postwar period.

Maclean's writer Anthony Wilson-Smith called the budget "the Liberals' first real attempt to deal with those issues since they came to power." What issues was he referring to? "How to remake an already-fragile Canada without fracturing it." They *knew* it was fragile. The Progressive Conservatives had collapsed in part due to the fractioning of Quebec supporters into the Bloc Québécois and activists from the western provinces flocking to the upstart Reform Party. The second referendum for Quebec sovereignty would take place in October 1995. Free trade's impacts were being felt. In

Canada's "already fragile" state, what did the Liberals believe needed to be done?

Martin didn't mince words. Canada is being tested, he said in the first ten seconds of the budget speech. "Our resolve, our values, our very way of life as Canadians are being tested," he proclaimed. Answering this test, he foretold his plan: "We can take the path — too well-trodden — of minimal change, of least resistance, of leadership lost. Or we can set out on a new road of fundamental reform, of renewal — of hope restored. Today, we have made our choice. Today, we take action."

Take the path of leadership lost? Poetry, kind of, but meaningless, so not exactly beautiful.

He was right though; they took action. They shrank the federal civil service by 45,000 jobs, primarily jobs that coordinated and administered federal programs and ensured that people were employed, had salaries, and could buy things like mortgages and cars. The budget included $25 billion in spending cuts to pensions, unemployment insurance, and arts and culture supports. Grain subsidies were slashed by $2.6 billion. Cuts to unemployment insurance, said Martin, would save taxpayers $700 million and reduced the number of people eligible for supports: just 30 percent of people who lost their jobs would qualify under the reformed program. This was a drop from 80 percent before 1995.[14] Wilson-Smith wisely notes that the impact of these cuts would take a while to bear out: "Over time, welfare programs, which are run by the provinces, will inevitably be reduced because the federal government is also cutting the amount of money it gives the provinces to help finance the program." Chrétien even hinted on CBC Radio that they might open the Canada Health Act to "eliminate guarantees of coverage for a number of medical services that now are offered for free."

The Chrétien-Martin budget embodied the technocratic obsession with deficits and debt that underpinned neoliberal ideology.

The first promises, indeed the first full ten pages of the budget speech, were focused on the debt, the deficit, structural adjustment, and program spending. The budget didn't comment on the things that programs do or on the people who rely on those programs or on the people who administer them. It was all about reducing the size of the government's budget. They promised to reduce government spending by $29 billion and reduce spending on social programs by just over $12 billion (or approximately $51.5 billion and $23 billion in 2023 dollars, respectively). Martin bragged that program spending would be lower in 1996–97 than at any time since 1951, when Canada's social safety net barely existed and there were 15 million fewer Canadians. The budget literally pulled money out of people's salaries and services — $5.5 billion to be exact — and transferred it to international banking institutions by way of financing the debt, robbing Peter to pay Paul (except here Peter is a guy who was just laid off of his factory job and Paul is a bank executive in the U.K.). Wilson-Smith writes, "The pleasure, not surprisingly, was most evident abroad, where international moneylenders reacted to the tough measures with satisfaction that translated into a slight rise in the value of the Canadian dollar — which ended the week at 71.09 cents (U.S.) — and a slight fall in interest rates."

There were other changes, too: they created a $975 fee to immigrate to Canada. But don't worry, promised Martin, anyone who couldn't pay the fee could get a loan. They cut $500 from Atlantic freight subsidies, which they said would actually improve transportation in eastern Canada, and then also promised to "modernize" highways in eastern Quebec and Atlantic Canada. The budget promised to sell the government's shares in Cameco and Canadian National, as well as the remaining 70 percent share in Petro-Canada. They also announced commercializing the Air Navigation System, which oversees commercial flight in Canada. And Martin promised that this was just the beginning — more privatization was on the table. Where Canada had had a national rail line, a national gas company, a joint-venture public uranium company, and an agency to manage air traffic, within a decade these would all be privatized and Canadians would be subject to the whims of the market, whether that meant watching air service out of Saskatoon vanish, watching the cost of gas go up as profits were paid out, or sitting on a GO Train waiting for a cargo train to pass by because the private rail operators have priority over the quasi-public operators of southern Ontario's commuter trains.

And finally, probably the most profound and fundamental promise made in that budget was to radically change how the federal government transferred money to the provinces. Whereas Brian Mulroney had looked at transfer payments and decided to lower the annual increases that funded them, Martin's approach was far more radical. Under the guise of allowing provinces the flexibility to innovate, Martin announced that his government would collapse the three envelopes of funding that Ottawa sent to the provinces into one. The Canada Assistance Plan, which existed to split the cost of social program administration between the provinces and federal government, was brought into the same transfer as health and post-secondary education to create the massive Canada Social Transfer. In so doing, they abolished a universal welfare program that had been in place since 1966.[15] Against the backdrop of a campaign gaining strength for Quebec to declare sovereignty from Canada, Martin explained that the federal transfers to the provinces had "a lot of unnecessary strings attached." To ensure that provinces still spent the money where it needed to be spent, the government would set national goals and expect the provinces to meet them. Martin announced that provinces must provide services to people with minimal provincial residency requirements and that the minister of human resources development would develop new "shared principles and objectives" for the Canada Social Transfer. It justified austerity in every province while at the same time downloading more expectations on the provinces.

This absolved the federal government from its direct responsibility to ensure that program spending was equitable and stable from region to region. Equalization payments, which Martin maintained, became the most significant hammer in the government's tool box when giving provinces the money needed to deliver services of equal quality. This "equalization" would be at the whim of the economy, and how well a province did in a particular year, confirmed through annual tax revenue, determined which provinces were haves and which were have nots. The budget also reduced the transfer by $4.5 billion and froze the transfer amount until 1996–97.

In 1991, Maude Barlow and Bruce Campbell wrote that financial inequities in Canada profoundly impact service delivery: "Newfoundland spent twice as much, relative to GDP, as Alberta to maintain a similar level of health care even before the Tories started to slash. It has now begun to cut back hospital beds and health-care staff."[16] Now, with the changes to these transfer payments, Newfoundland and Labrador would get more funding through equalization by dint of the fact there is less provincial wealth and not, say, because the province's tiny population lives on an island, making healthcare more costly to deliver. Yukon and the Northwest Territories had their transfers frozen at 1994–95 levels, which forced them to reduce the core expenditure amount by 10 percent.

The Liberals also formally got out of building social housing. From 1994 until 2004, the number of social housing units built by the federal government dropped to a tiny fraction of what it had been between 1966 and 1992. With the Canada Mortgage and Housing Corporation (CMHC), the banks, and the real estate sector, Canada's social housing planning shifted its priorities from including social housing builds directly funded and coordinated by government to incentivizing home ownership. People were encouraged to purchase cheap mortgages so that more of them could own their homes. The impact of this has been devastating, as some people win the lottery by selling homes they purchased for nearly nothing two decades ago while others are fully shut out of the housing market, with very few public housing options available to them.[17]

Paul Martin Jr. oversaw the deepest cuts to the Canadian state in the postwar period. Even Conrad Black called cuts made by Chrétien, Martin, and Stephen Harper "exemplary, if not slightly fetishistic."[18] It's no wonder that by the late 1990s, the federal government was finally turning out surpluses. The logic of the market, that everything needed to be done as cheaply as possible, had moved from free trade into government services. But despite their annual surpluses, the Liberals continued to divest money from the state. Polling showed that a majority of Canadians wanted to see surpluses reinvested in social spending, but that didn't matter; the Liberals knew in whose interest they governed. In 2000, Chrétien's government announced more than $100 billion in tax cuts. Like tax cuts made consistently since the mid-1980s, these favoured the wealthiest Canadians and made more changes that benefitted people who earned income from capital gains and stock options.[19]

The Fallout

Many Canadians take pride in the fact that our calm, even boring approach to radical change is measured. Not like the Americans. Not like *over there*. The promise in Canada's constitution of "peace, order, and good government" highlights one of the country's most fundamental beliefs: that peaceful, orderly, good governance is the best way to do anything. Revolutions are quiet. Radical reforms percolate through the peace, order, and good governance machine, easily passing under the guise of the normal operation of things. And so it should surprise no one that Canada created a crisis — its own "shock doctrine," to use Naomi Klein's theory — delivered by a man whom the press called "Mr. Dithers," a man whose "umms" and "ahhs" every eight seconds helped me learned how to edit the "umms" and "ahhs" out of someone's speech when I was in radio class in university. My podcast audience thanks you for that, Mr. Martin.

Consider this comment from David Frum, Canadian ex-pat, key ideological force within the Bush administration, and coiner of the term "axis of evil." In March 1995, in a forum published by *Harper's Magazine*, he said this: "Instead of cutting incrementally — a little here, a little there — I would say that on a single day this summer we eliminate three hundred programs, each one costing a billion dollars or less. Maybe these cuts won't make a big deal of difference, but, boy, do they make a point. And you can do them right away." The Chrétien-Martin budget had just dropped. Was Frum paying attention to the land of his birth? Or was he simply on the same page as the Liberals to the north?

While she doesn't mention Chrétien or Martin, Naomi Klein does briefly mention Canada's 1995 budget in her book *The Shock Doctrine*. She uses it to illustrate how corporate leaders manufactured the fury around the debt crisis, hoping that it could be used to justify a budget that Canadians would not normally accept. She cites the work of Linda McQuaig, who uncovered the fact that Canada's debt crisis was triggered mostly by interest rates set by the Bank of Canada. But thanks to a coordinated campaign by the C.D. Howe Institute and the Fraser Institute that aggressively pushed the line about Canada's "debt crisis" among journalists and within society in general, a full-blown crisis emerged in the minds of many Canadians. McQuaig interviewed Vincent Truglia, the senior analyst whose job it was to give Canada its credit rating for Moody's. He said "that he had come under constant pressure from Canadian corporate executives and bankers to issue damning reports about the country's finances, something he refused to do because he considered Canada an excellent, stable investment."[20] In 1993, the year the Liberals came to power, Canadians were in the tail end of a recession. Looking back in 2001, then governor of the Bank of Canada Gordon Thiessen said this in a speech to the Canadian Club of Toronto: "By the early 1990s, the realities of the new world economic order were becoming clearer to Canadian companies too. Only at that time, they were also coping with the fallout from the high-inflation years, especially the sharp drop in the prices of speculative investments and the burden of servicing large debts, as well as with declining world commodity prices." So what was the solution?

> Just as I believe that the restructuring in our private sector in the 1990s was impressive, I also think that Canadian governments (federal and provincial) responded forcefully and effectively in the mid-1990s to the need to cut fiscal deficits and slow down the accumulation of public sector debt. The overall government sector moved from a total deficit of close to $45 billion or 6 per cent of gross domestic product (GDP) in 1995, to a balanced position in 1997 and 1998, and to surpluses thereafter. Moreover, net public debt as a ratio of GDP fell from close to 104 per cent in the fiscal year 1995/96 to an estimated 80 per cent in 1999/2000. That is some adjustment!

And then coolly he added, "Overall, given the type and size of structural changes that had to be made, it is not surprising that, for much of the 1990s, unemployment rates in Canada remained high and incomes stagnated."

The reflection of Canada's former top banker reveals how bankers and business people saw the role of the Canadian state: it is not a body that exists primarily to help Canadians. Despite the fact that it is paid for by these same Canadians, the state is first in the service of capital. Canada had always had a cozy relationship with its corporations, but it wasn't until the 1990s that corporate capture of the postwar political space was complete. Corporations ran the show. They even, said Truglia, lobbied Moody's to downgrade Canada's rating: "It's the only country that I handle where, usually, nationals from that country want the country downgraded even more — on a regular basis. They think it's rated too highly."[21] Of course they do. When the misery of millions of Canadians can be reduced to "unemployment rates in Canada remained high and incomes stagnated," without actually describing what being forced into unemployment and managing with a stagnant income does to a person, a family, or a community, it's already clear on whose side the speaker finds himself.

The fallout from the 1995 Chrétien-Martin budget was immense. It impacted subsequent federal budgets and created shockwaves among the provinces. And those shockwaves created new, mini-shock-doctrine-esque "crises" in each province, exploited by politicians of all parties.

Fight Back?

One of the reasons why the 1995 budget was so effective was because it was perfectly timed and faced minimal protest. The budget dropped at the end of February 1995. Left-wing movements had been hyperfocused on free trade for years, and the Liberal decision to go ahead with free trade was deeply demoralizing. By the time 1995 rolled around, people were burnt-out. It wasn't just movements; there was barely any opposition mounted by the opposition NDP either. Wilson-Smith writes, "The only substantive criticism of the budget nationally came from the Reform Party — which called the budget 'cowardly' because it did not contain even tougher measures. That made it easier for the Liberals, even as they presented the toughest budget of any federal government in recent history, to present themselves as kinder, gentler cost-cutters." Some politicians, like Mike Harris, were shrewd in their response; Harris was able to use this budget to justify his own austerity program, the Common Sense Revolution.

It wasn't just that protesters were exhausted. During the 1990s, funding to special interest groups dried up. In the budget speech, Martin promised to cut what he called "interest group funding." Groups who could receive private funding could become eligible for matched public funding, but for others, "while they undoubtedly serve a worthy purpose, continued funding will not be possible due to our financial situation." This was part of a broader shift to defund social aid organizations and force them to chase project funding through individual grants, something that killed activism, especially activism against the state, in many movements.

Just a few weeks before the 1995 budget dropped, university and college students took to the streets of English Canada to hold the biggest protest in the history of English Canada's student movement. One hundred thousand students walked out of classes all across the country to oppose income-contingent student loans. These loan schemes entrenched inequality between students who could afford to pay their tuition fees in cash and students who needed to take out loans. At the same time, protests against cuts to social assistance were "larger than at any time since the Vietnam War," according to Seth Klein. In 1996, he wrote that throughout 1994, as a parliamentary committee toured Canada to hear from people about proposed cuts to social programs, "the hearings were dogged by protests; student, community and labour activists ... disrupted the proceedings in at least three cities."[22]

Alongside activists, religious leaders were also protesting the feds. Seth Klein quotes a public letter that Christian, Jewish, and Muslim religious leaders wrote to Chrétien a few weeks before the

1995 budget, saying that they had "a deep and growing concern with the current framework of the debate. In the midst of such an affluent society, the fundamental question is not how to cut our financial support for these … programs to reduce the deficit but rather how can we fulfill our responsibility to our neighbours in need through strengthened support of these programs."[23]

Dobbin wrote that once the budget was passed, there was little done to try to stop the inertia: "Most of the traditional social movement organizations are now moribund, their activists demoralized by governments' refusal to engage on policy issues, and their outmoded strategic approach in need of fundamental change."[24] Just as it had been true in the 1930s and 1940s, left-wing movements were critical to forcing governments to adopt people-centric policies. Looking back on the 1990s from 2015, Dobbin saw how badly damaged that decade left social movements and social movement organizing.

Charities and not-for-profits were especially harmed as a result of undoing the welfare state. As the groups who dealt directly with people who needed various services, many were best placed to see the impact these cuts had on average people. Thus, many of the loudest advocates for these people worked within the voluntary sector. But the combination of social cuts and the growing service demand on the voluntary sector rendered many activists incapable of being able to mount an effective fight against government cuts.[25] People were too busy dealing with the front-line impacts from social services cuts to put their energy into building the kind of fight that could have taken on federal politicians. The women's movement is a prime example of this: movement activists were expected to do more and more front-line service work, like helping people fleeing violence, accessing reproductive health services, navigating child services, delivering childcare services, and so on. As a result, they lost the capacity to build the kind of movements that had been able to influence power during the 1970s and 1980s. They just didn't have the time or the resources. The changes to funding in the voluntary sector were also intended to overload activists with the side effects of government cuts and then watch the most talented and creative activists dedicate their time to helping people find ways around systemic barriers, rather than organize to remove the barriers themselves. Neoliberalism doesn't just transform government and business; it also transforms activism and our relationships to one another.

These dizzying and compounding factors profoundly disoriented social movement organizers. Social movement structures were incapable of changing strategies to respond to radically differently politics. A solid argument or well-reasoned debate could not convince a politician owned by the corporate world to change his mind. Power was consolidating, parties were coalescing with less and less difference between their policies, and politics became poisoned by highly technocratic language that disenfranchised a lot of people.

The 1995 budget transformed popular understandings of federal fiscal policy by changing the very definition of a budget from something that funds services to an accounting exercise driven by foreign financial institutions, free trade, domestic banks, and corporate leaders. No more was the goal to save people from the shocks of unfettered capitalism. Now, government's principal reason to exist was to balance the books. It became harder for average people to understand the budget. They had to understand international finance, credit ratings, deficit budgeting, interest rates, and other highly technical concepts to be able to effectively intervene in the debate. They instead heard this refrain: if we don't get the deficit down, the cuts will go even deeper. The approach, at its most basic, made sense. But was this really what was happening?

In a technical paper written in 2010, economist Hugh Mackenzie pointed out that deficits are normal in years that follow a recession and that after every recession in Ontario since the mid-1980s, the deficit worked itself out as economic activity grew stronger, without a need to spend money specifically to reduce it. The same thing was apparent in the United States in the 1990s. He noted that the primary reason Canada balanced its books after 1995 was not because of Martin's deep spending cuts, but rather because GDP growth and interest rate reductions in the years that followed were strong.[26] With the 1995 budget and subsequent budgets focusing on technical promises like deficit reduction, left-wing researchers, often working in the orbit of the Canadian Centre for Policy Alternatives, found a new reason to exist: to cut through the bullshit.

Mulroney could take credit for the 1995 Liberal budget; his reforms a decade earlier made this budget possible. And Mulroney himself saw free trade as the gateway drug to the rest of the social reforms his government and his party supported. They didn't need to just win votes; they needed to shift how people understood politics, how they understood the role of the state, and what things they gave value to. In 2000 Mulroney explained it like this: "And so what began as a free trade agreement has wound up shaping attitudes, not only of my government and my party and people on the right, but it has forced the Liberals into a completely new set of policies which they adopted from us."[27] While Mulroney might be accused of overstating the influence he had on the politics of his longtime political opponents, what he said was borne out throughout the 1990s. The Liberals took the Conservative plan, put a kinder spin on it, and implemented cuts that were even more ruthless than those Mulroney was able to achieve.

· · ·

In a 2010 lecture prepared for the Pierre Elliott Trudeau Foundation, former Canadian Centre for Policy Alternatives president Duncan Cameron argued that Canada needed a new vision for how we define progress and economic success. After all, he noted, things that had been tried over the previous three decades hadn't exactly worked. He rattled off this list, citing Andrew Sharpe:

> inflation targeting (1991); zero-deficit philosophy and policy (mid-1990s); federal debt-to-GDP ratio target of 25 per cent over 10 years (1994); plans to hold program spending to below economic growth (on-going); Canada-U.S. Free Trade Agreement (1989), North American Free Trade Agreement (1994); Foreign Investment Review Agency (1985) replaced by investor-friendly Investment Canada (later merged into Industry Canada); federal privatization of Crown corporations, including CN, Petro-Canada, Nav Canada, Air Canada, Telesat, De Havilland, and Canadair; deregulation, including air transport, electricity, road transport, and telecommunications; Goods and Services Tax (GST) replaces the Manufacturers' Sales Tax (1991); reductions in the statutory federal corporate tax rate from 37.8 per cent in 1980 to 19.5 per cent in 2008, to go down to 15 per cent; reduced direct research and development performed by government; attempts to eliminate inter-provincial barriers to the movement of goods and people; labour-law regime that discourages unionization in emerging sectors, resulting in a significant decline in private sector union density.[28]

Politicians argued every time that each of these measures was intended to boost productivity, supposedly key to ensuring economic security for Canadians. But that was the greatest deception; as these reforms worked their way through the system, inequality rose, productivity never significantly increased, and Canadians today are worse off. The neoliberal experiments that started in the 1980s and kicked into overdrive in the 1990s did not achieve what Canadians were told they would achieve. But annual record profits suggest that these neoliberal experiments did achieve something big: a corporate takeover of Canada's democratic institutions was complete and public policies today serve businesses before they serve people. Unsurprisingly, the social safety net is now bent toward serving the corporate world, ensuring that people are kept at the right amount of desperate to agree to terrible working conditions.

To celebrate the twenty-fifth anniversary of the 1995 Liberal budget, the right-wing Fraser Institute published essays that reflected on that budget and how it echoed throughout the years. This was the victor celebrating the victory. It was 2020 and the essay series was launched on February 27 — twenty-five years to the day that the budget was released. It perhaps flew under the radar, thanks to national focus on an emerging virus — Quebec's first Covid-19 case was recorded on February 27, and two days later, the United States announced the first of what would eventually be nearly 1.2 million Covid-19 deaths. It was funny timing to celebrate the 1995 budget, considering how cuts from twenty-five years earlier had chipped away at provincial healthcare systems that, by the time we needed them to be robust and well-funded — well, they had collapsed. William Watson, writing to mark the Fraser Institute's anniversary series, offered *National Post* readers a version of history that, at one time, was solely the domain of the far right, but today is squarely mainstream:

> The question the current generation of Canadians
> now faces is whether deliberately departing from

the 1995–2015 political consensus favouring balanced federal budgets threatens a return to the potentially unstable debt dynamics of 1975–1995. The philosopher George Santayana famously said that those who cannot remember the past are condemned to repeat it. Strictly, it doesn't follow that those who do remember the past aren't also similarly condemned, but a good understanding of what did happen 25 and more years ago certainly cannot hurt. To that end, the papers in the Fraser Institute's new publication, which is available free online, make for socially instructive reading. It would be good if Finance Minister Bill Morneau downloaded a copy.

Whether or not Morneau downloaded a copy doesn't really matter. Just a few weeks later, he was overseeing the creation of the biggest social programs in a generation through the Canada Emergency Wage Subsidy (CEWS) and the Canada Emergency Response Benefit (CERB) — both programs that funnelled public money into private pockets, using the pandemic to boost the profits of some of Canada's biggest corporations. Morneau found a means that Martin couldn't have dreamed of: give people peanuts to fight over while the banks, telecommunications, grocery, and resource extraction industries make profits beyond their wildest dreams.

There was no similar essay series coordinated by the people who opposed the 1995 budget. There were no commemorations, funerals, dirges, or analyses. The will to fight back, to organize, to protest, collapsed under the weight of social services that could not provide service. In the twenty-five years since the 1995 budget, politics has grown bolder and corporations stronger. This was their victory — not ours.

CHAPTER 5

Provincial and Territorial Austerity Trends

During the transformation of social programs under neoliberalism and behind the politicking of Ottawa were ten provinces, two territories, hundreds of municipalities, and tens of millions of people who relied on programs supported by federal dollars. This federal money helped pay for everything from repaving highways to giving people access to a family doctor, from child welfare services to disability supports, from education at all levels to front-line service offices. Long gone were the days when paving highways was work that benevolent societies used the undeserving poor to do, paying them a poor day's wage in the process. The Canadian federation had matured.

While the territories and provinces are independent of the federal government, they all operate using the same neoliberal rationale. So while there are disagreements and squabbles, especially over limited resources, there have rarely been ideological clashes. Leaders tend, at minimum, to agree on basic principles: taxes are too high, government may or may not be too big but it certainly could be made to be more efficient, the deficit is public enemy number one, and the best path out of poverty is a job.

Indeed, while we were more than a century away from colonial "deserving poor" moralities, the same kind of proselytizing was repackaged in a modern neoliberal framework. Where there were disagreements, they were usually between ruthless right-wing politicians who didn't care if people couldn't afford to live and politicians who understood that it might look bad if they didn't at least appear to be helping people. It was the difference between a Ralph Klein, drunk and throwing change at people within a homeless shelter, and a Dalton McGuinty, smiling and announcing that they just had no other choice than to jack tuition fees up by 5 percent.

"At the end of the 1990s," the magazine *L'actualité* declares, "the obsession with *déficit zéro* [had] invaded the entire country."[1] *Déficit zéro* is what Quebecers called the obsession with balanced (or zero-deficit) budgets. By then, prioritizing deficits over services, markets over society, and corporations over people was just as pernicious at the provincial level as it was at the federal. *Déficit zéro* was brought to Quebec by former Mulroney Cabinet minister Lucien Bouchard later than it came to other provinces. The 1995 Chrétien-Martin budget changed Canada, and provinces responded to the downward pressure on their budgets by defunding social services and throwing the money at their own deficits or debts. Healthcare was especially battered by these funding cuts, the results of which are felt in every province and territory, in every hospital and doctor's office, to this day.

Provincial-Federal Relations

Provincial powers are enshrined in Canada's constitution, a document that never conceived of, and therefore didn't plan for, the sophisticated health and social systems that have evolved. Nor did the constitution anticipate the borderless reality of internet-reliant existence or free trade. Therefore, while broad powers like taxation or education are considered either federal or provincial responsibilities in the constitution, many responsibilities are determined not by the constitution itself, but instead through negotiations, changing attitudes, political needs, and the demands of the electorate. Federal-provincial relations have changed dramatically since 1867; the most important roles given to the federal government are now overshadowed by provincial responsibilities that have grown to be dominant forces in Canadians' lives, like healthcare and education.[2]

Federal-provincial relations have shifted over the years. The 1950s and 1960s were the era of co-operative federalism. The federal government often had willing allies at the provincial level when creating large, new national programs.[3] But as provinces matured during the 1970s and started to diverge from the political orientations and aspirations of the federal government, the relationship became more strained. The co-operative federalism era was replaced by an era that political scientists call executive federalism. Executive federalism brought provincial-federal relations into the public, and negotiations among political leaders happened more frequently in public. Conferences were held where first ministers or premiers of each province and territory would meet with the federal government and plans were hashed out accordingly. Provinces' capacities and aspirations to create their own programs grew. Quebec led the pack with the most ambitious projects of any province, designed to literally create a new nation state. Starting in the 1960s and fuelled by the Quiet Revolution, Quebec's government implemented reforms that were closely aligned to Keynesian philosophy, including founding many *sociétés d'état*, or state companies, a less eloquent but more independent way of referring to Crown corporations. The most important would be the *Caisse de dépôt et placement du Québec*, a state-run investment firm that today remains one of the most important financial institutions in the province.

During the era of executive federalism, tensions rose between the provinces and the federal government, and the relationship became politicized in a way that had not been the case before. With the added stress caused by financial crises near the end of the 1970s, provincial leaders found that their governmental capacity had grown such that they could publicly joust with the federal government for political gain. In the 1980s, the politicization of federal-provincial relations became an important part of how politics was done in Canada. Indeed, this politicization became more and more Canada's status quo.

The era of executive federalism came to a head thanks to Pierre Trudeau's leadership style. Trudeau routinely made political decisions without consulting with the provinces. When he created the National Energy Program (NEP) in 1980, he tried to give the federal government more control over resources located in Alberta. But for ten years, provincial leadership had been resisting Ottawa's influence in their affairs. The NEP was a nuclear bomb in Alberta, poisoning the relationship that Albertans and their government had with Ottawa. It didn't help that Trudeau only had two MPs in his government from west of Ontario. The Trudeau Liberals repatriated the constitution unilaterally, without first securing the participation and support of the provinces, and changed federal transfer payment financing without consulting the provinces. The federal government also shifted to deliver some programs directly. To heighten its visibility in service provision, it created more regional programs directly financed by the federal government, it strengthened regional representation in the Senate, and, by creating the Canada Health Act, it established national standards that provinces would be expected to adhere to or else be sanctioned.[4] What became understood as "political strings" — federal guarantees that the provinces wanted eliminated so they could put federal money into their own programs — were critical to the federal government's nation-building project. For Trudeau, that's what his last term was about: large national programs and initiatives to create a strong, unified country under the political hand of Ottawa. The provinces grew increasingly restless with this approach, so when Mulroney was elected, he was handed a Canadian federation with badly damaged provincial relationships. Mulroney's commitment to reconciliation, as stated in his first Speech from the Throne (again, not the reconciliation you're thinking of), meant that he would work to better manage conflicts with the provinces. And he had something that Trudeau's previous government didn't have: national representation. In his 1984 Throne Speech, Mulroney reminded Canadians that, unlike with the previous government, "all regions of the country are represented in a national government." National reconciliation was so important to Mulroney that it was the first issue he spoke about in that speech. He saw an opportunity in the growing frustration with Ottawa. He could transform federal-provincial relationships, even improve them, by cutting government spending in the name of harmony: "My government's management of federal-provincial relations will pursue three basic objectives: to harmonize policies of our two orders of government, to ensure respect for their jurisdictions, and to end unnecessary and costly duplication."

The federal government was the body that had the power to raise the money needed to pay for massive social programs, so every cut to provincial transfers impacted services. Talk of harmonization and duplication usually just meant that money would be reduced from one pocket and would need to be increased from another. As the federal government pulled back on its spending, provinces resisted federal influence in their programs.[5] This created what is today the greatest sport in contemporary Canadian politics: passing the buck. Provinces can always use the excuse that the federal government isn't supporting them enough, and the federal government can always use the excuse that the provinces are spending their money inefficiently or improperly. Every single closed emergency room, shuttered school, classroom with thirty-two kids, or form of disability support that forces people into poverty can be traced to these tensions that were fomented at the end of the 1980s and into the 1990s. It's good politics to pass the blame on to someone else. And the foundation of this strategy goes back to anti-tax politicians at the provincial, territorial, and federal levels defunding the state so that businesses could rush in and "save" failing social programs.

Provincial Neoliberalism

At first, neoliberalism wasn't forced onto the provinces by an emerging neoliberal federal government. It grew in the provinces in the same way that it grew in federal politics, and it similarly started with neoconservativism. Neoconservatives were rooted in many parts of Canada, and many politicians openly expressed neoconservative ideology. Just as the marriage of neoconservatism with softer liberal ideology proved to be an explosive combination for Western nations like Canada, the same was true for the provinces and territories. The only difference was that their budgets were smaller, their services touched people more directly, their contracts were slightly less lucrative, and they had to compete with eleven other jurisdictions if they were going to elbow their way to the top of the ladder in Canada.

Among the provinces and territories, neoliberalism as a hegemonic political force emerged first in western Canada. In Alberta, the oil price shocks and corresponding recessions of the 1980s gave Conservative governments the excuse to play around with neoliberalism even before it was introduced in federal programs. The 1981 recession was felt worse in Alberta than anywhere else in Canada. The province's overreliance on oil meant that there was little else to insulate the province's economy from the shockwaves of that recession if prices dropped (sound familiar?). Whereas the 1995

Chrétien-Martin budget needed to create a crisis for its deep cuts to be accepted (more or less), Alberta had a full-blown economic crisis. The demand for Alberta's oil dried up, triggering thousands of layoffs, bankruptcies, and business closures; falling real estate values; and an exodus of people. Oil companies were leaving the province, posing not just a direct threat to the economy but also an existential crisis for Albertans who identified themselves as oil people.

The government had two paths forward. One was to strengthen Alberta's social safety net and adapt its economy by diversifying it. But they did not do this. Instead, as if the oil itself was under threat, the government bailed out oil companies through tax cuts and through a program for the industry that cost the government $5.4 billion (approximately $17.4 billion in 2023 dollars). They even tried to entice Shell to embark on a new tar sands project that would have cost $14 billion (approximately $45.3 billion in 2023 dollars), with half of the cost covered by the governments of Alberta and Canada, but that project didn't go through. By 1987, unemployment in Edmonton had reached 11.1 percent and, of 521,205 residents, 24,000 were accessing welfare and food banks.[6]

The Alberta government had the money to keep Edmontonians from having to access food banks or to soften the blow of the economic downtown. It just didn't want to use money in that way. In 1982, premier Peter Lougheed gave corporations a tax and royalty break to the tune of $1.6 billion over three years (approximately $5.1 billion in 2023 dollars). Winston Gereluk, in his history of working people in Alberta, writes, "The annual report of the provincial Auditor General found that in the fiscal year that ended 31 March 1983, Alberta's corporate sector received $162 million more from Alberta taxpayers than it paid in taxes, royalties, and fees." By 1984, 1,400 workers had been laid off from government jobs. By 1986, Alberta had its first deficit, and to pay it down program spending was slashed by 6.3 percent, impacting schools, hospitals, and municipalities. Public liquor workers were laid off, provincial institutions like technical institutes and mental health hospitals were defunded, and services were contracted out and privatized. And despite the cuts, the deficit continued to grow. But people fought back; during this period, unions in Alberta responded with radical action and mass rallies, a level of activism that has perhaps never been seen since.

The path forged by Alberta soon became the norm for the rest of Canada. Austerity and bailing out the corporate sector while average people starve became the standard reaction to any crisis in every part of Canada. The useful part of the strategy of starving people to feed corporations is that it created feedback loops where this approach wasn't just preferred, it became necessary. The more that the state was defunded, the more that private operators swooped into help fund social services, whether through privatized, for-profit services or through innovations like volunteer-reliant food banks, and the economy came to rely on them more and more. And in times of crisis, the government *had* to bail out the corporations; otherwise whatever social services they did offer would vanish over-night as unprofitable. Neoliberal solutions gradually became com-mon sense, and anyone who called for markets to be decentralized or to organize differently to resist corporate power was derided and marginalized by people in power as promoting fantasy thinking or, using that infamous accusation, communism.

Ontario started the 1980s in a similar spot to Alberta but di-verged in the mid-1980s, thanks to a coalition government of the Liberals and the NDP. In 1975, Ontario's long-tenured Conservative government created a spending review program that included busi-ness people but no labour or social policy representatives. It con-cluded that spending on social programs was "out of control and threatened the economic future of Ontario."[7] Spending was cut just in time for the 1980 recession, which of course triggered a sharp rise in poverty rates. In addition to higher than normal unemployment, Ontario had an increase in child poverty, as did Edmonton at that time. Forty-two percent of those living in poverty were children. In 1986, the province restored funding for social assistance programs nearly fully to inflation-adjusted rates from between 1975 and 1981.[8] After a 1985 spring election gave the Conservatives a shaky minority of just four seats, that government didn't survive a confidence motion. A few weeks later, the Liberals emerged as the governing party thanks to a coalition with the NDP. The NDP's support was conditional on several issues and, as a result, the government expanded social assistance eligibility and increased rates to be higher than inflation.[9] In 1987, the Liberals won a majority government and created a program that allowed people receiving social assistance to also earn employment income without having their assistance reduced. However, it wouldn't take very long for these gains to be wiped away by more austerity policies.

The Social Credit government of Bill Bennett in British Columbia also made deep cuts in the early 1980s. Writing in the *Tyee*, labour journalist Rod Mickleburgh calls Bennett's government "a revolution from the right." Bennett himself personified an aggressive mix of neoconservatism and neoliberalism. On July 7, 1983, his government dropped twenty-six bills at once; they abolished rent controls, landlords no longer needed cause to evict tenants, the Human Rights Commission and the Employment Standards Branch were shuttered, and "the government tightened its grip over local school board budgets and community colleges, including course content." Bennett also declared war on unions, making it impossible to consider any issue beyond salaries and benefits in collective bargaining and allowing any public sector body — from government to health authorities — to fire people without cause.

The reaction from the labour movement and social movement organizations was swift. Mickleburgh writes that the reforms pushed people into organizing quickly and "brought B.C. to the verge of a general strike." The fightback was organized under the banner "Operation Solidarity." Workers staged wildcat strikes, and activists held massive rallies and events. In October 1987, eighty thousand people marched in Vancouver and twenty-five thousand marched in Victoria, and then cascading strikes among public sector workers, teachers, ferry workers, and municipal workers finally started to make Bennett nervous. The workers managed to secure some victories, but Operation Solidarity eventually fizzled out. Even still, it was powerful enough to damage Bennett's popularity, stop his neoconservative reforms, and keep neoliberal reforms at bay for a bit. Mickleburgh concludes, "The extent of the historic fightback also dampened public enthusiasm for his right-wing, neocon restraint program, few elements of which survive today. It also ensured Bennett would never be hailed a conservative folk hero, except perhaps by the Fraser Institute, as were Ronald Reagan and Margaret Thatcher."

Neoliberalism came to Manitoba in the 1980s, too. After his second election, Conservative Gary Filmon got started right away implementing an austerity agenda. His government, in power from 1988 to 1999, kept wages low and massively cut spending, leading to a rise in poverty.[10]

Going after unionized workers was, and is, a clever way to defund the state. Unionized workers are in the minority and so they're easy to demonize, especially if they make higher than average wages. But by placing a cap on how high wages can rise, Filmon's government was intervening in market forces that normally would allow workers to fight for higher wages, thereby depressing wage growth for unionized and non-unionized workers alike. Wage depression has the spin-off effect of reducing the amount of money that workers pay in taxes, as they pay taxes based on a percentage of their salaries. In BC, Bennett was ideologically motivated to take on unions because they stood for collectivity and community; something that neoconservatives oppose, but politicians across the country who might say that they are pro-union regularly fight to limit the wage increases of unionized workers if they have the chance.

The early 1990s found many Canadians looking to a party they had never tried before to form their provincial government. None of the NDP provincial platforms were particularly radical, so rather than bringing in radical socialist reforms, NDP activists instead appealed to a sense of fairness and community. But it was also an unfortunate moment for progressive parties to take office. The political winds had already begun to shift, and flying into those winds would prove to be a disaster for at least some of those parties. Starting in the 1990s, Canadians in three provinces showed that they were finally ready for NDP governments.

In 1990, the NDP took office in Ontario for the only time in its history, and the following year, they retook government in British Columbia and Saskatchewan as well. In Ontario, Bob Rae promised to invest in infrastructure and social services, but his election coincided with yet another deep recession that was felt across Canada.[11] While his first budget raised social assistance rates by 7 percent and shelter allowances by 10 percent and included other poverty-reduction measures that had been part of the Liberals' legislative priorities, Rae's government quickly decided to tighten its fiscal belt and shifted its political sights to the deficit, declaring war on unions.[12] At the same time, the Progressive Conservative federal government imposed a 5 percent cap on Canada Assistance Plan payments for Ontario, Alberta, and British Columbia. This decision cost Ontario alone an estimated $1 billion, and Rae was left needing to find money that was no longer there.[13]

The Saskatchewan NDP was elected in 1991, and in the nine years they had been out of office, the world and their own political ideology were no longer governed by the Keynesianism of the 1970s. Under Roy Romanow, the Saskatchewan NDP privatized Crown agencies, cut services, closed hospitals, and changed the tax regime to encourage private sector investment, especially in agriculture.[14] Romanow was advised by many of the same business people as the previous Conservative government. The finance minister from 1993 to 1997, Janice MacKinnon, explained how business leaders, at a meeting in 1992, had been very concerned that an NDP government might try to undo what had been started under previous Conservative premier Grant Devine and seek to restore the welfare state. She said that "business people needed to be reassured that we would not return to the 1970s with its high royalties and big government, but would create the right climate for investment." The policy statement released in fall 1992 promised to create a "competitive tax regime," promote public-private partnerships, and implement tax cuts for corporations. On taxes, the NDP set the tax reforms of Alberta's Conservative premier, Ralph Klein, as their own goal, pledging to reduce taxes on high income earners and reduce corporate taxes, all to stay "competitive" with the government next door.[15] The election of the BC NDP, also in 1991, was a surprise result; they hadn't been in power in sixteen years. With the days of Operation Solidarity nearly a decade in the rear-view mirror, NDP premier Mike Harcourt cut the public sector, reduced capital spending, decreased social assistance benefits, and divested program funding, leaving British Columbians to pick up the tab. Mulroney's promise of more provincial fiscal flexibility was coming true, though rather than investing in the state and its services, even NDP governments were pulled by neoliberal rationales.[16]

Together, these three social democratic parties were already lining up behind the same approach that would guide Paul Martin as he wrote the 1995 federal budget. There's no doubt that these provincial experiments helped to forge the path; the federal Liberals could already see how Canadians would react to these changes, thanks to Rae, Romanow, and Harcourt, and adjust their strategy accordingly. After all, they were chasing the same voters.

These were just three provinces. The NDP wouldn't be in power in Manitoba, the only other province with a history of NDP governments, for many more years, and the party's short tenures in Nova Scotia and Alberta would come about more than a decade later. But just as voters in these provinces reached to a party to respond to the challenges brought on by recession and free trade, other provinces, under similar conditions, chose leadership that would go in the opposite direction.

Reinforcing Social Segmentation

The neoliberal project may have come to the provinces before the 1990s, but it was federal political decisions made during that decade that made neoliberal politics, economics, and ideology far more powerful than they had been before. NDP governments had mostly failed to use social democracy to bring back the welfare-state days of previous years, and right-wing politicians became more brazen about imposing their vision of Canada on their provinces.

Voters in Alberta, after being hit hard by tanking oil prices and high interest rates, elected Ralph Klein in 1992. Klein and his provincial treasurer, Jim Dinning, convinced Albertans that provincial record-high debt was Alberta's primary problem. "Alberta has a spending problem, not a revenue problem," was a common refrain of both men, one that perhaps few noticed was borrowed from a speech delivered by Ronald Reagan to the National Association of Realtors in Washington in 1982 and reused by neoliberals across North America thereafter.[17] The welfare state was dying, and its death was being aided by a federal government that was trying to balance its budgets, putting even more pressure on the provinces to cut back their own spending.

Klein may have been the most famous face of this hard right turn in Canada, but when Mike Harris rolled into Ontario, he transformed his province by imposing something he called the Common Sense Revolution. Harris represented a break in the traditional governance of the Progressive Conservatives in Ontario. The party had been ideologically diverse enough to rule uninterrupted from 1943 to 1985, but they had since become a harsher right-wing party. Harris's Common Sense Revolution put the ideological underpinnings of neoliberalism into overdrive. He deftly used both Bob Rae's failures and the massive federal spending cuts in the 1995 budget to convince Ontarians to support his vision. This combination gave Harris more than enough political capital — including goodwill on the part of voters — to unleash a radical program of right-wing reform on the province. He cut taxes, cut welfare, privatized parts of the public sector, and relied on public-private partnerships to build massive capital projects. Responsibility to administer social programs was downloaded onto municipalities.[18]

Harris did not only revolutionize Ontario politics. His tenure demonstrated to politicians everywhere in the country that with effective branding and particular social conditions, moving politics to the right is easy. You just need to reinforce the deficit as the most important piece of public policy, identify people to blame for out-of-control spending (like teachers), and find ways to defund the state and outsource its functions to private corporations. Making such bold moves doesn't just change the course of politics in general; it can come with personal rewards, too. Harris was very much rewarded through board appointments — as well as literal awards — not the least of which was his appointment to the board at Chartwell, one of Canada's largest private, for-profit nursing home operators. During the first year of the Covid-19 pandemic, Harris made $223,000 from his involvement at Chartwell and nearly five hundred people died in Chartwell facilities from a Covid-19 infection.[19]

Ontario and Alberta may have moved quickly, but when neoliberal reforms reached Quebec, it was a sign of the changing times and put the nail in the coffin of social democracy in the 20th century. Many of the austerity measures that had appeared in other provinces during the 1980s and 1990s took longer to reach Quebec because the Parti Québécois was a social democratic party. But with a conservative in the premier's office in the late 1990s, a spending crisis triggered by the 1995 Chrétien-Martin budget, and neoliberal sentiment that had slowly been transformed into "common sense," it was only a matter of time before austerity reached Quebec as well.

Quebec society was not as easily convinced as people in other provinces were of the need for deficit spending. Rather than inventing a crisis or relying on groups like the Fraser Institute to popularize arguments in favour of deficit spending over social programs, Lucien Bouchard organized an economic and social summit. It was 1996, and his government had just been elected. Bouchard was a seasoned politician and an old friend of Brian Mulroney from law school. Mulroney had named him ambassador to France in 1985 and then environment minister in 1988. Bouchard was key to Mulroney's support in Quebec, but in 1990, when Bouchard declared that he was a sovereigntist and he supported the Parti Québécois, the two fell out and never spoke again.[20] In the aftermath, Bouchard founded the Bloc Québécois, and by 1993 he had amassed enough support from former Liberal and Conservative MPs that the Bloc became the official federal opposition. In 1995, Jacques Parizeau convinced Bouchard to take the reins of the provincial Parti Québécois. And so, one year after the failed referendum, Bouchard called a summit of business, union, political, and feminist leaders to forge a path toward balancing Quebec's budget.[21]

The summit gave Bouchard the cover he needed to make cuts under a party banner that had been socially democratic for most of its existence. His government pulled $4 billion from health and education spending, but they also introduced pay equity legislation, a pharmacare program, an income security policy, and Canada's first public daycare program.[22] Even though they created new programs to help people, the drive for balanced budgets would be codified that year. The law has been in effect since, with the exception of the years in which emergency orders related to Covid-19 trumped them.[23] As the Parti Québécois and then the Liberals and then the Coalition Avenir Québec chased balanced budgets, they imposed social service cuts to make up for the tax cuts that remained their real priority. The province's overall higher tax rates plus the presence of its own taxation agency have allowed the myth to linger that Quebec is the only province where taxes never dropped during the emergence of neoliberalism in Canada. But Bernard Landry cut taxes in 1998 by $850 million, though this was balanced by a hike in provincial sales tax. The next PQ finance minister, Pauline Marois, reduced taxes in 2001 by another $1.5 billion, and then in 2002, taxes were cut again, this time by $2 billion.[24] Many people point to this as the turning point when the PQ turned its back on social democracy. Just five years later, a new provincial party called Québec Solidaire would take the social democratic space that the old Parti Québécois once filled. The PQ would hold government for a brief 18 months in 2013, and then would be decimated.

By the 2000s, "deficit mania" was everywhere. Politicians convinced voters that a balance sheet was more important than funding and supports for marginalized people or paying for health and education services to avoid a generalized state of decline. Selling the deficit as an issue of primary concern for average people completely changed people's relationship with the state and what they felt they could reasonably ask for. Now, rather than simply calling for a policy to protect or promote something, people were expected to explain what the impact of this policy would have on a government's balance sheet. The provinces, where cuts to education, health, and social services funding were felt most acutely, drilled home the rationale that guided the federal government. This was especially damaging to people who came of age at this moment: the ones who had never known anything other than "We must balance the budget" and who accepted these talking points as reasonable and true. "How can we possibly afford lower tuition fees when the deficit is so big," I was asked as a twenty-year-old student activist. For the questioner, a fellow student, tuition fees presented an immediate difficulty. And yet he came of age in an era when his struggles to pay student fees, mortgaging his future to do so, still didn't add up to the pressing matter of any particular government deficit he was thinking of. For those of us who have been adults only during this paradigm, it is all we have ever known. Growing up in a world where neoliberalism was everywhere but the dominant narrative was that Canada was still a fair and progressive society was not just confusing — it was disenfranchising, too.

Do Canadians take stock of the psychological damage these politics have had on us? It's not possible to have revolutionary political change, left or right, without also stirring something deep within the minds of the people such change is impacting. From the late 1970s until 2000, when provincial and territorial governments, federal governments, and international markets fundamentally changed how we exist, our sense of self has also undergone a massive shift. Perceiving that shift is difficult, because it isn't always clear that a shift has happened. Many people, certainly those Conservative voters who still cling to the ideas of Red Toryism from another era, have in their minds an image of Canada that hasn't existed for decades. The resulting cognitive dissonance is profound. Canadians may say they're mad that their local hospital has closed because there's no emergency room doctor to staff overnight shifts. And yet they still vote for politicians who are keen to allow a private operator into that emergency room so that someone makes money off it and services still decline. Whether through contracting out; hidden user fees paid through the public insurance system; operators owned by hedge funds that sound like small, local agencies; or many other structures — these things have also changed us.

In 1997, the *New York Times* went to Prince Edward Island to talk to Islanders about Jean Chrétien and the changing times in Canada. Journalist Anthony Depalma wrote, "Canadians have come to grips with the economic and social burdens of the compassionate big government they created over the last half century. And many concluded, as did Mr. Chretien in the debate, that they cannot do as well as they once wanted to." By then, the federal government's 1995 budget was slowly being implemented. Things were changing in PEI. Confederation Bridge, which connects the island to the mainland, had opened days before this article was published. Despite Depalma's being a *New York Times* journalist (or perhaps because of it), his argument could have come directly from the Business Council on National Issues or the Fraser Institute: Canada doesn't have the money that it used to have, and therefore Canada's "compassionate big government" needs to be defunded. He quoted twenty-one-year-old Bryn MacCallun, pet shop manager and university student, who said, "It's not a question of whether or not Canada is changing; Canada has to change.... We have to be more realistic. We can't have everything." Depalma also talked to a deli owner in New Brunswick, Matthew MacDonald, who said, "In this election people are realizing that to save what we want to save we'll have to expect less of what we used to get," and that Canada had "a good ride for more than 40 years."

That "good ride for more than 40 years" line could have been cooked up in an executive board room in an office tower hundreds of metres above the plebes running around like ants in downtown Toronto. And lines like these probably were. With it came a concerted effort to push this language into the day-to-day lives of average people, to make it "common sense" to be regurgitated by a deli owner in New Brunswick or a university student in PEI. One year earlier, Seth Klein wrote that certain lines have become so common that they are assumed to be true. Like "Government is too big," "The government has been over-spending," "The government cannot get its financial house in order," "We have been living beyond our means." And then there's an array of household-related tropes that many people today will recognize as common, like "We must act now, as the cupboard is bare."[25] Or, as then Business Council on National Issues chair J. Edward Newall said in advance of the 1995 budget, "We are not paying our own way. You could say we're putting the tab for our present high living on our grandchildren's Visa cards."[26] These powerful tropes, repeated over and over again by local politicians, national politicians, and journalists, were part of a powerful campaign that fundamentally changed how Canadians think about their government and its priorities. Average people embraced messaging that led to their own suffering. And this was so clearly demonstrated in the crises that unfolded in doctors' offices, in waiting rooms, in hospital beds, and on the streets of this country.

Healthcare

As a massive program that is formally the responsibility of the provinces, health policy is a particularly important lens through which to see how the rationale of common sense neoliberalism has direct impacts. Between 1957 and 1977, before Canada had a formal system of medicare, the federal government sent money to the provinces and territories that would cover one-half of their health costs, both in hospitals and for doctors who worked outside of hospitals. Canada's public healthcare system started in Saskatchewan, when the government there extended provincial medical insurance to pay for doctors' services in 1962. The policy inspired the foundation of Canada's universal program, and the Medical Care Act passed in 1966. However, the act also bound the federal government — rather than the provinces or territories — to paying one-half of the costs that doctors incurred for their services outside of a hospital setting.

But medicare was never a stable program; it was always under threat of government cutback. In 1977, after twenty years of federal funding covering half the cost of services, the cost-sharing agreement was replaced with a block transfer payment, made up of a mixture of tax points and cash transfers. The addition of tax points allowed the federal government to reduce its tax rates while the provinces increased theirs. This was the beginning of downloading programs onto the provinces under the guise of "flexibility," divesting the federal government's responsibility for these programs to operate with a national scope.[27] This would start the ball rolling toward more disconnected provincial programs that would have to individually fight off privatization while the federal government's only role was to turn a funding tap on or off.

Private fees in healthcare became an increasingly greater problem as the provinces, territories, and federal government preferred to target spending and taxes over improving funding to public services. On September 3, 1980, Justice Emmett Hall chaired a second commission into the state of healthcare in Canada. The commission was created by the Progressive Conservatives, but the Liberals were in power by the time its report was completed. In his report, Hall underlined the need for social solidarity through tax collection to sustain the public healthcare system: "The Canadian people determined that they should band together to pay medical bills when they were well and income earning. Health services were no longer to be bought off the shelf and paid for at the checkout stand. Nor was their price to be bargained for at the time they were sought. They were a fundamental need, like education, which Canadians could meet collectively and pay for through taxes."[28] Indeed, the popularity of a public healthcare system that had existed forty years earlier had never subsided, which made the protest movement against the draft Canada Health Act all the more surprising.

The government tried to use the report from the Hall Commission to convince doctors and provinces to stop extra billing — billing for services on top of provincial fee guidelines — but it failed. Doctors started to protest and many started opting out of provincial health plans. The Parti Québécois legislated striking doctors back to work in 1982. Unions and other activists came out against doctors and protested extra billing. Polls showed that Canadians, overwhelmingly, not only supported the principle of medicare, but they actually identified its existence as fundamental to life in Canada. This popularity no doubt made the Canada Health Act possible; it came into effect on July 1, 1984. It tried to harmonize what was expected of provincial and territorial healthcare systems: healthcare needed to be available to people moving from region to region, it needed to be universal, it needed to be comprehensive, and it needed to be public. Without these principles, it couldn't be a truly national program that was universal. If people in Corner Brook received fewer services than those in Brandon, what good was a national piece of legislation? The Canada Health Act also prohibited extra billing and user fees for services covered under the act. It remains the most important piece of legislation for Canada's universal public health system today.[29]

Even though many provinces reduced their own taxes at the same time the federal government reduced transfer payments, they still demanded that federal money be restored to education and health spending. By 1998, at two different conferences, the provinces demanded that the federal government fully restore the money that had been cut from the federal transfer. At a meeting of the premiers in Quebec City in 1999, they formally made a call for the funding that had been cut in 1995 to be restored to what it had been in 1994–95. They asserted that healthcare needed to remain publicly funded and that services should be accessible to all. There were three priorities for healthcare in Canada: first, that it be sustainable, including being adequately and predictably funded; second, that staffing meet projected needs and IT systems be improved to ensure the health of all Canadians; and third, that there be clear roles and responsibilities established between the federal government and the provinces and territories.[30] In 2004, Paul Martin successfully negotiated a health accord that stabilized healthcare funding for the provinces and territories for the next decade. Built into the accord was a 6 percent escalator to capture the rising costs of healthcare delivery and increased demand on healthcare services as the population aged.

In 2011, Geoff Norquay, former policy adviser to Brian Mulroney and communications director for Stephen Harper, wrote that "some provinces have begun to manage down the growth in healthcare costs," mentioning Ontario, whose costs were rising by 4 percent, not 6 percent, and that they could be heading toward 3 percent or even 2 percent spending increases in the next few years. The call for stable healthcare spending was well and good, except, as Norquay pointed out, the provinces were all defunding their programs.[31] Stable funding to ensure consistent and quality service is one thing. Stable funding so that provinces can figure out how to reduce their own spending leaves average people no better off. In Manitoba, the Conservative government's healthcare cuts in 1996 saw the budget for The Pas Health Complex, a hospital and long-term-care facility that served the community and surrounding regions, reduced by 20 percent. In Nova Scotia, acute care beds were cut by one-third.[32] This is also the province where, from 1990 to 2001, Nova Scotians lost, on average, $3,600 in annual income and the poorest Nova Scotians lost 29 percent of their disposable income. The bottom 60 percent of Nova Scotian households had lower average incomes than in any other province.[33] Poverty and negative health outcomes are deeply intertwined, so the increasing rate of poverty in Nova Scotia put greater strain on the health system.[34]

During Mike Harris's tenure in Ontario, health spending didn't grow at the rate of inflation, and a combination of this plus spending cuts and a population needing more medical care as it aged left a hole of $4.1 billion in the province's budget by 2001. Using policies and generous compensation packages, Harris's government shed almost twenty-five thousand healthcare workers and set a target to close twenty-four thousand beds. In an 2001 alternative budget paper published by the Canadian Centre for Policy Alternatives, Bill Murnighan explained that Harris routinely blamed the federal government for the spending shortfalls in healthcare in the province, "But the big story — which neither level of government wants to highlight — is that in good economic times, and when blessed with soaring government revenue, they both made the same choice at the urging of the business lobby: to shift enormous amounts of public funds into tax cuts that largely benefit the wealthiest among us, rather than to restore social programs."[35]

In 2002, it was obvious that healthcare costs would increase as the baby boom generation aged and a bulge of individuals requiring more healthcare more regularly made its way through the system. That year, the healthcare costs related to Canadians aged sixty-five and older made up about 40 percent of combined provincial and territorial healthcare expenses. Drug costs were also rising, and overall spending on drugs amounted to 13.6 percent of total healthcare expenditures. Drug costs are a particularly pernicious problem, as drug pricing often maximizes profits for drug manufacturers, so public money goes right into their coffers.

The thing about a spiral is that bad logic begets bad logic, and soon you're unable to tell where the root of a problem lies. Take day surgery as an example. During the 1990s, workers' compensation boards aggressively pushed workers back to the workplace after an injury. One of the ways they did this was through expediting access to surgery, but at a cost. The workers were able to jump the line for surgery if it meant they would get back to work more quickly. By the late 1990s, fees for expedited surgery had increased by 500 percent in Alberta. In BC, expedited surgery costs were just over ten times what it would normally cost. One study found that expedited knee surgeries cost BC's workers' compensation board, WorkSafeBC, almost 375 percent more than surgeries performed in a public hospital. This study also found that people who had surgeries in the public system were actually back at work faster than those who had their surgeries expedited and done privately, as there were more side effects associated with expediting surgeries to pressure workers to go back to work as fast as possible.[36] Studies conducted in Ontario and Quebec in 2023 showed similar high payments in private clinics, just as Ontario premier Doug Ford and Quebec premier François Legault were expressing openness to giving private companies more access to the public healthcare system.

Canada's health system, while publicly funded, is massively private. A report from 2002 into various funding and delivery operations found that even though about 70 percent of healthcare in Canada was publicly funded, "almost all of this care" was delivered by private operators. That's a statistic I imagine would shock most Canadians. The key here, though, isn't that it's almost all privately delivered, but that it's privately delivered by for-profit organizations. Private, for-profit operators tend to chase the kinds of medical services that can be turned into profit: fast surgeries, cosmetic procedures, and so on. It leaves to the public and not-for-profit system the more complicated procedures, the ones that are far harder to generate profit from. While for-profit operators might operate comfortably in urban and suburban communities, where they are sure to turn a profit, it is far more difficult to convince them to operate in a rural or northern community, where the prospects of profits are far lower. A for-profit clinic that provides diabetic health services will send the more complicated patients to the not-so-local hospital because it cannot make money off the patient's services.[37]

• • •

Privatization has never actually been about efficiencies; that's simply its most powerful public relations talking point. It's a lie to equate the private sector with efficiencies as a way to justify profits. The lie has been turned into truth by a consistent war on reality waged by right-wing politicians, think tanks, business people, and public relations agencies like Earnscliffe, the agency that used to host Paul Martin Jr. in their boardroom when the finance ministry sought opinions rooted in public opinion polling.[38] Most galling is that the idea that the higher the profits, the more "efficient" a company is has become truth, even though it takes only a few minutes of critical thinking to realize all the ways in which that just isn't true in service delivery. Attacking "big government" was a favoured talking point in redefining "common sense" for the average person when it came to fiscal finance, and this happened in healthcare with privatization, too.

Applying market logic directly to the healthcare system isn't new. In 1983, an American company took over the small regional hospital in Hawkesbury, Ontario. The community needed to pay for a portion of the hospital's capital expenditures, and it put out a request for proposals to help raise the money and manage the construction. The only bid from a qualified agency came from American Medical International, a company that had a chain of 130 hospitals in thirteen countries. In exchange for the capital costs, the company would manage the hospital's non-clinical services for ten years. The hospital saved some money, specifically on IT systems, but the management contract wasn't renewed after that ten-year period, and the hospital changed back to being managed publicly, as a not-for-profit. Trying to operate the hospital on a for-profit basis didn't work.[39] But then, these systems rely on good governance, stable funding, and help to retain enough staff so that people don't work themselves to the edge. In Hawkesbury, they're still not getting this. On January 1, 2023, the hospital announced that it needed to close its emergency room for a few days because they didn't have the staff to keep it open.[40]

Public healthcare spending has always come under attack, whether through government cuts or underspending; doctors who wanted the right to charge more money; or market logic that artificially depressed workers' wages, cut beds, or made any number of other decisions that hurt the quality of care. At the same time, healthcare holds a vaunted place in Canadian society and identity. The fact that Canadians often put healthcare in the same pile as hockey and snow when they're listing off the things that make them Canadian shows that it can only be the people themselves who will permit this system to be dismantled.

But it's important to recall that these forces were not imposed on the provinces directly. Collusion among politicians and a combination of state compression policies created the conditions so that, in the words of Margaret Thatcher, there became no alternative. Today, when people complain or struggle against a system that feels like it's in perpetual failure, they're actually bumping up against a four-decade long project to create the system in crisis that is our current status quo. Like at so many other junctures in Canadian history, politicians could have chosen to invest in people or hand over control to the corporate world, and the provinces and territories alike chose the latter.

Healthcare is one of Canada's few remaining truly universal social programs, but their unified neoliberalism is leaving Canadians at the mercy of an underfunded, undersupported, understaffed system that is seemingly in constant crisis. We feel this most acutely with healthcare, but it touches all of what we imagine to still be part of our social safety net. Neoliberalism needs a docile population because no one would morally choose what it's actually offering: a system that enriches a few lucky individuals off of misery, suffering, and death. And Canadians are such nice people, aren't we?

CHAPTER 6

Canada's Reigning Status Quo

I magine that some provinces and territories had refused to operate under the same logic as the federal government. Maybe there would be parts of Canada where social services were completely different than in other places. Maybe there'd be a higher standard of living. But that hasn't happened. Every province and territory has absorbed neoliberal rationale. The federal arrangement has amplified neoliberal reforms, rather than operating as a bulwark against them, and the federal structure has become a principal argument for why these reforms cannot be resisted. Canada's federation has developed into a sophisticated network of buck-passing and lowering of expectations. Politicians always have someone else to blame for this program not working or that program being contracted out.

The reality is that government budgets are far more dependent on economic forces than they should be. With their constant cuts to stable state revenues like income and corporate taxes, governments have shackled themselves to the same economic system that is driving citizens into the ground. The old arrangement, in which governments provided at least some protection from boom and bust cycles, is long gone. We're closer than we have ever been to those years of "deserving" and "undeserving" poor, where a lucky few might receive some help and an unlucky many are abandoned and told to figure it out themselves. But worse still, we don't even have the religious organizations, extra time to volunteer, or collectivity to help out those people who are increasingly and ever more marginalized by the state.

From the Stephen Harper years, the 2008 financial crisis, massive bank and auto industry bailouts, and still more tax cuts, to the "sunny ways" of Justin Trudeau, things have gotten consistently worse for Canadians. Housing costs have exploded, collective debt has exploded, and the reliance on food banks has exploded. Income inequality has gotten far worse. The volunteer sector has tried to step in to fill the holes left by the transformed welfare state, but even not-for-profits and charities, which also operate through the neoliberal lens, are doing more than they can manage, ultimately creating an environment where the rich can launder their reputations by purchasing the right to post their names on hospital wings and university campuses. Government underfunding has given philanthropy a new heyday, as lower taxes mean that philanthropists have even larger net worths. They increasingly dictate social service priorities through massive donations. At the same time, Canadians are turning more and more often to personal donations, fuelled by platforms like GoFundMe, to pay for services that should be, and once were, paid for by our welfare state. We are very much on our own.

Politics Transforming

By the time Stephen Harper was elected in 2006, social services, more oriented to the market than ever before, were increasingly forced to extract things like "efficiencies," "revenues," and "synergies." But services were still there, if in name only, so people had not yet caught on to how drastically things had changed. It was still easy to live in the headspace of a decade earlier, a time when social programs were in trouble but not on life support, a time when, maybe, if we had just organized in the right way, or had gotten the right people elected, we could have made things better. While a majority of Canadians didn't elect Stephen Harper, enough did, and it gave him the power he needed to continue the transformation. Canadians had a prime minister who was uninterested in looking back. He forged ahead, solidifying changes that had been made in previous years, but added into the mix social conservative values in governance. This was often at odds with the perspectives held by most Canadians, including those who voted for him. Perhaps the biggest expression of the disconnect between the moment that people were living in and the moment that they thought they still lived in was when Harper prorogued Parliament in 2008 to avoid a confidence vote that threatened to bring down his minority government. Minority governments have fallen many times over the years — our government is structured in such a way to let this happen when needed — but this time Harper would use the system that had developed over the previous twenty years to stop government from functioning as it was designed to.

To try to bring down the government, the Liberals, Bloc Québécois, and NDP established a pact that would have allowed them to govern if the Conservatives lost confidence. It should have worked; if the Conservatives had lost a confidence vote, this coalition would have been given the chance to govern according to the democratic rules that govern Canada. But Harper was much smarter than that. He knew that he was governing in 2008, not 1988. So he demonized Jack Layton as "Taliban Jack," he scared Canadians by invoking the word "sovereigntist" when referring to the politics of the Bloc, and he gave space to Stéphane Dion to be humdrum and awkward. Harper then asked the governor general to close Parliament. In so doing, he bought himself enough time for the opposition coalition to collapse. The spontaneous anger that erupted across the country after Harper pulled that move divided Canadians between the ones who cared deeply about Canadian institutions and democracy and the ones who didn't. But the era in which Canadians could push politicians to actually do something was over. The campaign fizzled out, and Harper kept his government. The demands of the people were ignored. Their elected officials could govern with virtual impunity, like monarchs. That was the system as it had become.

I don't remember feeling like we had passed from one era to another, at the time. I was president of my student union that year and was very involved in the activism against Harper's decision but 2008 was an important turning point. Not only did Canada almost erupt into a constitutional crisis just so the prime minister could cling to power, but Canada also experienced a massive economic crisis. At the same time, a new generation of workers ostracized by the market and its various henchmen — media, business leaders, and so on — were infantilized and convinced they would never have any real power. These were the millennials. They may have had higher net worths than previous generations, but driving up that net worth was debt. Millennials had a higher debt-to-after-tax income level than any other generation at any point in their lives. And, compared with Gen X, millennials had much more income inequality within their generational cohort, primarily driven by housing costs and student debt.[1] While Gen Xers, the folks born between 1965 and 1980, grew up in the heyday of Canada's welfare state, the millennials were the neoliberal generation. They entered adulthood just in time to face a very neoliberal crisis.

When Harper prorogued Parliament, he demonstrated how politics had changed in Canada. Politicians could be openly hostile to the electorate — the people they were supposed to be representing. And with the financial crisis, many people discovered that the supports they thought had been in place for decades weren't sufficient anymore. The year Stephen Harper was elected, the economy was growing at a rate of about 3 percent of GDP annually, and fiscal surpluses were somewhere between $10 billion and $20 billion.[2] Like many Conservatives before him, Harper didn't actually manage to maintain these surpluses. Instead he created deficits through a combination of tax cuts for individuals and corporations and massive injections of funding to stabilize the economy during the 2008 financial crisis. In a similar callback to the Lougheed approach during the 1981 recession, the federal government rarely spent economic stimulus money on actual people. Corporations were the biggest winners. During the years that Harper was in power, the federal government spent money with the intention of preserving the system and entrenching a close relationship with businesses while adding $130 billion to Canada's accumulated deficit.[3]

These priorities were on full display when the federal government rushed to save the auto industry during the financial crisis. In North America auto sales plummeted, and in the United States the debt crisis led to fewer people taking on loans to pay for vehicles. Following the United States' lead, Canada floated $13.7 billion to the auto sector by buying stocks and offering loans. It took years before it became clear how much money the industry received and worse, didn't pay back. Nearly a decade later, in 2018, then finance minister Bill Morneau "quietly authorized" writing off bad debt from unpaid loans to Chrysler and General Motors. It is estimated that Canadians never saw about $3.7 billion of the money that had been loaned out.[4] Far less publicized than the auto bailout was the money that Canadian agencies loaned to the banks to save them from their own crisis. The federal government loaned huge sums of money to bail out Canada's banking system; the CMHC, the Bank of Canada, and the U.S. Federal Reserve injected massive sums into

Canadian banks. In total, the banks received about $114 billion: $26 billion to TD Bank, $25 billion each to the Royal Bank and Scotia Bank, $21 billion to CIBC, and $17 billion to BMO. At various points, CIBC, BMO, and Scotiabank were receiving more government support than the values of the banks themselves. At the same time, they collectively posted $27 billion in profit, none of which made it back to the government — or the citizens — who had paid to keep them afloat.[5]

Harper, with Minister of Finance Jim Flaherty (a former Ontario finance minister), continued what had been started decades prior. In 2012, they cut federal cash transfers from 6 percent annually to 3.9 percent annually. These changes would reduce health expenditures at the provincial level from 20.4 percent to 18.6 percent over the next decade. Adjusted for inflation, the federal government increased health transfers to the provinces by a measly average of 2.7 percent from 2008–09 to 2018–19, barely enough to keep up with the rising demand that an aging population of boomers placed on healthcare spending. But spending on social services also went down, from 13.6 percent to 13.3 percent, despite the aging and growing population.[6] The government continued to strip away these services bit by bit, leaning more to the strategy of slow and steady cuts than to imposing deep cuts all at once.

When Justin Trudeau's Liberals swept Stephen Harper's government out in 2015, many people who had been worried about the state of Canada under Harper breathed a sigh of relief. Trudeau promised to do politics differently, punctuated by his "sunny ways" branding. As the son of a prime minister, he was a closer mint ideologically to Paul Martin Jr., but his approach was kinder, gentler, and more feminist. At a campaign stop in Brampton, Trudeau asked, "Why does [NDP leader Thomas Mulcair] want to take billions of dollars out of the economy in a recession, and what public investments will he be cutting to do that?"[7] He asked this question while standing beside Paul Martin Jr. himself, a man who took billions of dollars out of the economy. But the damage was done: Trudeau accused Mulcair of choosing austerity over jobs, an accusation that went directly for Mulcair's jugular and the platform of the NDP. The NDP had been outflanked on the left by the Liberals.

During the Trudeau era, cash transfers rose, thanks especially to pandemic-related emergency relief funding. Total government cash transfer expenditures in 2008–09 were $47.1 billion, and they rose to $94.6 billion in 2023–24. In their press release announcing this new spending, the Liberals declared it to be a "record" sum and an increase by $7 billion over the year previous. But when you realize that the health transfer portion of this spending grows at the same rate as Canada's economy, increasing at the most by 9.3 percent annually, this "record" spending doesn't actually signal that Canadians are about to enter a new era of social program spending and expansion.[8] It is simply a band-aid solution, temporarily restoring what should have been in place already.

Social programs over the past thirty years haven't been destroyed; they have been rendered inefficient and disorganized. The increased presence of private operators, profit-making in the delivery of services, and the proliferation of private consultants in politics is a new normal that funding alone cannot fix. Neoliberalism hasn't simply been cutting and slashing services; it has been a transformation. Neoliberalism has destroyed our communities and our relationships, and it has made it even more difficult for collective forms of organizing to be oriented around anything other than profit-making. Think about operating a hospital emergency room at 80 percent capacity. One kind of logic would see this and say, "This is a place where the workers have time for breaks, can take time off without overburdening their co-workers, and can absorb seasonal viral surges, and where patients can see a doctor within the hour." But the prevailing, market-based approach says that unless this operating room is running at 100 percent all the time, it's a drain on public money. This is deadly, and it hides the fact that more funding, while needed, is going to enrich corporate bodies like never before, rather than getting to where it actually needs to go. This is the Catch-22 of the current system: the neoliberal transformation has been so effective that even badly needed new funding gets eaten up by a million different holes in the system created by private, for-profit operators, inefficiencies, or, still, tax cuts.

When you throw the provincial and territorial governments back into the mix, things get even cloudier. Thirty years of downloading responsibilities has meant that the provinces and territories have more power over social services. A fine thing, in theory, if these governments weren't also swimming in the congealed soup of neoliberalism and austerity. That historic investment into health announced by the federal government at the start of 2023 — $46.2 billion — raised many eyebrows.[9] As the pandemic started to wane, provincial governments were calling on Ottawa to give them more money, especially and most obviously for healthcare. The one problem, as Trudeau himself pointed out, is that provincial budgets were doing well. The pandemic triggered the Bank of Canada to increase interest rates, and the post-pandemic recovery was a boon for provincial coffers. More than half of the provinces had surpluses at the end of 2022, despite the overwhelming and increasing need for health spending, especially for mental-healthcare and for illnesses that either developed or were made worse by pandemic conditions.

Collectively, British Columbia, Alberta, Saskatchewan, New Brunswick, Newfoundland and Labrador, Yukon, Northwest Territories, and Nunavut had surpluses that totalled $20.3 billion. Alberta had the biggest surplus, at $12.3 billion, thanks in part to higher profits from the oil and gas industry. BC had $5.7 billion and Saskatchewan's surplus was $1.1 billion. But even the provinces that had deficits finished the year above where they had expected to be: Ontario had $7 billion more than they had anticipated, Quebec had $1.2 billion more, and Nova Scotia had $363.6 million more. The year earlier, many provinces had even bigger gains: Alberta had $22.2 billion more than they had anticipated, turning a deficit budget into one that posted a $3.9 billion surplus. Ontario, BC, Nova Scotia, and PEI all had surpluses in 2021.[10] And despite these hugely improved "portfolio positions," people on the ground suffered from lack of funding for services, healthcare, and other supports during one of the worst pandemics of the last hundred years.

Aside from BC's decision to create a $1 billion fund for municipal infrastructure projects, and New Brunswick promising to create a fund called the New Brunswick Advantage, provinces spent some of the money the way that public money is so often spent: on measures that defund the state. Ontario's Doug Ford did away with licence fees, New Brunswick instituted a tax break for people who earn between $142,000 and $162,000 per year, and Alberta funnelled its surplus into several initiatives, including paying down the provincial debt and temporarily eliminating tax on gasoline.[11,12] Sure, the money that created these surpluses was temporary and wouldn't necessarily be there in a year, but there was nothing stopping any politician from doing something with it that looked innovative or interesting but ultimately only makes the fundamental problem worse.

Ontario's Financial Accountability Office found that the Ontario government's spending forecast through to 2025–26 includes $22 billion that the government doesn't plan to spend; it will have $5.6 billion more, each year, than what the office projects it needs to spend.[13] This surplus is made possible not just by limiting public sector spending but also by refusing to allow workers to have wage increases of more than 1 percent (a policy that was struck down in court but that the government appealed). The government could apply the money to the provincial debt, could liquidate it through cash handouts to Ontarians, or could sit on it and let it collect interest. None of these options will stop the decline.

The money is there. The solutions, from free nursing education to cheaper housing, are there. The desire from the people is there. And yet people have discovered that our common sense is not the same common sense that drives the people who hold power. Their common sense, their rationality and decision-making, is rooted in other concerns. They don't exactly care if it's 2:00 a.m. and your baby's fever has triggered a seizure and you now have to drive more than an hour to get to an emergency room that has had to absorb twelve thousand more patients each year. They care that they're re-elected and that public money goes to the people and the systems that matter to them.

The State of the Union

Today Canadians owe almost $2 trillion in mortgage debt and $706.2 billion in non-mortgage debt. In 2022, the ratio of household debt to income hit a record high: for every dollar of disposable income, individuals had $1.85 in debt.[14] For households led by people aged 35 to 44, the debt-to-income ratio was 238.7 percent and for people aged 45 to 54 years, it was 223.4 percent.[15] This is especially concerning considering the relatively high interest rates and the fact that the more someone has to borrow, the more they have to pay to the banks. The collective net profit of Canada's big five banks in 2022 was $50.52 billion. In the third quarter of 2022, when average disposable income increased by $827 for the second income quintile, Statistics Canada found a drop in income for the lowest quintile of $455 on average. In 2023, the unelected Bank of Canada increased interest rates by more than 400 basis points in less than a year, pricing out the growing gap in income between the highest and lowest earners.[16]

And still the profits were not enough for the banking executives. In an article about banks' year ends for the *Globe and Mail*,

James Bradshaw quotes Royal Bank's CEO: "Chief executive officer Dave McKay warned there are still several warning signs in the economy. With inflation, a potential recession on the horizon and labour-market pressures driving costs higher, 'there's a higher level of uncertainty and therefore you have higher tail risk right now.'"[17] Higher uncertainty is one thing when you can't make it to the end of the month without running out of money. It's totally another when you've just finished your last year with a collective $50 billion in profits.

But there have been other market-driven changes, too. Free trade decimated Canada's manufacturing industry, killing one-quarter of all manufacturing jobs (557,000 jobs) between 2002 and 2013. Manufacturing jobs fell from being 15 percent of Canada's total jobs to 9.8 percent, and dropped again to 8.9 percent between 2013 and 2023.[18] Manufacturing jobs have traditionally been well-paying, full-time positions, and during the postwar period, much of Canada's social safety net was oriented toward workers in these jobs. The loss of manufacturing jobs has been accompanied by a rise in precarious, part-time, and low-paid service work, and so social supports built around well-paying, stable, and full-time jobs have been unable to support workers in part-time or non-standard work. And with those jobs went union coverage: the unionization rate dropped from 38 percent in 1981 to 29 percent by 2022. While the loss of manufacturing jobs played a big role in this, there was also a loss of union jobs in forestry, mining, and construction. There is a gender gap in union jobs as well: 31 percent of women had a unionized job in 2022, while only 26 percent of men had a unionized job. The biggest drop in union rates occurred in British Columbia, where the percentage of unionized employees fell by 15 percentage points from 1997 to 2022. On the other hand, Quebec's unionization rate barely changed during this same period.[19] A decline in union jobs puts downward pressure on wages: as workers lose their power to collectively bargain for higher pay, wages start to decline and profits rise more quickly. In the early 1990s, one study that compared Canadian and American wages found that Canada's higher unionization rate explained 40 percent of the wage differential between the two countries.[20] Unionization helped balance the market pressures on workers. Without it, wages will continue to decline.

One of the telltale signs that power within society has become unbalanced is record-high income inequality. Income inequality has risen steadily as wages have fallen, corporate profits have ballooned, CEO bonuses and payouts have soared, and more and more creative ways to shelter salaries from taxes have been introduced. During the Harper years, most Canadians saw their incomes shrink. Incomes among the top 1 percent of Canadians doubled between 1982 and 2018, from $308,911 to $615,670 (2019 dollars). But even in the 1 percent, income inequality pushed the highest income earners even higher. The average income gains of the top 0.01 percent increased by 189 percent, while everyone else in the 1 percent saw their incomes increase by 90 percent. This, of course, doesn't include money that is put into tax shelters and is therefore not reported at all. Income held in tax shelters called Canadian Controlled Private Corporations "more than doubled as a percentage of GDP between 2002 and 2014," suggesting that the true amount of income held by Canada's wealthiest people is even higher than what we can learn from income tax filings.[21] The poorer half of Canadians in 2014 had lower after-tax income than the poorer half of Canadians in the late 1970s, and taxes have been kept low to encourage wealth hoarding among Canada's elites; in 1943, average taxes for Canada's richest 0.01 percent peaked at 71 percent. In 2023, the tax rate for the same group was 33 percent.[22] At these rates, the gap between rich and poor will just keep getting bigger.

Wages rose rapidly from 1940 until they started to drop in 1980, and then they stagnated. A 2016 analysis of salaries co-written by Jean-Yves Duclos — before he was elected and given a seat in Trudeau's Cabinet — found that hourly compensation no longer rose: it stagnated and even declined from 1980 to 2010. The study controlled for educational attainment.[23] The only time that middle-class wages rose was during booms in the energy sector in Alberta, Saskatchewan, and Newfoundland and Labrador after 2000. When oil prices collapsed, so too did wages.[24]

And then there was Covid-19, a pandemic for which Canada was woefully unprepared. The pandemic created conditions that governments used to justify historic levels of spending. All of a sudden, the state had to step in to help Canadians weather the storm in a way never before needed in the country's history. Just under 30 percent of Canada's workforce either lost their jobs or most of their work hours. Workers in tourism, food services, and retail were the hardest hit, losing one million jobs in these sectors alone.[25] And these were services already characterized by generally low wages. To their credit, the government did not simply bail out corporate Canada while leaving individual Canadians to wallow in financial crisis. Aid that went to individuals, either directly through the Canada Emergency Response Benefit or indirectly through the CEWS, reached $175.5 billion. The CEWS, however, was still a windfall for corporate Canada — companies could access public money to help them keep employees on payroll. But when all was said and done, employers made out like bandits with the public money while average people had the screws turned on them with income tax "adjustments" from the Canada Revenue Agency (CRA).

Nearly all corporations who applied for CEWS money — 99.8 percent of them — were approved. The program paid out $100.7 billion to more than 440,000 employers. Twenty-four corporations with more than 5,000 employees got $2.4 billion alone. And none of it had to be returned. But CERB was clawed back from people the CRA deemed to be "ineligible," sounding insidiously like "undeserving." Except, there were many reasons for why someone could be found ineligible, like if they had applied for Employment Insurance (EI) in April 2020, if they had accidentally been paid twice (because the system had created a double application), or if they did originally meet the program's requirements but for some reason CRA didn't think so on review. People were forced to jump through bureaucratic hoops to try to hang on to what they could. People who were easily awarded CERB — because they couldn't make more than $500 per week —quickly saw their money absorbed by rising rent and food costs occurring during the same time.[26] Rather than providing stability during a global upheaval, these "initiatives" by the government only increased instability and uncertainty for people who needed it most.

The grace showed toward corporations was not extended to average people. The largest and fastest social program ever assembled in Canada's history ended up being the largest-ever cash transfer of public money into private funds. It also continued the rationale that has underpinned Canadian aid programs from the beginning, and kicked it into overdrive: people only deserve help if the help offered to them is tied to employment. CEWS literally required people to be employed to be given indirect Covid-19 support, and still it relied on the goodwill of their employer to administer it. The only other form of direct aid that anyone got was $600 given to disabled Canadians once, in March 2021. In the first quarter of 2023, while Canadians were forced to pay back $3.7 billion in pandemic aid that they were deemed "ineligible" to have received, corporations did not repay one cent of the $100.7 billion they had been given.

Income inequality is poison to social cohesion. As the distance between the rich and everyone else grows wider, average people no longer even see the excess and luxury that the 1 percent live in. They don't see the decisions made to protect this class of individuals, and it becomes even easier to tell average people that the main source of their economic hardship is other average people, the ones who look differently, pray differently, or live differently than they do. Income inequality kills social cohesion because we no longer share common spaces, whether those spaces are physical, like outdoor space, or involve accessing the same programs or services. This segregation means that we don't have equal access to programs or services or, because of neoliberal messaging that says targeted programs are better than universal ones, we don't feel like we have equal stakes in fighting for things to be improved. No longer does collective suffering due to weakened or broken services encourage collective action for change. Increased income inequality leads to higher rates of crime and violence, less economic growth, and the decline of the efficacy of representative democracy itself.[27] These are exactly the kind of conditions that make autocratic governing easier, regardless of the political party in power. The social conditions justify increased security spending; a rise in violent crime creates fear and panic among the population; and politicians can get away with promising to get tough on whatever results, without ever needing to attack what's really driving the misery and social breakdown. If we can no longer see what's causing the problem, we can't see how to fix it.

Pressure on the Voluntary Sector

Covid-19 exposed just how tenuous social service provision is in Canada. Every day there are stories of services being on the brink of collapse: from deaths in hospital emergency rooms to deaths in long-term care due to negligence. The old lies that Canadians told themselves about their caring and just society collapsed under the weight of our material conditions. When shelter encampments in cities and towns across Canada were broken up by violent police intervention, the rationale that reinforces the neoliberal status quo was on full display: the destitute in society should simply not exist. They should be nowhere, not in parks, not in homes, not on transit systems or in bus shelters. They should be nowhere, and, from Halifax to Montreal to Kitchener to Toronto to Winnipeg to Regina to Edmonton to Vancouver, the one state service that has never seen a budget cut in the neoliberal era — the police — was on hand to carry out these forced disappearances from public spaces.

Poverty grew worse as a result of the pandemic, and people who already lived in extreme poverty were given no direct or indirect help from government. There was no CEWS for someone who was unemployed, and there was no CERB for someone whose income in 2019 was lower than $5,000. To help the poorest Canadians, the federal government gave $100 million to food banks. The expectation was that people who were destitute could survive if extra funding went to food banks. The pressure this placed on food banks themselves was immense, and it demonstrated just how much this sector absorbed the negative impacts of neoliberalism. Any time a service was defunded by the state, what stepped up to fill that need was, more often than not, a charity, a not-for-profit, or another social group. But throwing money at a problem temporarily during a time of crisis doesn't help, as we have seen.

As the welfare state was forming from the 1950s to 1970s, it absorbed the role that many private and religious organizations had filled in the years before the world wars. As social service provision, whether through welfare or healthcare, increasingly became part of what Canadians understood as the role of the state, there was less pressure on — and less need for — private social services, including religious organizations, citizen collectives, or benevolent societies, to care for people.

When the first food bank opened in 1981, it was a response to the economic conditions in Alberta caused by the crash within the oil industry and the resulting job loss and fuel price increases. By the middle of the 1980s, there were seventy food banks across Alberta, and the province had the highest food bank usage of any province or territory.[28] The food bank model relies on volunteers to solicit, coordinate, gather, and sort donations, which are then distributed to food bank clients at locations across a given area. Eventually, food banks also came to rely on the grocery industry, both as locations where donated food could be dropped off and sources of food that was about to spoil. Food banks were a great solution for that changing time. As wages stagnated and people grew hungry, here was a system that relied on unpaid, volunteered labour and the unpaid, volunteered kindness of people to stock shelves so that others wouldn't starve. Why would the state ever consider creating its own food program after food banks started popping up all over Canada?

There was such need for food banks that, by 1985, they grew from that single food bank in Edmonton to ninety-four dotted across Canada. The welfare state couldn't protect people from the market shocks of the oil industry and stagflation. Food banks grew and became more complex. They started to hire CEOs and professionalize but also expanded into coordinating community gardens; skill-building services for their clients, like employment or educational opportunities; and other social programs.[29]

Food banks are far from the only example. Within the charitable and not-for-profit worlds, similar models have been applied to help people flee violence, help immigrants settle in new communities, provide refugees with the supports they need when landing in a new country, coordinate sport and leisure opportunities, and so on. There are also services like Meals on Wheels, medical visit support services, language training, and so many others. While very few of these run completely on volunteer labour, the lion's share of their work tends to fall on the shoulders of unpaid workers, baking inequality from the bottom to the top into these organizations.

If we were to judge how well the state is doing to protect its citizens through the lens of food banks, we would have a pretty clear view. Food insecurity is an important marker of income inequality and poverty. One in seven Canadians is food insecure, a stat that certainly isn't distributed equally across the population.[30] People receiving disability payments are more likely to be food insecure, as are people who live in remote regions, especially on reserves. Worse still, food insecurity has been baked into the core of Canada itself. To build Canada, colonial forces needed to make Indigenous Peoples food insecure to compel them to acquiesce to colonial demands. This included destroying local food systems that had existed on this land since time immemorial. Food insecurity remains fundamental to how Canada operates. Canada could have spent the CEWS money on buying fresh food for every Canadian in the bottom half of income brackets. The Ontario government could spend its extra $22 billion on sending staples like rice, flour, and eggs to every low-income person in the province. But it didn't and it won't. And while anyone might find themselves food insecure as a result of life circumstances at one point or another, in a system that's ableist and rooted in colonialism, disabled people are kept food insecure through inadequate disability funding supports and other barriers to accessing food, and some Indigenous Peoples are the most food insecure people living on this land. Northern First Nations, Inuit, and Métis people have five to six times higher rates of food insecurity than the Canadian national average, and almost 70 percent of Nunavummiut are food insecure.[31]

Food is as fundamental to life as water and shelter, and yet all of these are considered ancillary to what "matters": jobs, saving money, and investing money. But as a proxy for government failure, there are few better examples available than hunger. In 2015, one in seven Canadians lived in poverty; 14.5 percent of all children, or about 1 million, lived in poverty. Eight hundred thousand people accessed food banks.[32] By 2023, new records were being set at food banks all across Canada. In April 2023, the *Toronto Star* published an article with this headline: "Daily Bread Food Bank Usage Hits 40-Year High." It's a funny headline, because it suggests that there were other highs, maybe forty-one or fifty-five years ago, but what it really means is that Toronto's largest food bank has never had usage so high in its entire history. The food bank has only existed for forty years. Twenty-five percent of its clients are children. Thirty-three percent of its clients are full-time workers, and its food budget has exploded from $1.5 million annually to a stunning $1.8 million every month. The Daily Bread Food Bank saw a jump of 12,000 new clients every month for three years straight. In March 2023 alone, 270,000 users visited the Daily Bread. Journalist Santiago Arias Orozco put these stats to Karina Gould, then minister of Families, Children, and Social Development Canada, who said that while she was very concerned by these figures, "the federal government has stepped up in a really big way to support our most vulnerable Canadians" — which is, let's be clear, a bold-faced lie. And this from someone whose very job title includes "families" and "children."

In 2022, Food Banks Canada reported 1,462,795 visits to food banks across the country. That means that Toronto's Daily Bread Food Bank's March 2023 figure alone equals more than 18 percent of total food bank usage in all of Canada the year before. If food insecurity can be compared to bleeding, food banks are trying to stop an artery burst with a gym sock. If you were bleeding on the floor, you'd probably ask yourself "Why a gym sock? Why is this the only thing they have to help me?" And then you find out that, oh, the gym sock manufacturer is a wealthy and well-connected business person. It makes more sense to buy his gym socks than to do anything more fundamental like, say, cauterize the artery. And besides, the owner of the cauterization machine plant isn't friends with government.

Is this too cynical? Consider that the only measure in the 2023 federal budget that targeted the cost of living and, in its branding, food prices, was a change to GST rebates that gives 11 million Canadians up to $234 per year. The so-called grocery rebate will cost $2.5 billion and will evaporate into the profits of Canada's grocery and pharmacy chains faster than you can say "stop the bleeding."[33] Food banks have become a fundamental reaction to hunger. Their importance has grown with the rise in income inequality and the defunding of state services. The 1990s and 2000s saw a massive shift in the relationship between the state and charitable or non-profit organizations. While these organizations had always existed, more pressures, not seen for nearly a century, were downloaded onto them, as they were expected to help fill service gaps that the underfunding of the state created. Starting in 1993, the first three budgets of Jean Chrétien made favourable changes to the tax code to encourage people to spend their money to make up for a shortage of public funds. Whether these changes involved RRSP tax breaks or increasingly generous tax refunds for charitable donations, each was guided by the same approach: loosen up the tax burden on individuals and make it seem like they have increased freedom to decide what services they should spend their money on. It simply meant that Canadians, increasingly, had to decide which form of cancer they believed was most worthy of their money.

Tax reforms were not the only way in which the federal government changed how it interacted with the charitable and not-for-profit sectors. Government also shifted away from core funding. In 1999, the federal government moved toward grant funding, which was tied to a program or a project. It cut the lifeblood from many organizations and forced them to chase grants based on delivering a particular service or product to government. With the passage of NAFTA, competitive bidding became part of service-provision funding. So now charities not only had to figure out how to secure more private funding and still offer services, but they also had to respond to market-based approaches in their grant applications:

how could they provide the cheapest services, offer the greatest consumer choices, and give governments the best bang for their buck?[34] User needs increased at the same time they got more complex. Grants grew even more rigid, reporting requirements for grant money grew more intense, and contracts were, at best, for projects that lasted only a few years. This short-sightedness has created, and will continue to create, pressures on social services, as meagre as they are, and leave people scrambling as the norm.

As is the natural flow of things in Canada, the Liberals set up the pins only for the Conservatives to arrive and knock them down. Stephen Harper famously attacked the voluntary sector, especially charities and not-for-profits that were doing environmental or progressive work. Where the Liberals buried the sector under increased demands and more tenuous support, Harper attacked them directly. This caught a lot of organizations up in frivolous charity audits, the most notable of which targeted the Canadian Centre for Policy Alternatives, probably Canada's most effective research group for progressive public policy (indeed, just take a wander through the bibliography of this book). At the same time, charities and not-for-profits that were friendly to the government were given privileged access.

The late 1800s and early 1900s are sometimes called the golden age of philanthropy. In the United States, wealthy industrialists sought to build public monuments to their wealth both as a way of demonstrating their generosity after their deaths and as a testament to the "superior wisdom, experience, and ability" of the financial elites, as Andrew Carnegie put it.[35] John D. Rockefeller set up his famous foundation in 1913, a few months after the United States introduced personal income tax. Five years later, average Americans were urged, through tax deductions for charitable gifts, to make their own donations. It was not a coincidence that this golden era of philanthropy coincided with "a period of tight moral control, extensive worker exploitation, and the most violent elements of residential schools and the Indian Act."[36] These things naturally go together. When the whims of the wealthy define where money should be spent to help solve social problems, they will always choose the locations that will keep them in power. After all, the wealthy are the primary benefactors of a status quo that keeps most people struggling and a few people exceedingly well off. You cannot have generous philanthropic donors if you don't have extensive worker exploitation and violence; it's only through worker exploitation and violence that philanthropists can make massive sums of money to pay for charitable activities. It's perhaps not surprising, then, that some academics are saying that 1998–2052 is the real "golden age of philanthropy," as bequests to charities in the United States alone are estimated to be somewhere between $109 and $454 billion per year.[37]

Philanthropy is the glove on the hand of neoliberal policy — allow the rich to make incredible sums of money and they will direct some of their money into a hospital wing or a university lecture hall or whatever they hold dear to their hearts. Take, for example, billionaire Jim Pattison. He donated $30 million to help fund the redevelopment of the Royal Columbian Hospital in New Westminster, BC. The tower will have a catchy name: the Jim Pattison Acute Care Tower. But don't confuse it with the Jim Pattison Outpatient Care and Surgery Centre in Surrey (donation: $4 million)[38] or the Jim Pattison Children's Hospital in Saskatoon (donation: $50 million) or the Jim Pattison Medical Campus in Vancouver, thanks to a donation of $75 million, the largest donation ever made by a private citizen.[39] When he made this donation, *Global News* wrote this: "His personal generosity totals $110 million."[40] Pattison's incredible *personal* generosity, aided and abetted by depriving the state of taxes and starving its systems for money. Pattison is far from alone. Peter Munk's name adorns universities and hospitals across Canada, despite his company, Barrick Gold, being implicated in human rights abuses around the globe.

These vanity projects fill a need created by a defunded state. Politicians refuse to increase Canada's revenues through higher taxes on corporations, which opens the door for wealthy benefactors to throw their money around where *they* think it should go. Forget about a democratically elected government making the decisions they were elected to make. Philanthropic donations on the scale of those by Jim Pattison are meant to make us exceedingly grateful for the "generous" help provided. But a properly funded state and government-managed social services would make this "generosity" unnecessary.

The impetus behind philanthropy has seeped into the brains of average people, too. More and more, people now expect to see a GoFundMe link accompanying a devastating announcement: money to pay rent due to an accident and loss of work, money to replace items lost in a house fire, money for food to help someone living with a new diagnosis, money for children in the event that a parent passes away. GoFundMe has stepped in to fill the gaps that have been left by the state, and it is increasingly *expected* to be part of tragedy or disaster. It's the new community chest or religious organization that is there for people who have sudden need.

In a *New Yorker* feature published in 2019, GoFundMe's then CEO Rob Solomon said that his platform had increasingly become a healthcare company, due to how often people use it to fund their healthcare needs. He believed that universal healthcare is a human right and was never concerned that a universal healthcare program would kill the digital platform: "'In Canada, or the U.K., where care is more evolved, medical is still the largest category for us.... When you're sick and out of work, very often you have no income, and GoFundMe is a viable solution.'" Imagine what Woodsworth and Heaps would think today about the fact that their fight for disability and sickness insurance under Mackenzie King had, one hundred years later, turned into this. Solomon blamed the trend toward medical crowdfunding in the United States on income inequality and cast GoFundMe as a stopgap measure. "We're going to be the world's largest health-care company that isn't actually a health-care company—I think we *are*," he said. As 70 percent of the donations to the site are less than fifty dollars, these donations aren't the work of wealthy philanthropists. Everyone is expected to donate if someone they're close to sets up a GoFundMe page. And, as there is no tax advantage at all, it demonstrates just how little Canadians with moderate income actually care about the tax breaks that are built into the system to encourage them to make donations. At the most basic level, people are always willing to help, regardless of any perceived tax benefits. The same probably cannot be said for the wealthiest philanthropists. The system, designed so carefully to mimic and reinforce the market, is being exposed as weak in the face of individual, collective generosity.

Fast forward two years: the Covid-19 pandemic is in full force and GoFundMe's next CEO, Tim Cadogan, writes in *USA Today* that from March to November 2021, a Covid-related fundraiser was started every two minutes, and from the start of the pandemic, one in three fundraisers on his platform was related to Covid-19. In October 2021, the platform saw a rise in people creating GoFundMes just to pay their regular bills. In a few months, the category that the platform had to create for this kind of fundraiser grew to account for 13 percent of all GoFundMes. He concludes his article: "We are proud of the role that GoFundMe plays in connecting those in need with those who are ready to help. But our platform was never meant to be a source of support for basic needs, and it can never be a replacement for robust federal Covid-19 relief that is generous and targeted to help the millions of Americans who are struggling." Charity isn't new, and charity on digital platforms isn't new, either. What is new is the proliferation of campaigns to help people simply cover their basic needs. Paying for rent or electricity shouldn't be so extraordinary that people need to turn to an internet fundraising campaign, but GoFundMe is there so, why not? Like food banks, these stopgap solutions become, in and of themselves, an excuse for governments to continue ignoring the problem as long as they can.

I guess it's possible to see all of this in a positive light. Governments have failed, but thank goodness we have corporations ready to step up to the plate. A government that can't even account for the money it plans to spend, or a government that eschews the obvious policy decision to give a contract to a friend, needs the efficient and compassionate private sector. Whether that private sector help comes through technology that provides average people an easy way to give others money, or whether that private sector help comes from an agency that is helping keep children off the street doesn't matter, right? As long as the help is there? Right?

This is the rationale that underpins everything about our tenuous and fraying situation in Canada today. Rather than challenging politicians, we are told to accept the way things are. These are fatalistic, nihilistic times that show us, in no uncertain terms and at every step of our lives, that we are powerless. The people who hold power in this country tell us they use that power benevolently, sparingly, and in good faith. And sure, we should challenge things like the housing crisis or food insecurity, but we shouldn't dig too deep. If we scratch too far below the surface, what we will find are networks and networks of corporate structures, wrapped upon themselves one hundred times over, obscuring the start from the finish and making it impossible to see how we can start untangling them. It's easier to accept things as they are. Besides, I have a mortgage to pay. I have a ten-hour shift. I have to commute for two hours a day. I don't have time for this.

. . .

At the start of June 2023, *Global News* reported that Canadians should brace for long waits and closed emergency rooms as the summer rush collided with holidays. The article explains the pending woes like this: "Amidst a perfect storm of staffing shortages, escalating burnout rates and upcoming summer vacation time, Canada's health-care system is grappling with a mounting crisis that may lead to longer patient wait times and more emergency room closures, experts warn."[41] *Global News* blames the crisis conditions on understaffing and burnout related to the Covid-19 pandemic but fails to mention any of the history of defunding, privatization, contracting out, tax cuts, and neoliberal transformation, except to mention that the Trudeau government had made the biggest funding investment into healthcare since 2004. Good for them. "But," says Canadian Medical Association president Alika Lafontaine, "the funding has yet to flow to the front line and make an impact on the shortages that people will witness as we go into the summer." Lafontaine warns that 2023 will be worse than 2022, and 2024 will likely be worse than 2023. In 2022, Quebec temporarily closed six emergency rooms, three were closed in New Brunswick, Ontario closed fourteen, a third of rural Manitoba emergency rooms temporarily closed, and thirteen rural British Columbian hospitals shuttered for the equivalent of about four months.[42] The mayor of New Denver, British Columbia, Leonard Casley, blamed the crisis in rural British Columbia hospitals on a 2001 decision made by the BC Liberals to collapse fifty-two health authorities into five large administrative units, which took decision-making out of local hands.[43] Casley is right to remind people that today's crises were designed decades ago. Far from being a perfect storm of vacations, understaffing, and burnout, as the *Global News* article asserts, the real issue goes far deeper. It's not a perfect storm; it's a relentless storm that has never stopped brewing. Or, to bring it into summer terms, it's a forest fire that is exacerbated by actions that we know will only make it worse.

That's the legacy of Mulroney, Chrétien, Martin, Harper, Trudeau, and every provincial leader who chose defunding the state over increasing funding to match service demand. While billions can always be found for corporations to be bailed out, money for health and social services cannot. Transformed over decades by funding cuts, this damage isn't suddenly undone when there is a cash injection into the system. Nurses are still working too many hours and front-line workers are burning out and struggling financially themselves, trying to help clients who are ravaged by the system. These are structural issues that need structural solutions — solutions that cannot continue to support the income inequality and private investment that only serve to reinforce the problem. And so, as your cousin starts a GoFundMe to pay for the time off they need to recover from a bike accident, it's far past time to ask ourselves this: When will we choose to disrupt this relentless storm we've been living in for decades?

CHAPTER 7

The Way Forward

The welfare state is dead. Long live the welfare state!

If neoliberal ideology is a tug-of-war between neoconservative ideology and liberalism, well, liberalism has won. The welfare state has been fundamentally transformed under our noses, but it's still there. We can still go to the hospital, mostly for free. We can still send our children to school, mostly for free. We can still apply for EI and maybe get enough to pay for most of our rent. The death of the welfare state has been wildly exaggerated.

But exaggerated doesn't mean that it's intact. The changes were made slowly, deliberately, in such a way that it was easy to miss what was happening. Rather than finding out that our hospital now only takes Mastercard or that our doctor is employed by an American multinational, we hear about acute examples here and there: a friend who waited thirteen hours to get an X-ray, a parent who spent three days on a gurney in the hospital hallway, a cousin who is homeschooling their child because the conditions at school make the child agitated and violent, a psychologist employed by your cellphone company. The signs of decline are all around us, and there is certainly nothing to suggest that anything is getting better. And worse, neoliberalism's impact on our minds has made it hard to even perceive the decline, let alone understand what needs to happen to reverse it.

We are held hostage by the markets. Humans cannot win in a political battle over corporations without mounting a tremendous struggle. If we expect that politicians are acting in good faith and making decisions based on the health and well-being of the population, Canada's history demonstrates that it is always only one part of the population that matters. Maybe it's white men. Maybe it's white men who make more than $260,000. Maybe it's white men who make $600,000 and work on Bay Street. And so we must be honest with ourselves: something must be done. What keeps tripping us up isn't whether or not we need to organize. It's how.

We need to decentre markets first and foremost and then take significant steps to dismantle Canadian colonialism. That means Land Back, language education, and divestments. That means reparations. But beyond that, Canadians have two options in front of them to stop this decline: reform or revolution. Both options are full of possibilities and come with their own perils. Regardless of which we choose, there is an air war that we must win first. The rhetorical, philosophical campaign that plays out through words, whether from business leaders, politicians, or journalists, is an air war that we simply cannot lose. And to win will take everything we've got.

To Hell with the Markets

When you write anything that identifies all the problems that exist in the world, people inevitably say "Cool story, bro. What's the solution? How do we get out of this mess?" Well, this book is cleverly devised to be the first book in a series, and so, while I have laid out many of the problems that exist in the world, I've fallen short. Corporate interest, from real estate holdings to oil companies to telecommunications to media companies, will all make their appearance in the second book. Government and its march toward authoritarianism and away from responding to people's desires with the help of corporate power will appear in the third. But I can't leave you hanging here like this, can I?

Usually, when framed as questions and posed in public forums, problems are introduced in a way that suggests you don't actually have the answer. In November 2022, I addressed several hundred delegates at a convention about crumbling social conditions and the impact these conditions have on immigrants. After the talk, delegates had the chance to ask me questions. But rather than gliding up to a mic and asking a question directly, the delegates asked their questions through an app. It was an interesting experience. People who might have been otherwise too shy to ask pointed and tough questions were given an invisibility cloak to protect them as they asked their questions. And they did — they were more hostile than I usually expect after a talk. One of the questions was something to the effect of "You think you have all the answers. So how would you solve the housing crisis?"

It was a good question, though my talk wasn't about housing, so it was unfair for the questioner to expect me to have an answer. It also felt like a gotcha; there's no way I can produce an answer to such complex policy issues when placed on the spot. If there were easy answers, they would have been figured out, implemented, tested, and realized by now. Or so goes common sense. That's the thing about common sense, though, as Seth Klein studied in 1996. It feels like it makes sense. It does make sense. But only under a specific set of circumstances or beliefs or ideals. Today's common sense makes sense only if you're looking at it through the extremely narrow lens of neoliberalism.

If the past forty years that have led us to this moment have shown us anything, it is that the slow capture of common sense has been one of the primary goals of the corporate world. It took decades of work and tons of money, research reports, op-eds, management decisions, media cutbacks, and pro-landlord bias — all repeating the same tropes over and over again. It took lobbying, conferences, academic papers, and a consensus among all political parties to form what we consider to be common sense today. My goal is to drive a knife through the heart of this beast and show just how great the deception has been, that our inability to imagine bigger than what we have already is the result of this concerted war, a war that they've won and we've lost. But, in losing, we have not been destroyed, and we can still come back to fight again.

So what's the answer to fixing the housing crisis in Canada? Back at the conference talk, I spitballed: expropriate units from the largest private landlord companies, flood the market with public housing, place rent controls on units and legislate lower rents, tie rental payments to a percentage of someone's paycheque, and so on. Radical ideas in a sense, but also not really. There is one problem with these ideas though: they could all be criticized as being bad for the market. But really, after forty years of neoliberalism, *isn't it time for us to say to hell with the markets?*

Yes, we need to talk about solutions. And breaking with market pressure is just one solution. There are many, many other solutions, depending on what it is we want to fix within society. But the two most important things, the ones that touch everything above all else, are these: ending income inequality and limiting profit. Both can be done, but both would upset the neoliberal status quo in significant ways. "It would be complicated" is how an unbiased journalist might describe this. Complicated, maybe. But necessary if we have any hope of making things better for average people in this country.

On May 23, 2023, Aled ab Iorwerth, deputy chief economist of the CMHC, wrote a concerning report about how Canadians' levels of debt posed a dire risk to the country's economy. "Household debt in Canada has been rising inexorably," he wrote. In 2008, the year of the last major recession, household debt stood at 80 percent of Canada's GDP. Two years later it rose to 95 percent, and by 2021 it reached an astounding 107 percent. That means that Canadians owe 7 percent more than the total worth of our national economy. Three-quarters of that debt comes from mortgages, and it's the three middle quintile income brackets (second lowest, middle, and second highest) that have the highest mortgage liabilities as a share of their total assets. The CMHC, the agency that backstops Canadian mortgages, warns that this poses a significant threat to Canada's economy, as job losses and wage reductions will exacerbate debt. Ab Iorwerth argued, therefore, that Canada is in desperate need of "improved housing affordability."

Few societal chains are harder to break than debt, and few societal prisons are more confounding than debt. Debt constricts one's every move. For deciding to physically move — across town, across the ocean, to change jobs, to escape a bad situation, to join friends, to try something new, to start over, to hide, to celebrate — whatever the reason, debt makes movement difficult. And for movement that requires risk, nearly impossible. Unless, that is, you're cashing in your Toronto-sized mortgage debt, paying it off, and moving to an acreage near Regina. Debt forces people to take jobs they wouldn't normally take, accept working conditions and schedules they wouldn't normally agree to, eat food they wouldn't normally eat, sleep four hours when their bodies are crying out for eight. Debt defangs people's boldness and makes them docile, reticent, and afraid. It lulls them into believing they can't change anything about the world in which they live. Instead, life is oriented around two things: servicing that debt and expanding it. There's no time for revolutionary thought or ideas or trying something new or even something old. Debt fixes us in place. We cannot easily throw off our shackles, just as we cannot hope to live anywhere that has two bedrooms and costs six hundred dollars per month.

If we understand debt as fundamental to how power controls a population, then the solutions to this crisis become more obvious. Debt isn't just someone's personal expenses overshooting what they are able to pay. It's the result of a structural problem: on one side, wages are too low, and on the other, consumption costs are too high. Considering how much profit is baked into both sides of the ledger, average people find themselves under the thumbs of both managers who depress wages to boost their bottom lines and corporations who force us to pay more for our daily needs. This is what happens when you have an economy wholly oriented toward the market. The concerted efforts of the last forty years to orient Canada's economy toward the market and away from people have paid off. Not only has it been a success, but many Canadians will defend this status quo, even if they are themselves drowning in the debt that is a direct result of this system.

The flip side of debt is profits. One study done by the Competition Bureau Canada found that from 2000 to 2020, prices have been driven up due to a lack of competition across the economy.[1] And corporations systemically used the cover of post-pandemic inflation to boost their profits. *CBC News*'s Pete Evans quotes data from Europe that shows whereas from 2000 to 2022 corporate profits composed one-third of inflation, in 2023, the ratio rose to two-thirds. In Canada, where competition makes this even worse, a unit of labour increased by just over 10 percent, while profit per unit rose by 70 percent. For every dollar held by someone in debt, another entity is making a profit, whether that's through the prime interest rate, prime plus five, prime plus eight, or a total of 46.9 percent if you borrow from somewhere like Money Mart. The banks or lenders or loan sharks all profit from debt. And we're a society that runs off of debt; with record-high household debt to income, we grow more indebted every year, simply for the privilege of having a place to live where only a bank, and not a landlord, might kick us out someday.

There is only one way forward if we want to change course. It's obvious. It's the same path that was advocated by social reformers in the late 1800s, by socialists in the Regina Manifesto, by choruses of activists that have sung throughout the decades and whose stamp is affixed to every policy in this country that has provided more for people and done something good for them. We have to decentre the markets from our economy, and we need to build back democratic control of our governments and society. It isn't more complicated than that. No more allowing the markets to decide what gets value and what doesn't. No more tying government spending to market fluctuations. No more market rationales driving everything from where we live to how much we pay to live there to what we eat and so on. Capitalism is on a collision course with total destruction. Rosa Luxemburg is as right today as she was in 1915 when she plainly laid out the options that are before us all: we either advance into socialism or fall back into barbarism. Having tried various forms of barbarism for years, maybe it's time we try socialism.

Of course, this is easy enough to write. As I write this, cars whizz by my street-facing bay window, mostly carrying solitary human units to or from work — jobs they love, jobs they hate, jobs that stir in them no emotion at all, jobs they hold only because their debt is so high. Some of the people in these cars have passions; some would pursue nothing but their passions if they had the financial freedom and time to do so. Indeed, the opportunity cost of our status quo is enormous: money and time spent on commuting that could otherwise be spent on leisure, artists trapped in dead-end jobs, never having the freedom to honour the world with their talents. Chasing the dream of stability in a society where the foundations feel increasingly unsteady. Asphalt where there could be trees. Scowls of capitulation where there could be the contented faces of satisfied people.

How do we get from where we are now to that utopia I've just described, recognizing that Canada has been built, very intentionally, to be a place where radical change is not only opposed, but is derided as bad? Part of the answer is in those societal chains that must be broken: income inequality and debt. The more income inequality grows, the worse societal conditions are going to get. This is where barbarism really shines. People either fight for some small piece of what they think they're entitled to or they fight for the collective. Income inequality and debt create the conditions for people to not only uphold the status quo but even defend it if they are asked to. And that is thanks to this stubborn sense of "common sense" that tells us that the status quo is somewhere between good enough and the best we could ever hope for.

The other part of the answer lies in democratic control — the need for people to have control over what happens within their daily lives, their communities, and their societies. We have fallen so far away from anything that resembles democracy that this can be hard to conceive of for an average person. While expanding imaginations and showing people a new way forward is difficult work, pulling money out of the grubby hands of the rich will be far more difficult. But history shows us that both are very possible.

If we can only agree that the status quo is unsustainable, there are two types of ways forward. The first is a reformist way. This would fall closer in line with the tradition of social change in Canada. The other option is more radical: a revolution that breaks with Canada's status quo to stop the decline. To be sure, a radical option would be far more difficult, but the possibilities are also far more exciting and interesting and, frankly, inspirational. People can discover possibilities they have never dreamed of before. But regardless of which one of these options one chooses, the matter of colonialism needs to be dealt with first.

Regardless of the Way Forward

Reform versus revolution is a classic debate, one that is multifaceted and complex, and one that anyone who wants to see things start changing for the better for average people must engage in. But regardless, colonialism underpins every aspect of life in Canada, including our decline. It generates profits and tethers Canada to a market economy that's rooted in resource extraction. And, as reconciliation efforts to date have demonstrated, reformist decolonialism is not going to cut it. So what is there to do about colonialism? The answer is short: for our collective survival, the land, air, and water included, we have to dismantle it.

Colonialism never ended; it simply mutated. Reconciliation efforts going on while Indigenous women are still murdered or still go missing ring hollow. Making right the sins of the past, like residential schools or the Sixties Scoop, is impossible when there are more Indigenous children in care today than there have been at any time before. These problems aren't theoretical. They continue to destroy lives. In the daily Facebook posts of mothers and fathers and cousins and friends desperately searching for their loved ones; in the cries for help, whether for financial help or safety or care or service needs; in the broken asphalt, the melting ice roads, the defrosting runways; in the house fires, the mercury poisonings, the plastics found in food — these are the greatest problems facing Canada right now. And these problems are directly connected to Canada's colonial social safety net.

In 1920, as a committee of the House of Commons was considering whether or not to make residential school mandatory for "Indian" children aged 5 to 15, Deputy Superintendent of Indian Affairs Duncan Campbell Scott laid out his vision to explain why he believed participation in these institutions needed to be mandatory: "I want to get rid of the Indian problem. I do not think as a matter of fact, that this country ought to continuously protect a class of people who are able to stand alone. That is my whole point. Our objective is to continue until there is not a single Indian in Canada that has not been absorbed into the body politic, and there is no Indian problem and there is no Indian question, and no Indian Department and that is the whole object of this Bill."[2] The bill passed. School was fundamental to Scott's vision, and the horror of this institutional system remains alive and very present for the many survivors and their families to this day and beyond.

Sure, there has been evolution — the residential schools have closed down and Indigenous children now attend public school like non-Indigenous children, but how far, really, has the model evolved? Just 55 percent of First Nations people have finished high school. Among Inuit people, that number is even lower: 44.5 percent.[3] Household income, whether they live in crowded housing, on or off reserve, or with one versus two parents, impacts how likely an Indigenous youth is to finish high school. Education itself is a factor, but so, too, are all the other ways we would judge someone's quality of life: good housing, dependable income that can cover for more than just necessities, and so on.

It is fundamental to understand that the social safety net was intended to give white Canadians what they needed to populate, mine, exploit, and develop Canada from a colony into a grown-up country. We must understand the connection between the public school system and residential schools because we have never endeavoured to reconcile how tightly woven colonial and white supremacist ideals are in education in this country. The same goes for healthcare and social services. The social safety net was used to establish a white Canada while coordinating genocide among Indigenous Nations, from whose land every bit of wealth that exists in the country today is made possible. Regardless of whether Canadians choose reform or revolution as their path forward, there is no getting around this: the only way that we can ensure a future that is safe, prosperous, and joyous for all people in this land is to start with divesting parts of Canada back to Indigenous communities and to pay commensurately for everything we have stolen and continue to steal. And let me be clear, I say this as someone who has benefitted immensely from white supremacy. The inheritances, the family members who give jobs to their relations, the parents to pay for mortgage down payments, the debt-free access to university education — all the white people stuff so many of us assume to be normal needs to be dismantled if we are going to rebalance the scales of justice and fairness in this country.

There is no reform option here. The revolution has to be fundamental and bold. And this will take a combination of measures, measure that have been building in parallel with neoliberalism, from the Royal Commission on Aboriginal Peoples in 1991 to the Calls for Justice of the Final Report into Murdered and Missing Indigenous Women and Girls following the national inquiry begun in 2016. But, critically, these changes cannot be implemented in a way that seeks to defend Canada's status quo — Canadians keep trying to maintain things as they are while attempting reconciliation, and that's why we keep failing so badly. It requires that power from the government of Canada and the provinces be divested and that Indigenous communities be given the resources they need to build their own services, protect and grow their languages, and build a prosperity that Canada has always refused to allow.

It also goes beyond Calls to Action toward what can be summed up as Land Back. Canada must relinquish land. Determining how much, where, how, and to whom is a process the country must engage in if there is any hope at a just future. There are too many Canadians who think these issues are a side note, however critical or important, to issues that plague the health system or social services, but they aren't. They are deeply entwined, and we cannot solve these problems without getting to the root of what drives so much misery in Canada — the food insecurity, housing insecurity, personal and community insecurity, and desperate poverty that Canada continues to impose on Indigenous people. It means restoring free travel and pouring money and resources into language education. And yes, in the process of all of this, directly confronting the racism that would meet a project like this.

In 2015, political leader and member of the Secwépemc Nation Arthur Manuel wrote, "It is no accident that protecting the land was the first issue that mobilized Idle No More. In the struggle to protect the land, Indigenous peoples are the first and last line of defence."[4] Idle No More started as teach-ins in Saskatoon held to show what Canada was losing as Stephen Harper planned to loosen protections of most of Canada's freshwater pathways. Understanding the common sense connection between life and land, air, and water is fundamental, and Indigenous movements rooted in Land Back — justice, civil rights, self-determination, nation building, language strengthening, and traditional practices — are bringing back to Indigenous people what has been stolen and turned into economic profit by Canada. But all of this poses an existential threat to Canada itself. As Indigenous people reclaim what is theirs, Canadians will undoubtedly be forced to ask themselves on what basis they even have a claim to this territory. When strong Indigenous cultures, economies, and politics pose a threat to access to oil and gas, mining, or logging exploitation, we see very clearly why Canada's status quo exists: regardless of the horrors and depraved living conditions of so many, economically and politically, misery serves Canada very well.

It isn't just existential, of course. If Canada is ever to fully atone for its colonialism, it will cost all the money that oil companies make from exploiting Dene, Cree, and Métis lands in the north and west. Or the money that mining companies are lining up to make as Ontario develops the so-called Ring of Fire. Or Coastal

GasLink in British Columbia. Or the money made off poisoning waterways cared for by the Wolastoqey. Or new mines that threaten Mi'kmaq or Anishinaabe traditional territory. Or, or, or, or, or. But, as Melissa Brittain and Cindy Blackstock wrote in a literature review published in 2015, "The government pattern of trying to save money by providing inequitable and flawed services to Aboriginal peoples has persisted, regardless of the availability of solutions and the financial situation of the country." The continued theft and exploitation of land while consistently underfunding Indigenous communities is colonization. Experiments in underfunding are then brought to the entire system. If leadership thinks that underfunding doesn't cause too much harm, it gets adopted into the mainstream system. If it causes harm, the colonial mindset says "That's okay — let's just keep this formula for Indigenous people." This is a pattern that needs to be smashed if we, all of us, have any hope of ever trying to change our current trajectory through either policy reforms or revolutionary ideas.

The Reformist Way Forward

The most attractive way forward for many progressives is reformist: changes that could provide fast relief to some people, that aren't too complicated, that could be implemented immediately, or that would require a straightforward policy change. These are the kinds of solutions we hear most about from journalists and politicians — they tend to be easier and faster and rarely disrupt the status quo. And sometimes that's fine; getting food to someone quickly is a priority if they're starving. There's no reason to throw the baby out with the bathwater, many people will argue, and rather than tearing down things that have been built over decades, why not try to reform them in such a way that we can start turning things around. You know, give people small victories so they get ready and have the energy to fight for the big ones.

Because really, even small victories take a lot of work to implement today. So the voices that call for Canadians to fight for reforms have the benefit of urgency. Take EI as an example. In 2019, just before the start of the Covid-19 pandemic, Canada had 1.15 million unemployed workers. But only a small number of them — 453,130 — were receiving EI, not even half. The Liberals have been promising to overhaul EI for years, and they had made some changes to the program, especially when massive unemployment from the pandemic forced them to. They made temporary changes like eliminating the waiting period before you can receive benefits, requiring fewer qualifying work hours (you must have worked 420 hours over three years, down from up to 700) and setting a new minimum benefit. But it's still a broken system. The Liberals have *promised* to make significant changes to the program. They swear they're good for it.

Recent Liberal temporary reforms significantly boosted the ranks of individuals receiving EI — the number of workers receiving regular benefits under the temporary changes was 75 percent, up from 40 percent, on average, before the pandemic.[5] So there's little question that their reforms are helping more people. The program covers only 55 percent of lost earnings, though, still forcing many people into poverty. Increasing that rate to at least the median rate among industrial countries, which is 65 percent, would have a big impact on the financial security of unemployed Canadians. Or Canada could restore the previous rate of 67 percent from before 1994. Though, to compare, in 1971, individuals with dependents received 75 percent of their earnings. There should also be a scale that caps how much they receive. The higher a wage goes above the maximum insurable earnings cut-off of $60,300, the less a percentage of their earnings someone will receive. So someone who lost a job paying $80,000 would be eligible to receive only 41 percent of their previous salary from EI.[6] The federal government could once again finance the program as it did when it was created in 1940 — pay for all administrative costs plus kick in 20 percent. The federal government has also promised that their reforms will include ways to get freelancers and gig workers onto EI. We're waiting.

These reforms help people, no question. But there are more significant reforms that could help people, too. The minimum wage could be increased to force employers to pay people enough so they can afford to live. There could be minimum-hours legislation to ensure that part-time workers get the hours they need instead of the zero-hour contracts that are becoming more and more common. In parallel, there is also the question of a maximum wage. The NDP has taken this approach and promised to implement a wealth tax of 1 percent on family income above $10 million a year. Plus they would increase the top marginal tax rate from 33 percent to 35 percent and increase the capital gains inclusion rate from 50 percent to 75 percent. That means that only 25 percent of profits extracted from capital gains would remain untaxed under the NDP plan. This could generate more than $12 billion annually, if the rich didn't respond to the policy changes by stashing their money somewhere else to shelter it from taxes.[7]

Housing is another policy area where minor reforms would make a big difference. If Canada needs to build 3.5 million units of affordable housing by 2030, which is the estimate as of late 2022, then the only question is who will build these units the fastest and of the highest quality. At least a quarter need to be reserved for people with very low or no incomes. None of the national parties is currently promising this many new units — making this reform one that feels radical. Politicians need to catch up to where housing advocates have been for a long time, and the rapid creation of new housing, including low- or no-income housing, is one of the most pressing policy demands in Canada right now. The federal government needs to get back into building social housing. There also need to be changes made in zoning policies, especially in areas that have been zoned for single-family housing. That will open up market spaces to townhouses, multiplex apartments, and other units that aren't either single detached houses or skyscrapers. And again, developers need to be forced to ensure that a quarter of these units are reserved for low- or no-income residents, with guarantees that will last for more than a couple of years.[8]

One of the reasons why the housing crisis in Canada is worse than nearly anywhere else in the world is because of the influence of corporations, who treat housing as a commodity rather than as something that everyone has a basic human right to access. Canada's largest seven real estate trusts own 145,000 rental units. Together, they have dodged paying $1.5 billion in taxes through tax breaks facilitated by neoliberal governments. The magazine *Corporate Knights* breaks down how the tax loopholes are starving the state from much-needed revenue while also driving income inequality: "How fair is it that someone can buy a house in 2015 for $500,000 as an investment (not a principal residence), gather $18,000 a year in rent, sell it for $1.2 million in 2022, pay 25% in capital gains tax on half of the increased value, and walk away with a $612,500 gain?" Loans could be linked to the rentable value of a property, rather than the speculative value, which would help deflate some of the inflation that is built into the housing market, and capital gains taxes should be increased to 100 percent.[9]

Then there is the entire health and social services world. Paying workers more, giving workers more control over the workplaces, and allowing the people who see the problems close-up every day to make the changes they know are necessary would all move the needle in the right direction. Increasing the number of physicians or integrated health teams that can care for individuals is critical, considering how many Canadians report not having — at minimum — a family doctor. To relieve pressure on emergency rooms,

Canadians need to have access to non-emergency healthcare, whether through clinics or the family doctor's office, so that the ER is not their only recourse for accessing care. Service provision and disability supports need to be better funded, especially programs like provincial disability allocations, which currently force people into poverty to the point that some individuals consider medical assistance in dying (MAID) as an alternative to their ongoing struggles. Increasing disability allowance rates and eligibility would go a long way to helping many people, as would ending clawbacks on earnings for disabled people, who have higher than average costs for their daily needs.[10] In Saskatchewan, where it was found that 60 percent of all calls made to the Saskatchewan Income Support program are flat-out ignored, reforms that boost resources should have the specific aim of building in respect for clients.[11] Similar ableism and disrespect are built in to all provincial and territorial systems and cause thousands of people needless grief while they deal with systems that were never built to care about the person or their needs.

In education, large class sizes and a lack of supports for complex mental health challenges could be fixed with more teacher and re-source workers, whose salaries should be higher and whose education and training should be free. Canada is in the midst of implementing a national childcare program. Ensuring that this is implemented universally is absolutely critical and will help families with young children ease the incredible financial burden of paying for childcare. And at universities and colleges, student fees should be free and housing should be significantly subsidized so that students are not rejected from the system based solely on their inability to pay.

If income inequality remains the most pernicious problem facing Canadians, then attacking it should also be a priority. While that can be done through all of these reforms, it needs to happen alongside policy changes to redistribute money beyond making adjustments to the tax system. Union membership should be encouraged, and joining a union should be made easy. All provinces and territories should outlaw the use of scab labour during a labour dispute, making negotiations the only way forward for both workers and their employers. As workers get better organized and demand more money from their employers, they will cut into employers' profits, thereby reducing how much money is paid out to shareholders or bequeathed to tax-sheltered foundations. Average people are far more likely to spend the money in their pockets in local cafés or stores than are the ultra-wealthy, who are much more likely to hoard their money offshore and look at it from time to time when they're feeling lonely or sad. While one research paper from the Bank of Canada rejects the notion that income inequality is spiking higher now — though it is higher today than it has been in forty years — even they concede that government spending and policy measures are key to tackling income inequality, something that worries them because it is negatively correlated with economic growth: "Government transfers to households and the progressive nature of the personal income tax system in Canada have significantly reduced the level of income inequality and mitigated its increase during recessions."[12]

In the face of many complex, deep, and concerning problems, the one thing that Canada has no shortage of is solutions. For every issue, in every sector, for every source of someone's pain, there are multiple ways forward. More money. Better management of social services. More responsive services. More democracy. Financial incentives to get people to volunteer more. Income supplements for food. Removing the GST from more essential items. And on and on and on. Indeed, the voices from the ground, struggling against every single issue that plagues Canada, say exactly what steps could be taken to improve their situations. This is why it's so easy to construct a manifesto these days. It isn't ideas we're short on; it's will.

But will isn't simply the will to fix minor issues. It's also the will to see these issues as interconnected. The second you find a particular thread to pull, you realize that everything is connected. You start pulling and before you know it, you have a string that stretches across housing affordability, social services, mental health supports, addiction healthcare and services, profit gouging, and the list of isms that characterize the life of anyone who is marginalized in this country.

The Radical Way Forward

But how much do reforms help when the thread you've pulled keeps going and going and going? EI can only be reformed so much. Unless there is a fundamental change in how we care for people who are unemployed, there will be infinite excuses, consultations, calls to action, forums, focus groups, reports, and roundtables suggesting all manner of changes necessary for the program. That's the thing about modern Canada: so much of its infrastructure is self-replicating. Bad programs beget bad programs, and eventually, you're scraping off another layer of wallpaper that had been painted over three times. If we go back to the truth that Canada is a colonial nation that continues to do colonial things, then the reforms that we can identify as necessary for this country will always stop before we hit something real — they'll always stop before we upset the status quo.

Canadians had a glimpse of that in 2020, as the federal government created the CERB and the CEWS. Both programs had revolutionary potential in that tens of billions of dollars were sent to Canadians to try to keep them afloat during a historic moment. Except governments everywhere constrained all of the pandemic responses to very specific ends: narrowly helping a narrow group of people and not, under any circumstances, upsetting the status quo. Not upsetting the status quo meant ensuring that there would be no permanent improvements made to anyone's lives. So rather than giving people what they needed to survive the pandemic, escape rising domestic violence, and deal with increasing behavioural issues among children, personal crises, or whatever, Canadians were given the smallest amount of money that would make sure they remained chained to this very system, while the biggest corporations hit paydirt yet again.

Even though there isn't much appetite among politicians to have serious discussions about reforms — they instead prefer to talk about talking about reforms — there is at least space for these conversations. Corporations and lobby groups alike talk about how they would fix things like extreme poverty or gendered violence, and their voices are regularly welcomed on mainstream platforms, whether in media or at conferences, organizations like the Canadian Club, or professional not-for-profits. Reforms are so popular to talk about that even on mainstream television channels, it's rare to hear a real debate over solutions because our problems are well-known and hard to argue with. Debates about the problems rarely depart from everyone agreeing that we have a problem. This becomes fuel for the far right; because massive change is too taboo to entertain in this country, it finds currency in rising extremist movements. Remember Harper calling Layton "Taliban Jack" as a strategy to distract from his constitutional problems? These movements are dominated by the far right, proto-fascists who have the ear of only one mainstream political party: the Conservatives.

And so it's difficult to have sober and serious conversations about radical change. There is very little space in Canada — no mainstream space and very little alternative space — to talk about massive change with a mass audience. The kinds of changes that would make a banking executive tug at his collar or the CEO of a telecommunications company feel his stomach drop.

But radical thought has always existed in Canada, and the blueprint that was written in 1933 by the Co-operative Commonwealth Federation remains as relevant today as it was back then. Consider this from their preamble: "Power has become more and more concentrated into the hands of a small irresponsible minority of financiers and industrialists and to their predatory interests the majority are habitually sacrificed. When private profit is the main stimulus to economic effort, our society oscillates between periods of feverish prosperity in which the main benefits go to speculators and profiteers, and of catastrophic depression, in which the common man's normal state of insecurity and hardship is accentuated."[13] And that was written ninety years ago.

Indeed, profit drives everything. Profit is the reason we don't give people necessities for free as a matter of course, but instead force them to line up at the food bank. Profit is why the housing market is out of control. Profit and the rationale that creates profit are why public services have been mismanaged to the point of disaster, as group after group takes charge of them and applies market principles to care industries, extracting "cost savings" from someone whose job is to remove a catheter, take a blood sample, and monitor someone's oxygen levels. Profit is insidious and creates a cyclical "logic": my salary is too low and I have no pension because my boss wants profit, so I can't afford to retire. To pay for retirement, I have invested too much money into the house I live in that I plan to sell when I retire, so I need the housing market to remain inflated so that when I sell this house, I have the money I need to pay off my mortgage and also retire. The money that I have saved needs to earn me as much interest as possible because I don't make enough money in my job to afford my expenses, so I need to invest in the highest yield stocks and bonds, the very stocks and bonds that are extracting high rents from people living in their hedge fund–owned apartment block. And on and on. Pull the thread, the yarn doesn't stop.

Capitalism is slippery. With every new reform, capitalism has evolved to swallow it up and turn it into something that helps the markets above all else. We could sit around and argue how best to untangle this yarn — put that loop over this thread here, shuttle the ball through this hole, place the thread back over itself here — or we could just get the scissors and cut through to what we need. Reframing the question with what scissors, where to cut, and so on, is collective work that we are very capable of doing. That is, if we find the necessary space to have these conversations boldly, soberly, and publicly.

The social safety net is incompatible with commodification. At every instance when a government hacked at it, it was done in the service of the markets. Whenever someone rushed in to fix a hole or save a program, there was someone else who stood to make money off the decline of well-funded, progressive measures. And so, if we have any hope at all of stopping this decline, we have to decommodify the necessities of life. Of that there is little question. Decommodifying food, housing, and social services is critical to ensuring that people can have what they need to survive without having vultures looming over them looking for how to extract profit from the things they need to live. In Berlin, a city where about 85 percent of people rent, Berliners voted in favour of expropriating all rental units owned by private landlords who own more than three thousand of them. They would then be incorporated into the city's social housing. The vote didn't trigger action, however. Berlin's city government has not put the results into action. They have either been stalling or doing their due diligence to "examine their options."[14]

Just as debt constricts people's choices, so do their fears about being able to afford retirement someday. We need public pensions to help get us out of the circular thinking imposed by the logic of investments that underpins everything from private, for-profit long-term care to the inflated real estate market. If every Canadian was given enough money to live out their retirement, there would be no need for anyone to try to maximize their savings with investments that — you guessed it — serve the market. By the same token, all businesses should pay into a public pension, open to scrutiny and public review, that will guarantee enough money for their employees when they retire. Healthcare has to be free and expanded to include eye care, dental care, physiotherapy and massage therapy, and mental-health supports. Education should be free, from childcare right through to a Ph.D. if someone wants to pursue one. And Canada needs to rapidly divest from oil, gas, and mining and develop internal industries that actually produce goods. If we have any hope of transitioning to a greener economy, the sooner we get on with building our own transition, the sooner we'll avoid having the transition forced upon us by catastrophic climate change. Yes, sometimes even radical ideas are common sense.

Fighting Neoliberalism

To change anything in Canada requires a concerted, multifaceted effort to change culture, ideas, and popular understandings of why things are the way they are. The right wing has shown us how to do this. All you need is a rotating door of politicians and business people who sit on the same boards, operate the same companies, or hold the same Cabinet positions. Then have think tanks, funded by the richest oil, gas, and mining companies, flood the public sphere with literature, arguments, rhetorical frames, and so on, and repeat them on national tribunals. This is easy because no *Globe and Mail* editor is going to refuse the contribution of someone from RBC or Shell. And then you create a national council that brings together the most powerful business leaders. They lobby international players to make sure everyone sings from the same song sheet. Policies are floated. If they land like a lead balloon, change course, but always do it fast enough so the average person doesn't notice.

It's easy.

It's easy if you are rich and powerful and have access to resources and national media outlets. That's all it takes. When we're up against a system that tells us what is good, what is right, what is immoral, and what should outrage us, it's *very hard* to pierce through the rhetoric, especially when we have no power, relative to the country's top CEOs, politicians, and other decision-makers.

But *very hard* does not mean impossible. In being crushed, we have stopped a lot of the critical work of movement building that would be very easy to restart. We still have institutions that could be doing the kind of work that can change narratives. There's no reason, for example, why the Canadian Labour Congress or provincial labour federations couldn't organize one-day student conferences akin to the ones the Fraser Institute has organized since the early 1990s. There's no reason why labour bodies couldn't put out a statement to respond to every sneeze, grunt, or fart coming out of Ottawa, always bringing the sneeze, grunt, or fart back to working people. There are channels we can use to popularize revolutionary ideas. We could take advantage of the collapse of mainstream, for-profit news and build alternatives — there are some organizations on the left with the kind of money needed to do this well, especially with the collapse of the print industry.

The problem is that the institutional left in Canada has been the most stuck in time of all of us, and because they are stuck, it's hard for many of the people in the bureaucracy to claw to the top of the hole in which they work and see the sky. Between government and committee meetings, between focus groups and negotiations, between surveys and emailers, neoliberalism has weighed down these groups as well, but they rarely stop to consider what is harming our ability to do fundamental organizing and what is helping. There aren't enough left-wing organizations that aren't already wholly committed to reform. Too many think that tinkering here and there is going to end extreme poverty in this country. It will not. If we're all distracted enough to believe we are making progress, we will never build the popular support required for wide-scale, massive change. It's a classic strategy of distraction, and far too many people who have the power to fight for massive change have bought into it.

We are in dire need of changing the narrative. It's not sufficient to allow ourselves to have these crises named and defined for us — we have to name them and define them ourselves. I have called the housing situation a crisis throughout these pages, and I am reminded of Ricardo Tranjan, author of the book *The Tenant Class*, who writes, "A housing system that serves all but one group is not in a state of crisis; it is one based on structural inequality and economic exploitation."[15] Nothing is a crisis when a system is simply doing what it was set up to do.

• • •

We have to build power that can meaningfully confront both political ideology and capitalist demagogues in this country. Duncan Cameron argues, "In Canada, as elsewhere, the business counter-revolution was economic. Its aim was to change the way in which surpluses are shared by investors and workers, between the people who own the businesses and take the profits and the people who do the work and create the value." Indeed, the fight to wrestle profits away from workers required an incredible effort to do away with religious conditioning that says greed is sin and replace it with the belief that greed is not only good, it's necessary. Cameron argues that this could not have happened without businesses dominating Canada's political system: "To change the economics you have to change the politics; that is the lesson of the business counter-revolution. And politics is the only way to gain democratic control of the economic agenda."[16] Reading this and thinking about the NDP is enough to send someone into a spiral of despair. But more support for the NDP isn't what Cameron is calling for. To change the status quo requires us to actually do politics, and we can look to the past to see ways in which doing politics was successful: wide-scale, radical organizing among disenfranchised workers happened at the same time that movements of farmers, union members, and progressive religious leaders came together over common concerns. The CCF brought forth movement demands, not to ultimately throw them aside and sell out, but to bring socialist ideas to the political arena. Their role in creating the best elements of the welfare state is undeniable. We cannot lobby or work-with-government ourselves out of this decline. It will take organizing on our own terms, across issues and across regions, to really build the kind of power necessary to stop this decline. But it will also take radical demands. Reforms are a dead-end street, and the stakes are too high for us to waste time finding ourselves at the bottom of a fenced-off cul-de-sac, scratching our heads and wondering how Google Maps could have led us astray.

Conclusion

In March 2021, Canadians were eagerly awaiting their first doses of a Covid-19 vaccine. Most Canadians would have access to their first dose by the time July 2021 rolled around. Vaccine clinics were set up inside convention centres, ferry terminals, parking lots, gyms — anywhere where a lot of people could be brought in, processed, stabbed with a needle, observed for twenty minutes, and then sent on their way. These clinics showed the incredible potential that Canada's healthcare industry has: when we deem it important or necessary, we can do amazing things.

Also in March 2021, Canada passed the biggest change to healthcare policy in a generation. Parliament agreed to expand MAID to anyone with a grievous and irremediable condition and whose death was not reasonably foreseeable. MAID had been legal since 2016 but only for those whose death was reasonably foreseeable. Now, anyone with a grievous and irremediable health condition could apply to the state to have the state end their lives. Hailed by some as a humane policy that engendered the most fundamental type of self-determination, it was panned by others as being modern eugenics. On one side were people who were afraid to die without having the option to pull the plug themselves. On the other were people who had already fallen through the cracks in the medical system. They were yelling as loud as they could: this will push people to an early grave.

Since the policy was expanded, many, many people have said publicly that they feel like they're being pushed into an end-of-life decision they don't want. Nearly every week in 2023, another story emerged of someone who has applied for MAID because they're afraid of losing their apartment, they don't have the access to medical support that they need, or they're desperate for help that they can't access. A medical condition that is grievous and irremediable is exacerbated when an individual cannot get the disability support services they need. From public assistance rates that legislate disabled people into poverty to a shortage of personal care workers that makes it difficult to ensure someone can get the help they need; from a lack of accessible transportation options to rents that are too high; from social isolation to feeling like a burden on loved ones — all of these issues are made far worse by a person's state of health and access to social services. If someone could live in an accessible apartment, have the personal help they need, have enough money to afford good and healthy food and enough left over for savings, life would look much better. The mental toll that comes with fighting for services from a system oriented to make someone money rather than keep someone alive is enormous. When the government passed expanded MAID, it signalled that it is easier for someone to die than it is for the same person to pay for the services they need to live well.

There is no better issue that encapsulates the current moment than expanded MAID. Politicians, knowing that expanded MAID will save the healthcare system money, have run toward expanding suicide rather than running toward changing the healthcare system. The federal government could have quadrupled income supplements for disabled people. They could have mandated that no landlord charge a rent higher than a third of a province or territory's low-income supplement. They could have mandated that air conditioning be installed in every low-income apartment in the country. Instead, they gave people with already strained resources quick access to ending their lives. After all, when someone is not able to work, they may be part of the "deserving" poor, but their worth to a market-oriented society drops considerably. If the argument is that all people should have the ability to end their lives if they believe that death is preferable to life, why is suicide legal for someone who has a permanent disability and not for everyone else? Or is that what's coming?

Expanded MAID, which the Liberals want to expand further for people whose sole underlying illness is mental illness (despite groups like the Canadian Association for Suicide Prevention arguing that there is no scientific evidence that demonstrates that suicidal thoughts cannot be abated with the right treatment) and to mature minors, is the natural outcome of the death march called neoliberalism. Give people total freedom: freedom to profit, to exploit others, to accumulate as much capital as they can, to end their lives. It's the most intense and narrow freedom the markets can allow. And we can never be free of the markets; we owe our lives to the markets.

When Maude Barlow and Bruce Campbell wrote *Take Back the Nation*, they were principally concerned with how free trade and emerging political decisions to defund the state would destroy Canada as they knew it back in 1991. While fears about a U.S. takeover dominated their pages, the idea that assisted suicide would become one of the biggest healthcare policy decisions of the past forty years was nowhere in the book. It wasn't contemplated — assisted suicide wasn't legal at all. Their concerns were deeply coloured by the context in which they lived, and they assumed that the biggest threat to Canada was U.S.-style politics. Regardless of whether those politics came directly from the U.S. or they came by way of corporate control, they posed a threat to the existence of the Canada they knew. Indeed, the first sentence of the book was a dire warning: "Canada faces extinction as an independent nation." The threats were regional rivalries within Canada, the "long-unresolved conflict between the French- and English-speaking peoples of Canada," and "the lure of closer economic and political ties to the United States." The appearance of all three crises, plus the emergence of free trade, could spell the end of Canada, they warned.

Barlow and Campbell were right to be concerned, and both would go on to become leading activists and researchers warning about everything from the threats of deregulation, like in the rail industry, which led to the incineration of Lac-Mégantic and the deaths of forty-seven people, or the corporate threat to Canadian waters. But what neither saw clearly in 1991 was that the threat came primarily from within: that Canadian politicians and business people posed a greater threat to Canada than did anything that might come from the United States. That free trade wouldn't destroy Canada; it would mutate into something far more grotesque. That, as manufacturing was hollowed out, Canadian politicians would say the only way to build anything anymore is to hand massive sums of public money directly to companies to bribe them to operate here. When Canada offered $13 billion to Volkswagen to build an electric vehicle plant, a new era was born again. The state is defunding itself for the pleasure of having a few thousand jobs in southwestern Ontario, for an amount of money that eclipses what it spent to bail out the auto industry or the airline industry. When competitor Stellantis saw the deal, they stopped the construction of their electric vehicle battery plant until Canada agreed to pony up similar money; the $1 billion the government had offered was not nearly enough.[1]

Defunding the state, reconceptualizing services as business ventures rather than collective care, allowing corporations to increase their prices under the cover of inflation — these all have obvious impacts. Life is more expensive. Services are crumbling. We lose democratic control. But what's less obvious is that they also have a psychological impact on us. We feel tired, isolated, and burnt-out. Teachers cry in the lunchroom. Nurses cry in their cars. Personal care workers rush from person to person, never able to form a relationship with the people they work with. Men are told to chase good jobs that sap the resources from our land and then are told that if those resources were ever to end, it would pose not just a threat to their livelihoods but an existential threat to their identities. We feel powerless. We've forgotten how to organize. We grow increasingly desperate.

But we can't lose hope. We have to understand that these feelings are the intended result of the policies that have dominated Canadian politics for forty years. The balance has been tipped; the markets control everything and everything is in service to the markets. Understanding these as intentional forces allows us to make the necessary connections and, critically, build the pieces necessary to fight against them and take Canada back from the markets.

We are on the cusp of a new paradigm shift. Neoliberalism has been around for forty years and has evolved to look much different than it did when it first came to Canada. The material conditions of neoliberalism have been transformed, and so the political outcomes are radically different than what people like Barlow and Campbell were worried about back in 1991. The good news for everyone concerned about this new paradigm shift is this: there has never been a better time to disrupt the status quo.

I feel like I've left so much out of this book. I could have turned out an entire book about housing, healthcare, or any of the big issues that appear in these pages. But, as we say in French, in order to *mettre la table*, or set the table, for a discussion about Canada in decline, we have to start at the foundation. The foundation of any country is the rights of its people — who has them, who does not, and what we get from these rights. As citizens, we have a collection of rights and responsibilities. On paper, we can flex our rights to advocate for better protections, more resources, and more complete services. But in reality, our ability to flex anything has been stymied by the forces that have hacked the social safety net to bits. To understand the break between citizens and their leverage over their governments, we have to talk about corporate capture of democratic institutions. Corporate control has always been an important force in Canadian politics, but since the 1980s, corporations have consolidated control over all aspects of Canadians' lives. Canadians exist as mere units of profit, whether for the Weston family, for Rogers Communications, for Suncor or Coastal GasLink, for Canadian Pacific or the Irvings. Understanding the interplay between corporate control over government, our economy, and society in general is no small part of the puzzle of understanding Canada. And that is the next volume in this series.

Acknowledgements

One afternoon, I found myself on Whyte Avenue in Edmonton with a few hours to kill. It was September, warm and sunny. I had a talk that evening sandwiched between beers on a patio and a surprise Joel Plaskett show. All of that plus sleep in just seventeen hours before my flight home.

It was on that patio that I wrote the outline for this series, Canada in Decline. Pitching a multivolume book in this market is an act of pure optimism, and I'm lucky that Kwame Fraser is an optimistic guy. My deepest thanks to everyone at Dundurn for believing in this project, especially my editor, Meghan Macdonald.

Thanks also to everyone who generously gave me their attention over the period that I wrote this book. Speaking to crowds in Orillia, Waterloo, Saint John, Bracebridge, Halifax, Banff, Toronto, Peterborough, Huntsville, Edmonton, Ottawa, and Montreal helped crystalize many of the ideas contained herein.

This book would not have been possible without the Canadian Centre for Policy Alternatives. Thanks to them, Canadians know so much more about their country and their government. They serve a fundamental role in helping us understand what's wrong with Canada, and how it could be made right.

To everyone who has sent me a kind word to remind me that I don't exist in a void, thank you for your solidarity. Thanks for every beer, decaf coffee, and sandwich that you bought for me. I hope I can return the kindness if I haven't yet.

And to my family, the primary audience for that process of crystallization: my eternal gratitude.

Notes

Introduction

1   Pierre Bourdieu, "The Essence of Neoliberalism," *Le Monde Diplomatique*, December 1998, mondediplo.com/1998/12/08bourdieu.

2   Margaret Thatcher, "Interview for *Woman's Own*," interview by Douglas Keay, October 31, 1987, transcript, Margaret Thatcher Foundation, margaretthatcher.org/document/106689.

3   William K. Carroll, "Social Democracy in Neoliberal Times," in *Challenges and Perils: Social Democracy in Neoliberal Times*, eds. William K. Carroll and R.S. Ratner (Black Point, NS: Fernwood, 2005), 13.

4   Bourdieu, "The Essence."

5   Carroll, "Social Democracy," 12.

6   Cynthia J. Cranford, Leah F. Vosko, and Nancy Zukewich, "Precarious Employment in the Canadian Labour Market: A Statistical Portrait," *Just Labour* 3 (Fall 2003): 8.

7   Francis Fong, *Navigating Precarious Employment in Canada: Who Is Really at Risk?* (Toronto: Chartered Professional Accountants Canada, 2018), 11.

8   "Canadians with Disabilities Twice as Likely to Report Low Quality Employment Than Those Without Disabilities," *At Work*, no. 112, May 3, 2023, iwh.on.ca/newsletters/at-work/112/canadians-with-disabilities-twice-as-likely-to-report-low-quality-employment-than-those-without-disabilities.

9   "Household Debt Level Rises as Interest Rates Bite into Cash Flow," *CTV News*, June 14, 2023, ctvnews.ca/canada/household-debt-level-rises-as-interest-rates-bite-into-cash-flow-1.6440924.

10   "Household Debt."

11   At least according to the 2016 census.

12   Carroll, "Social Democracy," 12.

13   "President Reagan's Meetings with Prime Minister Mulroney in Canada on March 18, 1985," Reagan Library, posted August 28, 2017, YouTube video, 11:56, youtube.com/watch?v=Fn78kjABPQc. Quoted material occurs at 10:19.

Chapter 1: From Before Confederation to 1945

1   Thébault, Fréderic, "Descendez-vous des Filles du Roy?" *Geneanet*, June 3, 2022. journaldemontreal.com/2018/05/07/les-millions-de-descendants-des-filles-du-roi.

2   Peyton Carmichael and Peter R. Elson. "A Short History of Voluntary Sector–Government Relations in Canada (Revisited)," *Philanthropist Journal*, April 12, 2022, 5, thephilanthropist.ca/2022/04/a-short-history-of-voluntary-sectorgovernment-relations-in-canada-revisited.

3   Carmichael and Elson, 5.

4   Carmichael and Elson, 5.

5   Stuart K. Jaffary, "Social Security: The Beveridge and Marsh Reports," *The Canadian Journal of Economics and Political Science* 9, no. 4 (1943): 473. jstor.org/stable/137442.

6   As quoted in "The Paupers of New Brunswick," *Allicor's Blog*, June 6, 2012, allicor42.typepad.com/blog/2012/06/the-paupers-of-new-brunswick.html.

7   Carmichael and Elson, "A Short History," 7.

8   Judith Fingard, "The Relief of the Unemployed Poor in Saint John, Halifax and St. John's, 1815–1860," *Acadiensis* 5, no. 1: 33. journals.lib.unb.ca/index.php/Acadiensis/article/view/11393.

9   As quoted in Fingard, "Relief," 43.

10 Carmichael and Elson, "A Short History," 13.

11 Carmichael and Elson, 5.

12 Jake Cuneo, "Changing of the Guard: The Evolution of Catholic Trade Unionism in Quebec, 1907–1960," *Undergraduate Review* 16 (2021), vc.bridgew.edu/cgi/viewcontent.cgi?article =1494&context=undergrad_rev.

13 As quoted in "Halifax Poor Man's Friend Society," MemoryNS, accessed November 8, 2023, memoryns.ca/halifax-poor-mans -friend-society.

14 *The Report of the Halifax Poor Man's Friend Society: 1820* (Halifax: Halifax Poor Man's Friend Society, 1820), 14, canadiana.ca/view /oocihm.8_01145_1/16.

15 *The Report*, 15.

16 C.S. Clark, *Of Toronto the Good — A Social Study: The Queen City of Canada as It Is* (Montreal: The Toronto Publishing Company, 1898), 77.

17 Fingard, "Relief," 36.

18 Fingard, 36.

19 Carmichael and Elson, "A Short History," 6.

20 Arthur Manuel, "Indigenous Rights and Anti-Colonial Struggle," in *Canada After Harper*, ed. Ed Finn (Toronto: Lorimer, 2015), 248.

21 Carmichael and Elson, "A Short History," 10–11.

22 "The Legacy of Egerton Ryerson," *Foundations of Education*, Brock University, last modified August 28, 2023, foundations.ed.brocku.ca /week07/2.

23 "The Legacy of Egerton Ryerson."

24 Carmichael and Elson, "A Short History," 10.

25 Christopher Rutty and Sue C. Sullivan, *This Is Public Health: A Canadian History* (Ottawa: Canadian Public Health Association, 2010), cpha.ca/sites/default/files/assets/history/book/history-book -print_all_e.pdf.

26 Kevin Plummer, "An Unsettling Prairie History: A Review of James Daschuk's *Clearing the Plains,*" *Active History,* December 5, 2013, activehistory.ca/blog/2013/12/05/an-unsettling-prairie-history-a -review-of-james-daschuks-clearing-the-plains.

27 Carmichael and Elson, "A Short History," 6.

28 "Finance and War Production," *Canada and the First World War,* Canadian War Museum, online exhibit, accessed November 8, 2023, warmuseum.ca/firstworldwar/history/life-at-home-during-the-war /the-war-economy/finance-and-war-production.

29 Martin Robin, *Radical Politics and Canadian Labour, 1880–1930* (Kingston: Industrial Relations Centre, Queen's University, 1968), 134–37.

30 Carmichael and Elson, "A Short History," 5.

31 Barry Wright, Eric Tucker, and Susan Binnie, "Introduction: War Measures and the Repression of Radicalism," in *War Measures and the Repression of Radicalism, 1914–1939,* eds. Barry Wright, Eric Tucker, and Susan Binnie, vol. 4, *Canadian State Trials* (Toronto: Osgoode Society for Canadian Legal History and University of Toronto Press, 2015), 3-41.

32 "Civilian Reintegration," *Canada and the First World War,* Canadian War Museum, online exhibit, accessed November 8, 2023, warmuseum.ca/firstworldwar/history/after-the-war/veterans /civilian-reintegration.

33 Eric Story, "Coming Home: Veterans, Pensions and the Canadian State After the Great War," *Active History,* January 23, 2018, activehistory.ca/blog/2018/01/23/coming-home-veterans-pensions -and-the-canadian-state-after-the-great-war.

34 Ian Angus, *Canadian Bolsheviks: The Early Years of the Communist Party of Canada* (Vancouver: Vanguard Publications, 1981), 16–17.

35 Lorraine Boissoneault, "Bismarck Tried to End Socialism's Grip — By Offering Government Healthcare," *Smithsonian Magazine,* July 14, 2017, smithsonianmag.com/history/bismarck-tried-end -socialisms-grip-offering-government-healthcare-180964064.

36 Canadian Museum of History, *The History of Canada's Public Pensions,* online exhibit, accessed October 23, 2023, historymuseum .ca/cmc/exhibitions/hist/pensions/cpp-a15-ip_e.html.

37 Carmichael and Elson, "A Short History," 16.

38 Zhengxi Lin, "Employment Insurance in Canada: Policy Changes," *Perspectives* (Summer 1998), 42–47, www150.statcan.gc.ca/n1/en/pub/75-001-x/1998002/3828-eng.pdf.

39 Co-operative Commonwealth Federation, "Full Text: The CCF's Regina Manifesto," *Canadian Dimension*, May 7, 2018, canadiandimension.com/articles/view/the-regina-manifesto-1933-co-operative-commonwealth-federation-programme-fu.

40 Charles A. Deshaies, "The Rise and Decline of the Cooperative Commonwealth Federation in Ontario and Quebec During World War II, 1939–1945" (Ph.D. diss., University of Maine, 2019), digitalcommons.library.umaine.edu/cgi/viewcontent.cgi?article=4204&context=etd.

41 Hermina P. Ropel-Morsky, "William Lyon Mackenzie King: The Corporate Man" (master's thesis, McMaster University, 1978).

42 As quoted in Nicole S. Bernhardt, "Racialized Precarious Employment and the Inadequacies of the Canadian Welfare State," *Journal of Workplace Rights* 5, no. 2 (April–June 2015), journals.sagepub.com/doi/epub/10.1177/2158244015575639.

Chapter 2: Postwar Boom to 1970s Bust

1 Carroll, "Social Democracy," 9.

2 As quoted in Michael Horn, "Leonard Marsh and the Coming of a Welfare State in Canada," *Histoire sociale/Social History* 9, no. 17 (1976): 197–204.

3 Jaffary "Social Security," 581.

4 Jaffary.

5 Jaffary, 590.

6 Antonia Maioni, "New Century, New Risks: The Marsh Report and the Post-War Welfare State in Canada," *Policy Options*, August 1, 2004, policyoptions.irpp.org/fr/magazines/social-policy-in-the-21st-century/new-century-new-risks-the-marsh-report-and-the-post-war-welfare-state-in-canada.

7 Horn, "Leonard Marsh."

8 Horn.

9   Maioni, "New Century."

10 Horn, "Leonard Marsh."

11 Horn.

12 A.E. Grauer, "Canada's Program of Social Security. The Marsh Report and the Report of the Advisory Committee on Health Insurance," *Public Affairs* 6, no. 4 (1943): 181–87.

13 Grauer, 186.

14 Mike Burke, Colin Moores, and John Shields, "Critical Perspectives on Canadian Public Policy," in *Restructuring and Resistance: Canadian Public Policy in an Age of Global Capitalism*, eds. Mike Burke, Colin Moores, and John Shields (Black Point, NS: Fernwood, 2000), 11.

15 Murray Dobbin, "Canada's Progressive Politics Need Renewal," in *Canada After Harper*, ed. Ed Finn (Toronto: Lorimer, 2015), 305.

16 Bernhardt, "Racialized Precarious Employment."

17 "The Arrival of Displaced Persons in Canada, 1945–1951," Parks Canada, February 15, 2016, canada.ca/en/parks-canada /news/2016/02/the-arrival-of-displaced-persons-in-canada-1945-1951 .html.

18 G. Jared Toney, "Locating Diaspora: Afro-Caribbean Narratives of Migration and Settlement in Toronto, 1914–1929," *Urban History Review* 38, no. 2 (Spring 2010), doi.org/10.7202/039676ar.

19 Edward Dunsworth, "Welcome to Canada: A Story from the First Year of the Seasonal Agricultural Workers Program," *Active History*, April 11, 2019, activehistory.ca/2019/04/welcome-to-canada-a -story-from-the-first-year-of-the-seasonal-agricultural-workers -program.

20 Stephanie Procyk, *Understanding Income Inequality in Canada, 1980–2014* (Toronto: United Way Toronto and Neighbourhood Change Research Partnership, October 2014), neighbourhoodchange.ca/documents/2015/02/understanding -income-inequality-in-canada-1980-2014.pdf.

21 Carroll, "Social Democracy," 10.

22 As quoted in Bernhardt, "Racialized Precarious Employment."

23 Carroll, "Social Democracy," 12.

24 Duncan Cameron, *Getting It Wrong, Making It Right: Creativity and Public Policy in Canada* (Montreal: Pierre Elliott Trudeau Foundation. Summer 2010).

25 Daniel Béland, Michael J. Prince, and R. Kent Weaver, "From Retrenchment to Selective Social Policy Expansion: The Politics of Federal Cash Benefits in Canada," *Canadian Journal of Political Science* 54, no. 4 (2021).

26 Jen St. Denis, "Why Can't We Build Like It's the 1970s?" *Tyee*, April 22, 2022, thetyee.ca/Analysis/2022/04/22/Why-Cant -We-Build-Like-1970s.

27 Wayne Simpson, Greg Mason, and Ryan Godwin, "The Manitoba Basic Annual Income Experiment: Lessons Learned 40 Years Later," *Canadian Public Policy*, 43, no.1 (2017), umanitoba.ca/media /Simpson_Mason_Godwin_2017.pdf.

28 Travis Tomchuk, "Manitoba's Mincome Experiment," Canadian Museum for Human Rights, August 10, 2022, humanrights.ca /story/manitobas-mincome-experiment.

29 Lars Osberg, *From Keynesian Consensus to Neo-Liberalism to the Green New Deal* (Canadian Centre for Policy Alternatives, March 2021), 11, policyalternatives.ca/publications/reports/75 -years-of-income-inequality-canada.

30 Jim Stanford, "The Three Key Moments in Canada's Neoliberal Transformation," Rabble.ca, April 8, 2014, rabble.ca/columnists /three-key-moments-canadas-neoliberal-transformation.

31 Gordon Thiessen, "Canadian Economic Performance at the End of the Twentieth Century," speech, Canada Club, June 2, 1999, London, U.K., bankofcanada.ca/1999/06 /canadian-economic-performance-end-twentieth-century/.

32 Burke, Moores, and Shields, "Critical Perspectives," 12.

33 As quoted in Béland, Prince, and Weaver, "From Retrenchment."

34 Laurie Monsebraaten, "Report Reveals Alarming — and Growing — Racialized Income Divide in GTA," *Toronto Star*, May 6, 2019, thestar.com/news/gta/report-reveals-alarming-and-growing -racialized-income-divide-in-gta/article_25db2e5c-b55f-552d-8685 -f65ec146716a.html.

35 Burke, Moores, and Shields, "Critical Perspectives."

36 Burke, Moores, and Shields.

37 John Maynard Keynes, "The World's Economic Outlook," *Atlantic*, May 1932. theatlantic.com/magazine/archive/1932/05/the-worlds-economic-outlook/307879.

38 As quoted in Canadian Museum of History, *Making Medicare*, historymuseum.ca/cmc/exhibitions/hist/medicare/medic-4h02e.html.

Chapter 3: The Paradigm Shift

1 Yves Saint-Pierre and Patricia Tully, "Downsizing Canada's Hospitals, 1986/87 to 1994/95 — Archived," Statistics Canada, April 21, 1997, www150.statcan.gc.ca/n1/en/catalogue/82-003-X19960043023.

2 Kristie Jones, "Canada Ranks Last on Number of Hospital Beds, Wait Times," *Hospital News*, October 3, 2019, hospitalnews.com/canada-ranks-last-on-number-of-hospital-beds-wait-times.

3 Rebecca Graff-McRae et al., *Alberta in Context: Health Care Under NDP Governments* (Edmonton: Parkland Institute, January 2019), d3n8a8pro7vhmx.cloudfront.net/parklandinstitute/pages/1677/attachments/original/1548954492/albertaincontext.pdf.

4 Graff-McRae et al.

5 Congressional Budget Office, *Effects of the 1981 Tax Act on the Distribution of Income and Taxes Paid* (Washington, DC: Congress of the United States, August 1986), cbo.gov/sites/default/files/99th-congress-1985-1986/reports/doc20a-entire.pdf.

6 "Reaganomics: Economic Policy and the Reagan Revolution," Ronald Reagan Presidential Foundation and Institute, accessed November 9, 2023, reaganfoundation.org/ronald-reagan/the-presidency/economic-policy.

7 James Orlando, "Canadian Inflation: A New Vintage," TD Bank, April 27, 2022, economics.td.com/ca-inflation-new-vintage.

8 "Average Incomes of Families and Unattached Individuals, Canada, 1951–1995," Canadian Council on Social Development, last updated June 18, 2018.

9   "Brian Mulroney Wins Stunning Landslide Victory in 1984,"
    CBC Archives, June 21, 2018, cbc.ca/archives/brian-mulroney-wins
    -stunning-landslide-victory-in-1984-1.4675926.
10 Maude Barlow and Bruce Campbell, *Take Back the Nation*
    (Toronto: Key Porter Books, 1991), 11.
11 Barlow and Campbell, *Take Back*, 87.
12 Barlow and Campbell, 79.
13 Barlow and Campbell, 77.
14 St. Denis, "Why Can't."
15 Barlow and Campbell, *Take Back*, 79.
16 Barlow and Campbell, 84–86.
17 Barlow and Campbell, 127.
18 Barlow and Campbell, 128.
19 Barlow and Campbell, 74.
20 Barlow and Campbell, 75.
21 As quoted in Barlow and Campbell, 77.
22 Barlow and Campbell, 100.
23 Barlow and Campbell, 79.
24 Barlow and Campbell, 86–87.
25 Carmichael and Elson, "A Short History."
26 Linda McQuaig, *All You Can Eat: Greed, Lust and the New
    Capitalism* (Toronto: Penguin, 2001), xii.

Chapter 4: Neoliberal Retrenchment

1   McQuaig, *All You Can Eat*, 47–48.
2   McQuaig, 47.
3   Marjorie Griffin Cohen, "The Lunacy of Free Trade," in *Crossing
    the Line: Canada and Free Trade with Mexico*, ed. Jim Sinclair
    (Vancouver: New Star Books, 1992).
4   "Canada: Exports, Percent of GDP" [data from World Bank],
    TheGlobalEconomy.com, accessed November 9, 2023,
    theglobaleconomy.com/Canada/exports.
5   McQuaig, *All You Can Eat*, 48.
6   Dobbin, "Canada's Progressive Politics," 296.

7   McQuaig, *All You Can Eat*, 54

8   Cohen, "Lunacy."

9   Kim Richard Nossal, "The Mulroney Years: Transformation and Tumult," *Policy Options*, June–July 2003, policyoptions.irpp.org /wp-content/uploads/sites/2/assets/po/the-best-pms-in-the-past-50 -years/nossal.pdf.

10 Stanford, "The Three Key Moments."

11 Cohen, "Lunacy."

12 Anthony Wilson-Smith, "Martin's 1995 Budget," *Maclean's*, March 17, 2003, thecanadianencyclopedia.ca/en/article/martins-1995-budget.

13 Statistics Canada, "Personal Debt," *Perspectives on Labour and Income*, January 2007, www150.statcan.gc.ca/n1/en/pub/75-001-x /commun/4235072-eng.pdf.

14 Cameron, "Getting It Wrong."

15 Cameron, "Getting It Wrong."

16 Barlow and Campbell, *Take Back*, 75.

17 St. Denis, "Why Can't."

18 Conrad Black, *The Canadian Manifesto* (Toronto: Southerland House, 2018), 83.

19 McQuaig, *All You Can Eat*, xii.

20 Naomi Klein, *The Shock Doctrine* (Toronto: Vintage, 2008), 309.

21 Klein, 309.

22 Seth Klein, "Good Sense Versus Common Sense: Canada's Debt Debate and Competing Hegemonic Projects" (master's thesis, Simon Fraser University, 1996), 1–2, core.ac.uk/download/pdf/56371213 .pdf.

23 Klein, "Good Sense," 104.

24 Dobbin, "Canada's Progressive Politics," 297.

25 Carmichael and Elson, "A Short History."

26 Hugh Mackenzie, *Deficit Mania in Perspective*, Ontario Budget 2010 Technical Paper (Ottawa: Canadian Centre for Policy Alternatives, February 2010).

27 As quoted in Ed Finn, "Let's Make Canada the Great Country It Could Be," in *Canada After Harper*, ed. Ed Finn (Toronto: Lorimer, 2015), 16–17.

28 Cameron, "Getting It Wrong."

Chapter 5: Provincial and Territorial Austerity Trends

1   Jean-Philippe Cipriani, "Un épouvantail nommé déficit," *L'actualité*, September 6, 2022, lactualite.com/politique/un-epouvantail -nomme-deficit/

2   Jack Stilborn and Robert B. Asselin, *Federal-Provincial Relations*, Political and Social Affairs Division, May 1, 2001, publications. gc.ca/collections/Collection-R/LoPBdP/CIR/9310-e.htm.

3   Stilborn and Asselin.

4   Stilborn and Asselin.

5   Stilborn and Asselin.

6   Winston Gereluk, "Alberta Labour in the 1980s," in *Working People in Alberta*, ed. Alvin Finkel (Edmonton: Athabasca University Press, 2012).

7   Glynis Maxwell, *Poverty in Ontario: Failed Promise and the Renewal of Hope* (Community Development Halton and Social Planning Network of Ontario, 2009), 6, spno.ca/images/pdf/Poverty-in -Ontario-Report.pdf.

8   Maxwell.

9   Maxwell.

10   Todd Scarth, "Moves Made to Reduce Inequality," Canadian Centre for Policy Alternatives, May 11, 2000, policyalternatives .ca/publications/reports/moves-made-reduce-inequality.

11   Jessica K. Gill, "Unpacking the Role of Neoliberalism on the Politics of Poverty Reduction Policies in Ontario, Canada: A Descriptive Case Study and Critical Analysis," *Social Sciences* 10, no. 12: (2021), 485, doi.org/10.3390/socsci10120485.

12   Graff-McRae et al., *Alberta in Context*.

13   Maxwell, *Poverty in Ontario*.

14   Graff-McRae et al., *Alberta in Context*.

15   John W. Warnock, "The CCF-NDP in Saskatchewan," in *Challenges and Perils: Social Democracy in Neoliberal Times*, eds. William K. Carroll and R.S. Ratner (Black Point, NS: Fernwood, 2005), 88.

16   Graff-McRae et al., *Alberta in Context*.

17   David Weigel, "'It's Not a Revenue Problem. It's a Spending Problem,'" *Slate*, April 18, 2011, slate.com/news-and-politics/2011/04 /not-a-revenue-problem-a-spending-problem-tracing-the-history -of-a-republican-talking-point.html.

18 Maxwell, *Poverty in Ontario*.

19 Nora Loreto, *Spin Doctors: How Media and Politicians Misdiagnosed the COVID-19 Pandemic* (Halifax: Fernwood, 2021), 58.

20 Canadian Press, "Lucien Bouchard Says 'Wounds' Remain with Brian Mulroney," *CBC News*, August 21, 2014, cbc.ca/news /politics/lucien-bouchard-says-wounds-remain-with-brian -mulroney-1.2742836.

21 Karl Rettino-Parazelli, "Vingt ans plus tard, le Québec est toujours en quête du déficit zéro," *Le Devoir*, November 24, 2015, ledevoir .com/economie/456078/vingt-ans-plus-tard-le-quebec-est-toujours -en-quete-du-deficit-zero.

22 Rettino-Parazelli.

23 Cipriani, "Un épouvantail."

24 Francis Vailles, "Une première depuis un quart de siècle?" *La Presse*, November 21, 2017, plus.lapresse.ca/screens/464943fe-749d-4662 -9572-f52f1900f9be|_0.html.

25 Klein, "Good Sense," 22.

26 Klein, "Good Sense," 23.

27 "Canada's Health Care System," Government of Canada, last updated September 17, 2019, canada.ca/en/health-canada/services /health-care-system/reports-publications/health-care-system /canada.html.

28 As quoted in Canadian Museum of History, *Making Medicare*, historymuseum.ca/cmc/exhibitions/hist/medicare/medic-7h04e.html.

29 Government of Canada, "Canada's Health."

30 Stilborn and Asselin, *Federal-Provincial Relations*.

31 Geoff Norquay, "The Death of Executive Federalism and the Rise of the 'Harper Doctrine,'" *Policy Options*, December 1, 2011, policyoptions.irpp.org/magazines/the-year-in-review/the-death-of -executive-federalism-and-the-rise-of-the-harper-doctrine-prospects -for-the-next-health-care-accord/.

32 Joe Chidley, "Medicare Threatened by Funding Cuts," *Maclean's*, December 2, 1996, thecanadianencyclopedia.ca/en/article /medicare-threatened-by-funding-cuts.

33 Colin Dodds and Ronald Colman, *Income Distribution in Canada* (GPI Atlantic, Nova Scotia, July 2001), gpiatlantic.org/pdf /incomedist/incomedist.pdf.

34 Andrew Longhurst, "At What Cost? Ontario Hospital Privatization and the Threat to Public Health Care," Canadian Centre for Policy Alternatives, November 2023, policyalternatives.ca /sites/default/files/uploads/publications/Ontario%20 Office/2023/11/AtWhatCost-FINAL-November%202023.pdf; Tina Yazdani and Meredith Bond, "New Data Shows For-Profit Clinics Charging Significantly More for Surgeries," CityNews, last modified May 1, 2023, toronto.citynews.ca/2023/05/01/ for-profit-clinics-charging-significantly-surgeries/.

35 Bill Murnighan, *Selling Ontario's Health Care: The Real Story on Government Spending and Public Relations* (Canadian Centre for Policy Alternatives, April 2001), 9, policyalternatives.ca/sites/default /files/uploads/publications/Ontario_Office_Pubs/on_healthcare. pdf.

36 Colleen Fuller, "Health Care: A Public Right or Private Option?" in *Canada After Harper*, ed. Ed Finn (Toronto: Lorimer, 2015), 190.

37 Raisa B. Deber, *Delivering Health Care Services: Public, Not-For-Profit, or Private?* (Commission on the Future of Health Care in Canada, August 2002), publications.gc.ca/collections/Collection /CP32-79-17-2002E.pdf.

38 Cameron, "Getting It Wrong."

39 Deber, *Delivering Health Care.*

40 Krystine Therriault, "Closure of Hawkesbury General Hospital ER," *Seaway News*, January 1, 2023, cornwallseawaynews.com /local/closure-of-hawkesbury-general-hospital-er.

Chapter 6: Canada's Reigning Status Quo

1 Andrew Heisz and Elizabeth Richards, "Economic Well-Being Across Generations of Young Canadians: Are Millennials Better or Worse Off?" *Economic Insights*, Statistics Canada, April 18, 2019.

2 Kevin Page, "Fiscal Management and Parliamentary Democracy," in *Canada After Harper*, ed. Ed Finn (Toronto: Lorimer, 2015), 313.

3 Page, 313.

4 Dean Beeby, "Federal Government Quietly Writes Off Loan — But Won't Reveal Sum or Say Who Got It," *CBC News*, June 26, 2018,

cbc.ca/news/politics/loans-canada-account-finance-auto-sector
-bailout-2009-gm-chrysler-1.4722529.

5   David Macdonald, *The Big Banks' Big Secret* (Canadian Centre for
Policy Alternatives, April 2012), policyalternatives.ca/sites/default
/files/uploads/publications/National%20Office/2012/04/Big
%20Banks%20Big%20Secret.pdf.

6   Yves Giroux, Carleigh Busby, and Robert Behrend, *Federal Support
Through Major Transfers to Provincial and Territorial Governments*,
Office of the Parliamentary Budget Officer, September 3, 2020,
pbo-dpb.gc.ca/web/default/files/Documents/Reports/RP-2021-020
-S/RP-2021-020-S_en.pdf.

7   "Canada Election 2015: Justin Trudeau Accuses Tom Mulcair
of 'Austerity' over Balanced Budget Pledge," *CBC News*, August
25, 2015, cbc.ca/news/politics/canada-election-2015-justin
-trudeau-accuses-tom-mulcair-of-austerity-over-balanced-budget
-pledge-1.3202773.

8   "Federal Government Announces Record Transfers to Provinces and
Territories," Department of Finance Canada, December 16, 2022,
canada.ca/en/department-finance/news/2022/12/federal-government
-announces-ecord-transfers-to-provinces-and-territories.html.

9   Justin Trudeau, "Working Together to Improve Health Care for
Canadians," Prime Minister's Office, February 7, 2023, pm.gc.ca
/en/news/news-releases/2023/02/07/working-together-improve
-health-care-canadians.

10 Theresa Wright, "Here's How Much Provinces Have In
Surplus While Demanding More Federal Health Cash,"
Global News, February 16, 2023, globalnews.ca/news/9488839
/health-funding-provinces-surpluses-budget-gains-numbers.

11 Lisa Johnson, "Alberta's Continuing Gas Tax Holiday Has Cost
$850 Million Since April: Toews," *Edmonton Journal*, December
20, 2022, edmontonjournal.com/news/politics/albertas-continuing
-gas-tax-holiday-has-cost-850-million-since-april-toews.

12 Wright, "Here's How Much."

13 Canadian Press, "Ontario Will Have $22.6B in 'Excess Funds'
That Could Be Used on Programs or Debt, FAO Says," *CBC*

News, June 13, 2023, cbc.ca/news/canada/toronto/ontario-excess
-funds-fao-1.6874664.

14 Canadian Press, "Debt-to-Disposable-Income Ratio Eases Down
from Record 185%," *CBC News*, June 13, 2022, cbc.ca/news
/business/statscan-household-debt-1.6486665.

15 "Distributions of Household Economic Accounts for Income,
Consumption, Saving and Wealth of Canadian Households, Third
Quarter 2022," Statistics Canada, January 19, 2023, www150
.statcan.gc.ca/n1/daily-quotidien/230119/dq230119b-eng.htm.

16 Erik Hertzberg and Sarina Yoo, "Bank of Canada Expected
to Raise Interest Rates One More Time, Capping at 5%,"
Financial Post, June 23, 2023, financialpost.com/news/economy
/bank-of-canada-raise-interest-rates-once-more-cap-5-percent.

17 James Bradshaw, "Canada's Big Six Banks Reported Fourth-
Quarter Earnings This Week. Here's What You Need to Know,"
Globe and Mail, December 2, 2022, theglobeandmail.com
/business/article-earnings-canada-big-six-banks.

18 Andrew Jackson, "The Economy: Whose Interests Are Being
Served?" in *Canada After Harper*, ed. Ed Finn (Toronto: Lorimer,
2015), 109.

19 René Morisette, *Unionization in Canada, 1981 to 2022*,
Statistics Canada Economic and Social Reports, November 23,
2022, www150.statcan.gc.ca/n1/en/pub/36-28-0001/2022011
/article/00001-eng.pdf?st=P8EiQxOB.

20 Lynne Fernandez, "Unions: Their Role in Democracy and
Prosperity," in *Canada After Harper*, ed. Ed Finn (Toronto:
Lorimer, 2015), 134.

21 Osberg, *From Keynesian*, 14.

22 Trish Hennessy, "Tax Cuts: Part of the Problem, Not the Solution,"
in *Canada After Harper*, ed. Ed Finn (Toronto: Lorimer, 2015), 170.

23 Osberg, *From Keynesian*, 22.

24 Osberg, 25.

25 Osberg.

26 Nora Loreto, "CERB/CEWS: No Oversight for the Rich,
Little Forgiveness for the Poor," *Maple*, December 9, 2022,

readthemaple.com/cerb-cews-no-oversight-for-the-rich-little
-forgiveness-for-the-poor/

27 Ichiro Kawachi and Bruce P. Kennedy, "Socioeconomic
Determinants of Health: Health and Social Cohesion: Why Care
About Income Inequality?" *BMJ* 314, no. 7086 (April 5, 1997):
1037-40, doi.org/10.1136/bmj.314.7086.1037.

28 Gereluk, *Working*.

29 Krista McCracken, "Food Insecurity and the 'Temporary'
Relief of Food Banks," *Active History*, August 17, 2015,
activehistory.ca/2015/08/food-insecurity-and-the-temporary-relief
-of-food-banks.

30 "Hunger Count 2023," Food Banks Canada, accessed November
10, 2023, foodbankscanada.ca/hungercount.

31 "Affordable Food in the North," Food Secure Canada, last
updated July 24, 2023, web.archive.org/web/20230202183034
/https://foodsecurecanada.org/resources-news/news-media/we-want
-affordable-food-north.

32 Finn, "Let's Make Canada," 7.

33 Rachel Aiello, "Liberals' Grocery Rebate Bill Fast-Tracked
Through House with All-Party Backing," *CTV News*, April 19,
2023, ctvnews.ca/politics/liberals-grocery-rebate-bill-fast-tracked
-through-house-with-all-party-backing-1.6362550.

34 Fuller, "Health Care," 186–187.

35 As quoted in Thomas J. Billitteri, "Donors Big and Small
Propelled Philanthropy in the 20th Century," *Chronicle of
Philanthropy*, January 13, 2000, philanthropy.com/article/donors
-big-and-small-propelled-philanthropy-in-the-20th-century.

36 Carmichael and Elson, "A Short History," 12.

37 Ian Hay and Samantha Muller, "Questioning Generosity in the
Golden Age of Philanthropy: Towards Critical Geographies of Super-
Philanthropy," *Progress in Human Geography* 38, no. 5 (2014), doi.org
/10.1177/0309132513500893.

38 Kenneth Chan, "Jim Pattison Donates $30 Million to New
Royal Columbian Hospital in New Westminster," *Daily Hive*,
November 30, 2022, dailyhive.com/vancouver/jim-pattison
-acute-care-tower-royal-columbian-hospital-donation.

39 "Jim Pattison Makes Record $75 Million Donation to St. Paul's Foundation," The New St. Paul's Hospital, Providence Health Care, March 29, 2017, thenewstpauls.ca/jim-pattison-makes -record-75-million-donation-st-pauls-foundation/.

40 Jon Azpiri and Simran Gill, "B.C. Billionaire Jim Pattison Makes Canadian History," *Global News*, March 28, 2017, globalnews.ca /news/3340099/b-c-billionaire-jim-pattison-makes-canadian-history.

41 Katie Dangerfield, "Doctors Warn of Summer ER Crunch in Canada: 'A Lot of Waiting by Patients,'" *Global News*, June 2, 2023, globalnews.ca/news/9738218/er-wait-times-canada-summer.

42 Akshay Kulkarni, "Emergency Rooms in Rural B.C. Were Closed for Equivalent of Around 4 Months in 2022, Data Shows," *CBC News*, December 27, 2022, cbc.ca/news/canada/british-columbia /bc-er-closures-2022-1.6689970.

43 Dangerfield, "Doctors Warn."

Chapter 7: The Way Forward

1 Craig Lord, "Competitiveness on a 'Clear Decline' in Canada as Profits Rise: Report," *Global News*, October 19, 2023, globalnews.ca /news/10035678/competition-bureau-prices-profit-markups-canada.

2 As quoted in Melisa Brittain and Cindy Blackstock, *First Nations Child Poverty: A Literature Review and Analysis*, First Nations Children's Action Research and Education Service, 2015, fncaringsociety.com/sites/default/files/First%20Nations%20Child %20Poverty%20-%20A%20Literature%20Review%20and %20Analysis%202015-3.pdf.

3 Simon Landry, Audrey Racine, and Mohan B. Kumar. "Childhood Factors Associated with the Completion of a High School Diploma or Equivalency Certificate or Higher Among First Nations Children Living off Reserve, Métis and Inuit Children," Indigenous Peoples Thematic Series, Statistics Canada. April 6, 2023, www150.statcan. gc.ca/n1/pub/41-20-0002/412000022023002-eng.htm.

4 Manuel, "Indigenous Rights," 257.

5 Angelo DiCaro, "As Pandemic Rages, It's Time to Fix EI for Good," *Unifor News*, February 18, 2021, unifor.org/news/all-news/pandemic -rages-its-time-fix-ei-good.

6 Ricardo Chejfec and Rachel Samson, *Building a Package of Compromise Solutions for EI Reform*, Institute for Research on Public Policy, December 7, 2022, irpp.org/research-studies/building-a-package-of-compromise-solutions-for-ei-reform.

7 Nick Boisvert, "How the Main Federal Parties Plan to Tax the Wealthy," *CBC News*, September 16, 2021, cbc.ca/news/politics/tax-platforms-federal-election-1.6177278.

8 Guy Dauncy, "Six Ways to End Canada's Affordable Housing Crisis," *Corporate Knights*, October 27, 2022, corporateknights.com/category-buildings/six-ways-to-end-canadas-affordable-housing-crisis.

9 Dauncy.

10 "Our Demands," ODSP Action Coalition, accessed November 10, 2023, odspaction.ca/page/our-demands.

11 Drew Postey, "More Than 60% of Sask. Income Support Calls Ignored, Auditors Report Reveals," *CTV News*, June 6, 2023, regina.ctvnews.ca/more-than-60-of-sask-income-support-calls-ignored-auditors-report-reveals-1.6429562.

12 Sarah Burkinshaw, Yaz Terajima, and Carolyn A. Wilkins, *Income Inequality in Canada*, Bank of Canada, July 26, 2022, bankofcanada.ca/wp-content/uploads/2022/07/sdp2022-16.pdf.

13 Co-operative Commonwealth Federation, "Regina Manifesto."

14 David Braneck, "Berliners Voted for a Radical Solution to Soaring Rents. A Year on, They Are Still Waiting," *Euronews*, September 26, 2022. euronews.com/my-europe/2022/09/26/berliners-voted-for-a-radical-solution-to-soaring-rents-a-year-on-they-are-still-waiting.

15 As quoted in Matt Henderson, "'Housing crisis' a product of class struggle," *Winnipeg Free Press*, June 17, 2023, winnipegfreepress.com/arts-and-life/entertainment/books/2023/06/17/housing-crisis-a-product-of-class-struggle.

16 Duncan Cameron, "The NDP and the Making of a Citizens' Party," in *Challenges and Perils: Social Democracy in Neoliberal Times*, eds. William K. Carroll and R.S. Ratner (Black Point, NS: Fernwood, 2005), 143.

Conclusion

1 "Canada Finance Minister: Stellantis Investment 'Is Coming,'" *Reuters*, June 14, 2023, reuters.com/business/autos-transportation /canada-finance-minister-stellantis-investment-is-coming-2023-06-14.

Bibliography

ab Iorwerth, Aled. "Risks to Canada's Economy Remain High as Household Debt Levels Continue to Grow." *Housing Observer*, Canada Mortgage and Housing Corporation, May 23, 2023. cmhc-schl.gc .ca/blog/2023/risks-canadas-economy-remain-high-household-debt -levels-continue-grow.

Aiello, Rachel. "Liberals' Grocery Rebate Bill Fast-Tracked Through House with All-Party Backing." *CTV News*, April 19, 2023. ctvnews.ca /politics/liberals-grocery-rebate-bill-fast-tracked-through-house -with-all-party-backing-1.6362550.

Angus, Ian. *Canadian Bolsheviks: The Early Years of the Communist Party of Canada*. Vancouver: Vanguard Publications, 1981.

Atwood, Margaret. *Payback: Debt and the Shadow Side of Wealth*. Toronto: House of Anansi Press, 2008.

Azpiri, Jon, and Simran Gill. "B.C. Billionaire Jim Pattison Makes Canadian History." *Global News*, March 28, 2017. globalnews.ca /news/3340099/b-c-billionaire-jim-pattison-makes-canadian -history.

Barlow, Maude, and Bruce Campbell. *Take Back the Nation*. Toronto: Key Porter Books, 1991.

Beeby, Dean. "Federal Government Quietly Writes Off Loan — But Won't Reveal Sum or Say Who Got It." *CBC News*, June 26, 2018. cbc.ca/news/politics/loans-canada-account-finance-auto-sector -bailout-2009-gm-chrysler-1.4722529.

Béland, Daniel, Michael J. Prince, and R. Kent Weaver. "From Retrenchment to Selective Social Policy Expansion: The Politics of Federal Cash Benefits in Canada." *Canadian Journal of Political Science* 54, no. 4 (2021): 809–29.

Bernhardt, Nicole S. "Racialized Precarious Employment and the Inadequacies of the Canadian Welfare State." *Journal of Workplace Rights* 5 no. 2 (April–June 2015). journals.sagepub.com/doi /epub/10.1177/2158244015575639.

Billitteri, Thomas J. "Donors Big and Small Propelled Philanthropy in the 20th Century." *Chronicle of Philanthropy*, January 13, 2000. philanthropy.com/article/donors-big-and-small-propelled -philanthropy-in-the-20th-century.

Black, Conrad. *The Canadian Manifesto*. Toronto: Sutherland House, 2018.

Boissoneault, Lorraine. "Bismarck Tried to End Socialism's Grip — By Offering Government Healthcare." *Smithsonian Magazine*, July 14, 2017. smithsonianmag.com/history/bismarck-tried-end-socialisms -grip-offering-government-healthcare-180964064.

Boisvert, Nick. "How the Main Federal Parties Plan to Tax the Wealthy." *CBC News*, September 16, 2021. cbc.ca/news/politics/tax -platforms-federal-election-1.6177278.

Bourdieu, Pierre. "The Essence of Neoliberalism." *Le Monde Diplomatique*, December 1998. mondediplo.com/1998/12/08bourdieu.

Bradshaw, James. "Canada's Big Six Banks Reported Fourth-Quarter Earnings This Week. Here's What You Need to Know." *Globe and Mail*, December 2, 2022. theglobeandmail.com/business /article-earnings-canada-big-six-banks.

Braneck, David. "Berliners Voted for a Radical Solution to Soaring Rents. A Year on, They Are Still Waiting." *Euronews*, September 26, 2022. euronews.com/my-europe/2022/09/26/berliners-voted-for-a -radical-solution-to-soaring-rents-a-year-on-they-are-still-waiting.

"Brian Mulroney Wins Stunning Landslide Victory in 1984." *CBC Archives*, June 21, 2018. cbc.ca/archives/brian-mulroney-wins -stunning-landslide-victory-in-1984-1.4675926.

Brittain, Melisa, and Cindy Blackstock. *"First Nations Child Poverty: A Literature Review and Analysis."* First Nations Children's Action Research and Education Service, 2015. fncaringsociety.com/sites /default/files/First%20Nations%20Child%20Poverty%20-%2A %20Literature%20Review%20and%20Analysis%202015-3.pdf.

Brock University. "The Legacy of Egerton Ryerson." *Foundations of Education*. Last modified August 28, 2023. foundations.ed.brocku .ca/week07/2.

Burke, Mike, Colin Moores, and John Shields. "Critical Perspectives on Canadian Public Policy." In *Restructuring and Resistance: Canadian Public Policy in an Age of Global Capitalism*, edited by Mike Burke, Colin Moores, and John Sheilds, 11–23. Black Point, NS: Fernwood, 2000.

Burkinshaw, Sarah, Yaz Terajima, and Carolyn A. Wilkins. *Income Inequality in Canada*. Bank of Canada. July 26, 2022. bankofcanada.ca/wp-content/uploads/2022/07/sdp2022-16.pdf.

Cadogan, Tim. "GoFundMe CEO: Hello Congress, Americans Need Help and We Can't Do Your Job for You." USA Today, February 11, 2021. usatoday.com/story/opinion/voices/2021/02/11 /gofundme-ceo-congress-pass-covid-relief-desperate-americans -column/4440425001.

Cameron, Duncan. *Getting It Wrong, Making It Right: Creativity and Public Policy in Canada*. Montreal: Pierre Elliott Trudeau Foundation, summer 2010.

———. The NDP and the Making of a Citizens' Party." In *Challenges and Perils: Social Democracy in Neoliberal Times*, edited by William K. Carroll and R.S. Ratner, 137–50. Black Point, NS: Fernwood, 2005.

Canada. *Senate Debates*, April 14, 1980 (Jeanne Sauvé, Governor-General, Speech from the Throne). primarydocuments.ca /senate-debates-speech-from-the-throne.

———. *Senate Debates*, November 5, 1984 (John Bosley, Governor-General, Speech from the Throne). poltext.org/sites/poltext.org /files/discoursV2/Canada/CAN_DT_XXXX_33_01.pdf.

"Canada Election 2015: Justin Trudeau Accuses Tom Mulcair of 'Austerity' over Balanced Budget Pledge," *CBC News*, August 25, 2015. cbc.ca/news/politics/canada-election-2015-justin-trudeau-accuses-tom-mulcair-of-austerity-over-balanced-budget-pledge-1.3202773.

Canadian Council on Social Development. "Average Incomes of Families and Unattached Individuals, Canada, 1951–1995." Last updated June 18, 2018. ccsd.ca/factsheets/fs_avgin.html.

Canadian Museum of History. *The History of Canada's Public Pensions*. Online exhibit. Accessed October 23, 2023. historymuseum.ca/cmc/exhibitions/hist/pensions/cpp1sp_e.html.

———. *Making Medicare: The History of Health Care in Canada, 1914–2007*. Online exhibit. April 21, 2010. historymuseum.ca/cmc/exhibitions/hist/medicare/medic00e.html.

Canadian Press. "Debt-to-Disposable-Income Ratio Eases Down from Record 185%" *CBC News*, June 13, 2022. cbc.ca/news/business/statscan-household-debt-1.6486665.

———. "Lucien Bouchard Says 'Wounds' Remain with Brian Mulroney." *CBC News*, August 21, 2014. cbc.ca/news/politics/lucien-bouchard-says-wounds-remain-with-brian-mulroney-1.2742836.

———. "Ontario Will Have $22.6B in 'Excess Funds' That Could Be Used on Programs or Debt, FAO Says." *CBC News*, June 13, 2023. cbc.ca/news/canada/toronto/ontario-excess-funds-fao-1.6874664.

Canadian War Museum. *Canada and the First World War*. Online exhibit. Accessed November 8, 2023. warmuseum.ca/firstworldwar.

"Canadians with Disabilities Twice as Likely to Report Low Quality Employment Than Those Without Disabilities." *At Work*, no. 112, May 3, 2023. iwh.on.ca/newsletters/at-work/112/canadians-with-disabilities-twice-as-likely-to-report-low-quality-employment-than-those-without-disabilities.

Carmichael, Peyton, and Peter R. Elson. "A Short History of Voluntary Sector–Government Relations in Canada (Revisited). *Philanthropist Journal*, April 12, 2022. thephilanthropist.ca/2022/04/a-short-history-of-voluntary-sectorgovernment-relations-in-canada-revisited.

Carroll, William K. "Social Democracy in Neoliberal Times." In *Challenges and Perils: Social Democracy in Neoliberal Times*, edited by William K. Carroll and R.S. Ratner, 7–22. Black Point, NS: Fernwood, 2005.

Chan, Kenneth. "Jim Pattison Donates $30 Million to New Royal Columbian Hospital in New Westminster." *Daily Hive*, November 30, 2022. dailyhive.com/vancouver/jim-pattison-acute-care-tower-royal-columbian-hospital-donation.

Chejfec, Ricardo, and Rachel Samson. *Building a Package of Compromise Solutions for EI Reform*. Institute for Research on Public Policy, December 7, 2022. irpp.org/research-studies/building-a-package-of-compromise-solutions-for-ei-reform.

Chidley, Joe. "Medicare Threatened by Funding Cuts." *Maclean's*, December 2, 1996. thecanadianencyclopedia.ca/en/article/medicare-threatened-by-funding-cuts.

Cipriani, Jean-Philippe. "Un épouvantail nommé déficit." *L'Actualité*. September 6, 2022.

Clark, C.S. *Of Toronto the Good, The Queen City of Canada as It Is*. Montreal: The Toronto Publishing Company, 1898.

Cohen, Marjorie Griffin. "The Lunacy of Free Trade." In *Crossing the Line: Canada and Free Trade with Mexico*, edited by Jim Sinclair, 14–25. Vancouver: New Star Books, 1992.

Congressional Budget Office. *Effects of the 1981 Tax Act on the Distribution of Income and Taxes Paid*. Washington, DC: Congress of the United States, August 1986. cbo.gov/sites/default/files/99th-congress-1985-1986/reports/doc20a-entire.pdf.

Cook, Tim. "Mackenzie King and the War Effort." In *The Canadian Encyclopedia*. Historica Canada. Last updated February 19, 2016. thecanadianencyclopedia.ca/en/article/mackenzie-king-and-the-war-effort.

Co-operative Commonwealth Federation. "Full Text: The CCF's Regina Manifesto." *Canadian Dimension*, May 7, 2018. canadiandimension.com/articles/view/the-regina-manifesto-1933-co-operative-commonwealth-federation-programme-fu.

Cranford, Cynthia J., Leah F. Vosko, and Nancy Zukewich. "Precarious Employment in the Canadian Labour Market: A Statistical Portrait." *Just Labour* 3 (Fall 2003): 6–22.

Cuneo, Jake. "Changing of the Guard: The Evolution of Catholic Trade Unionism in Quebec, 1907–1960." *Undergraduate Review*, 16 (2021): 139–54. vc.bridgew.edu/cgi/viewcontent .cgi?article=1494&context=undergrad_rev.

Dangerfield, Katie. "Doctors Warn of Summer ER Crunch in Canada: 'A Lot of Waiting by Patients.'" *Global News*, June 2, 2023. globalnews.ca/news/9738218/er-wait-times-canada-summer.

Dauncy, Guy. "Six Ways to End Canada's Affordable Housing Crisis." *Corporate Knights*, October 27, 2022. corporateknights.com /category-buildings/six-ways-to-end-canadas-affordable-housing-crisis.

Deber, Raisa B. *Delivering Health Care Services: Public, Not-For-Profit, or Private?* Commission on the Future of Health Care in Canada, August 2002. publications.gc.ca/collections/Collection/CP32-79 -17-2002E.pdf.

Depalma, Anthony. "Canada, No Longer Riding High, Votes Today, Resigned to Austerity." *New York Times*, June 2, 1997, A6.

Department of Finance Canada. "Federal Government Announces Record Transfers to Provinces and Territories." December 16, 2022. canada.ca/en/department-finance/news/2022/12/federal -government-announces-record-transfers-to-provinces-and- territories.html.

Deshaies, Charles A. "The Rise and Decline of the Cooperative Commonwealth Federation in Ontario and Quebec During World War II, 1939–1945." Ph.D. diss., University of Maine, 2019. digitalcommons.library.umaine.edu/cgi/viewcontent .cgi?article=4204&context=etd.

DiCaro, Angelo. "As Pandemic Rages, It's Time to Fix EI for Good." *Unifor News*, February 18, 2021. unifor.org/news/all-news /pandemic-rages-its-time-fix-ei-good.

Dobbin, Murray. "Canada's Progressive Politics Need Renewal." In *Canada After Harper*, edited by Ed Finn, 288–310. Toronto: Lorimer, 2015.

Dodds, Colin, and Ronald Colman. *Income Distribution in Canada.* Nova Scotia: GPI Atlantic, July 2001. gpiatlantic.org/pdf /incomedist/incomedist.pdf.

Dunsworth, Edward. "Welcome to Canada: A Story from the First Year of the Seasonal Agricultural Workers Program." *Active History,* April 11, 2019. activehistory.ca/2019/04/welcome-to-canada-a -story-from-the-first-year-of-the-seasonal-agricultural-workers -program.

Evans, Pete. "Companies Are a Lot More Willing to Raise Prices Now — and It's Making Inflation Worse." *CBC News,* November 5, 2023. cbc.ca/news/business/inflation-profit-analysis-1.6909878.

Fernandez, Lynne. "Unions: Their Role in Democracy and Prosperity." In *Canada After Harper,* edited by Ed Finn, 131–52. Toronto: Lorimer, 2015.

"Finance Minister: Stellantis Investment 'Is Coming.'" *Reuters,* June 14, 2023. reuters.com/business/autos-transportation/canada-finance -minister-stellantis-investment-is-coming-2023-06-14.

Fingard, Judith. "The Relief of the Unemployed Poor in Saint John, Halifax and St. John's, 1815–1860." *Acadiensis* 5, no. 1: 32–53. journals.lib.unb.ca/index.php/Acadiensis/article/view/11393.

Finn, Ed. "Let's Make Canada the Great Country It Could Be." In *Canada After Harper,* edited by Ed Finn, 12–35. Toronto: Lorimer, 2015.

First Nations Health Authority. "Our History, Our Health." Accessed November 8, 2023. fnha.ca/wellness/wellness-for-first-nations /our-history-our-health.

Fong, Francis. *Navigating Precarious Employment in Canada: Who Is Really at Risk?* Toronto: Chartered Professional Accountants Canada, 2018.

Food Banks Canada. "Hunger Count." Accessed November 10, 2023. foodbankscanada.ca/hungercount.

Food Secure Canada. "Affordable Food in the North." Last updated July 24, 2023. web.archive.org/web/20230202183034 /https://foodsecurecanada.org/resources-news/news-media /we-want-affordable-food-north.

Frum, David, Frank I. Luntz, and James P. Pinkerton. "A Revolution, or Business as Usual?" *Harpers Magazine*, March 1995. harpers.org /archive/1995/03/a-revolution-or-business-as-usual-2.

Fuller, Colleen. "Health Care: A Public Right or Private Option?" In *Canada After Harper*, edited by Ed Finn, 175–92. Toronto: Lorimer, 2015.

Gereluk, Winston. "Alberta Labour in the 1980s." In *Working People in Alberta*, edited by Alvin Finkel, 109–40. Edmonton: Athabasca University Press, 2012.

Gill, Jessica K. "Unpacking the Role of Neoliberalism on the Politics of Poverty Reduction Policies in Ontario, Canada: A Descriptive Case Study and Critical Analysis." *Social Sciences* 10, no. 12 (2021): 485 .doi.org/10.3390/socsci10120485

Giniger, Henry. "Canadian Government Is Defeated On No-Confidence Budget Motion; Prime Minister Clark, in Office 6 Months, Is Expected to Resign Today — Sought to Increase Fuel Prices." *New York Times*, December 14, 1979. nytimes .com/1979/12/14/archives/canadian-government-is-defeated-on -noconfidence-budget-motion-prime.html.

Giroux, Yves, Carleigh Busby, and Robert Behrend. *Federal Support Through Major Transfers to Provincial and Territorial Governments.* Office of the Parliamentary Budget Officer, September 3, 2020. pbo-dpb.gc.ca/web/default/files/Documents/Reports /RP-2021-020-S/RP-2021-020-S_en.pdf.

TheGlobalEconomy.com. "Canada: Exports, Percent of GDP" [data from World Bank]. Accessed November 9, 2023. theglobaleconomy .com/Canada/exports.

Government of Canada. "Canada's Health Care System." Last updated September 17, 2019. canada.ca/en/health-canada/services/health -care-system/reports-publications/health-care-system/canada.html.

Graff-McRae, Rebecca, Trevor Harrison, Ian Hussey, and Larissa Stendie. *Alberta in Context: Health Care Under NDP Governments.* Edmonton: Parkland Institute, January 2019. d3n8a8pro7vhmx .cloudfront.net/parklandinstitute/pages/1677/attachments/original /1548954492/albertaincontext.pdf.

Grauer, A.E. "Canada's Program of Social Security: The Marsh Report and the Report of the Advisory Committee on Health Insurance." *Public Affairs* 6, no. 4 (1943): 181–87.

Halifax Poor Man's Friend Society. *The Report of the Halifax Poor Man's Friend Society: 1820.* Halifax: Halifax Poor Man's Friend Society, 1820. canadiana.ca/view/oocihm.8_01145_1/16.

Hay, Ian, and Samantha Muller. "Questioning Generosity in the Golden Age of Philanthropy: Towards Critical Geographies of Super-Philanthropy." *Progress in Human Geography* 38, no. 5 (2014): 635–53. doi.org/10.1177/0309132513500893.

Heisz, Andrew, and Elizabeth Richards. "Economic Well-Being Across Generations of Young Canadians: Are Millennials Better or Worse Off?" Economic Insights, Statistics Canada. April 18, 2019.

Heller, Nathan. "The Hidden Cost of GoFundMe Health Care." *New Yorker*, June 24, 2019. newyorker.com/magazine/2019/07/01/the-perverse-logic-of-gofundme-health-care.

Henderson, Matt. "'Housing Crisis' a Product of Class Struggle." *Winnipeg Free Press*, June 17, 2023. winnipegfreepress.com/arts-and-life/entertainment/books/2023/06/17/housing-crisis-a-product-of-class-struggle.

Hennessy, Trish. "Tax Cuts: Part of the Problem, Not the Solution." In *Canada After Harper*, edited by Ed Finn, 159–71. Toronto: Lorimer, 2015.

Hertzberg, Erik, and Sarina Yoo. "Bank of Canada Expected to Raise Interest Rates One More Time, Capping at 5%." *Financial Post*, June 23, 2023. financialpost.com/news/economy/bank-of-canada-raise-interest-rates-once-more-cap-5-percent.

Horn, Michael. "Leonard Marsh and the Coming of a Welfare State in Canada." *Histoire sociale/Social History* 9, no. 17 (1976): 197–204.

Houle, Sébastien. "60 ans depuis la première élection de Jean Chrétien: «On peut dire que j'ai eu un certain succès»." *Le Nouvelliste*, April 7, 2023. lenouvelliste.ca/2023/04/08/jean-chretien-60-ans-apres-sa-premiere-election-on-peut-dire-que-jai-eu-un-certain-succes-1f020c4f9a1279ced75225d01ac7ded8.

"Household Debt Level Rises as Interest Rates Bite into Cash Flow." *CTV News*, June 14, 2023.

Jackson, Andrew. "The Economy: Whose Interests Are Being Served?" In *Canada After Harper*, edited by Ed Finn, 95–112. Toronto: Lorimer, 2015.

Jacobs, Jane. *The Question of Separatism: Quebec and the Struggle Over Sovereignty*. Montreal: Baraka Books, 1980.

Jaffary, Stuart K. "Social Security: The Beveridge and Marsh Reports." *Canadian Journal of Economics and Political Science* 9, no. 4 (1943): 571–92.

Johnson, Lisa. "Alberta's Continuing Gas Tax Holiday Has Cost $850 Million Since April: Toews." *Edmonton Journal*, December 20, 2022. edmontonjournal.com/news/politics/albertas-continuing -gas-tax-holiday-has-cost-850-million-since-april-toews.

Jones, Kristie. "Canada Ranks Last on Number of Hospital Beds, Wait Times." *Hospital News*, October 3, 2019. hospitalnews.com /canada-ranks-last-on-number-of-hospital-beds-wait-times.

Kawachi, Ichiro, and Bruce P. Kennedy. "Health and Social Cohesion: Why Care About Income Inequality?" *BMJ* 314, no. 7086 (April 5, 1997): 1037–40. doi:https://doi.org/10.1136/bmj.314.7086.1037.

Keynes, John Maynard. "Economic Possibilities for Our Grandchildren." *Essays in Persuasion*. New York: W.W. Norton & Co., 1963.

———. "The World's Economic Outlook." *Atlantic*, May 1932. theatlantic.com/magazine/archive/1932/05/the-worlds-economic -outlook/307879.

Klein, Naomi. *The Shock Doctrine*. Toronto: Vintage, 2008.

Klein, Seth. "Good Sense Versus Common Sense: Canada's Debt Debate and Competing Hegemonic Projects." Master's thesis, Simon Fraser University, 1996. core.ac.uk/download/pdf/56371213.pdf.

Kulkarni, Akshay. "Emergency Rooms in Rural B.C. Were Closed for Equivalent of Around 4 Months in 2022, Data Shows." *CBC News*, December 27, 2022. cbc.ca/news/canada/british-columbia /bc-er-closures-2022-1.6689970.

Landry, Simon, Audrey Racine, and Mohan B. Kumar. "Childhood Factors Associated with the Completion of a High School Diploma or Equivalency Certificate or Higher Among First Nations Children Living off Reserve, Métis and Inuit Children." Indigenous Peoples

Thematic Series, Statistics Canada, April 6, 2023. www150.statcan
.gc.ca/n1/pub/41-20-0002/412000022023002-eng.htm.

Larochelle, Catherine. "L'histoire des pensionnats de l'Ouest est une
histoire québécoise." *Histoire engagée*, June 8, 2021. histoireengagee
.ca/lhistoire-des-pensionnats-de-louest-est-une-histoire-quebecoise.

Lin, Zhengxi. "Employment Insurance in Canada: Policy Changes."
Perspectives, Summer 1998. 42–47. www150.statcan.gc.ca/n1/en
/pub/75-001-x/1998002/3828-eng.pdf.

Lord, Craig. "Competitiveness on a 'Clear Decline' in Canada as Profits
Rise: Report." *Global News*, October 19, 2023. globalnews.ca
/news/10035678/competition-bureau-prices-profit-markups-canada.

Loreto, Nora. "CERB/CEWS: No Oversight for the Rich, Little
Forgiveness for the Poor." *Maple*, December 9, 2022.

———. *Spin Doctors: How Media and Politicians Misdiagnosed the
Covid-19 Pandemic*. Halifax: Fernwood, 2021.

Macdonald, David. *The Big Banks' Big Secret*. Canadian Centre for
Policy Alternatives, April 2012. policyalternatives.ca/sites/default
/files/uploads/publications/National%20Office/2012/04/Big
%20Banks%20Big%20Secret.pdf.

Mackenzie, Hugh. *Deficit Mania in Perspective*. Ontario Budget 2010
Technical Paper. Ottawa: Canadian Centre for Policy Alternatives,
February 2010.

Maioni, Antonia. "New Century, New Risks: The Marsh Report and
the Post-War Welfare State in Canada." *Policy Options*, August 1,
2004. policyoptions.irpp.org/magazines/social-policy-in-the-21st
-century/new-century-new-risks-the-marsh-report-and-the-post
-war-welfare-state-in-canada.

Maltais, Pierre-Alexandre. "Des millions de Québécois sont des
descendants des Filles du roi." *Le Journal de Montréal*, May
7, 2018. journaldemontreal.com/2018/05/07/les-millions
-de-descendants-des-filles-du-roi.

Manuel, Arthur. "Indigenous Rights and Anti-Colonial Struggle."
In *Canada After Harper*, edited by Ed Finn, 246–59. Toronto:
Lorimer, 2015.

Martin, Paul. "Budget Speech." Speech, Ottawa, February 27, 1995. publications.gc.ca/collections/Collection/F1-23-1995-1E.pdf.

Maxwell, Glynis. *Poverty in Ontario: Failed Promise and the Renewal of Hope.* Community Development Halton and Social Planning Network of Ontario, 2009. spno.ca/images/pdf/Poverty-in-Ontario-Report.pdf.

McCracken, Krista. "Food Insecurity and the 'Temporary' Relief of Food Banks." *Active History,* August 17, 2015. activehistory.ca/2015/08/food-insecurity-and-the-temporary-relief-of-food-banks.

McIntosh, Andrew, and Stephen Azzi. "Constitution Act, 1982." In *The Canadian Encyclopedia.* Historica Canada. Last updated April 24, 2020. thecanadianencyclopedia.ca/en/article/constitution-act-1982.

McQuaig, Linda. *All You Can Eat: Greed, Lust and the New Capitalism.* Toronto: Penguin, 2001.

MemoryNS. "Halifax Poor Man's Friend Society." Accessed November 8, 2023. memoryns.ca/halifax-poor-mans-friend-society.

Mickleburgh, Rod. "1983: The Year BC Citizens and Workers Fought Back." *Tyee,* July 6, 2018. thetyee.ca/Opinion/2018/07/06/Year-BC-Citizens-Workers-Fought-Back.

Monsebraaten, Laurie. "Report Reveals Alarming — and Growing — Racialized Income Divide in GTA." *Toronto Star,* May 6, 2019. thestar.com/news/gta/report-reveals-alarming-and-growing-racialized-income-divide-in-gta/article_25db2e5c-b55f-552d-8685-f65ec146716a.html.

Morisette, René. *Unionization in Canada, 1981 to 2022.* Statistics Canada Economic and Social Reports, November 23, 2022. www150.statcan.gc.ca/n1/en/pub/36-28-0001/2022011/article/00001-eng.pdf?st=P8EiQxOB.

Morley, J.T. "Co-operative Commonwealth Federation (CCF)." In *The Canadian Encyclopedia.* Historica Canada. Last updated March 26, 2021. thecanadianencyclopedia.ca/en/article/co-operative-commonwealth-federation.

Murnighan, Bill. *Selling Ontario's Health Care: The Real Story on Government Spending and Public Relations.* Canadian Centre for Policy Alternatives, April 2001. policyalternatives.ca/sites/default/files/uploads/publications/Ontario_Office_Pubs/on_healthcare.pdf.

Nossal, Kim Richard. "The Mulroney Years: Transformation and Tumult." *Policy Options*, June–July 2003. policyoptions.irpp.org /wp-content/uploads/sites/2/assets/po/the-best-pms-in-the-past-50 -years/nossal.pdf.

ODSP Action Coalition. "Our Demands." Accessed November 10, 2023. odspaction.ca/page/our-demands.

Organisation for Economic Co-operation and Development. *Linking Indigenous Communities with Regional Development*. OECD Rural Policy Reviews. Paris: OECD Publishing, 2019.

Orlando, James. "Canadian Inflation: A New Vintage." TD Bank, April 27, 2022, https://economics.td.com/ca-inflation-new-vintage.

Orozco, Santiago Arias. "'There Is No Sign of Relief': Daily Bread Food Bank Usage Hits 40-Year High." *Toronto Star*, April 4, 2023. thestar.com/news/gta/2023/04/04/there-is-no-sign-of-relief-daily -bread-food-bank-usage-hits-40-year-high.html.

Osberg, Lars. *From Keynesian Consensus to Neo-Liberalism to the Green New Deal*. Canadian Centre for Policy Alternatives, March 2021. policyalternatives.ca/publications/reports/75-years-of -income-inequality-canada.

Page, Kevin. "Fiscal Management and Parliamentary Democracy." In *Canada After Harper*, edited by Ed Finn, 311–22. Toronto: Lorimer, 2015.

Parks Canada. "The Arrival of Displaced Persons in Canada, 1945–1951." February 15, 2016. canada.ca/en/parks-canada/news/2016/02/the -arrival-of-displaced-persons-in-canada-1945-1951.html.

"The Paupers of New Brunswick." *Allicor's Blog*, June 6, 2012. allicor42 .typepad.com/blog/2012/06/the-paupers-of-new-brunswick.html.

Plummer, Kevin. "An Unsettling Prairie History: A Review of James Daschuk's Clearing the Plains." *Active History*, December 5, 2013. activehistory.ca/blog/2013/12/05/an-unsettling-prairie-history-a -review-of-james-daschuks-clearing-the-plains.

Postey, Drew. "More Than 60% of Sask. Income Support Calls Ignored, Auditors Report Reveals." *CTV News*, June 6, 2023. regina.ctvnews .ca/more-than-60-of-sask-income-support-calls-ignored-auditors -report-reveals-1.6429562.

Procyk, Stephanie. *Understanding Income Inequality in Canada, 1980–2014*. Toronto: United Way Toronto and Neighbourhood Change Research Partnership, October 2014. neighbourhoodchange.ca /documents/2015/02/understanding-income-inequality-in-canada -1980-2014.pdf.

Providence Health Care. "Jim Pattison Makes Record $75 Million Donation to St. Paul's Foundation." The New St. Paul's Hospital, March 29, 2017. thenewstpauls.ca/jim-pattison-makes-record-75 -million-donation-st-pauls-foundation.

Reagan, Ronald. "Inaugural Address." Speech, Washington DC, January 20, 1981. reaganfoundation.org/media/128614/inaguration.pdf.

Reagan Library. "President Reagan's Meetings with Prime Minister Mulroney in Canada on March 18, 1985." Posted August 28, 2017. YouTube video, 11:56. youtube.com/watch?v=Fn78kjABPQc.

Rettino-Parazelli, Karl. "Vingt ans plus tard, le Québec est toujours en quête du déficit zéro." *Le Devoir*, November 24, 2015. ledevoir .com/economie/456078/vingt-ans-plus-tard-le-quebec-est-toujours -en-quete-du-deficit-zero.

Robin, Martin. *Radical Politics and Canadian Labour, 1880–1930*. Kingston: Industrial Relations Centre, Queen's University, 1968.

Robinson, Greg, and Andrew McIntosh. "Internment of Japanese Canadians." In *The Canadian Encyclopedia*. Historica Canada. Last updated September 17, 2020. https://www.thecanadianencyclopedia .ca/en/article/internment-of-japanese-canadians.

Ronald Reagan Presidential Foundation and Institute. "Reaganomics: Economic Policy and the Reagan Revolution." Accessed November 9, 2023. reaganfoundation.org/ronald-reagan/the-presidency /economic-policy.

Ropel-Morsky, Hermina P. "William Lyon Mackenzie King: The Corporate Man." Master's thesis, McMaster University, 1978.

Rutty, Christopher, and Sue C. Sullivan. *This is Public Health: A Canadian History*. Ottawa: Canadian Public Health Association, 2010.

Sacks, Adam J. "Why the Early German Socialists Opposed the World's First Modern Welfare State." *Jacobin*, May 12, 2019. jacobin.com/2019/12 /otto-von-bismarck-germany-social-democratic-party-spd.

Saint-Pierre, Yves, and Patricia Tully. "Downsizing Canada's Hospitals, 1986/87 to 1994/95 — Archived." Statistics Canada, April 21, 1997. www150.statcan.gc.ca/n1/en/catalogue/82-003-X19960043023.

Scarth, Todd. "Moves Made to Reduce Inequality." Canadian Centre for Policy Alternatives, May 11, 2000. policyalternatives.ca /publications/reports/moves-made-reduce-inequality.

Simpson, Wayne, Greg Mason, and Ryan Godwin. "The Manitoba Basic Annual Income Experiment: Lessons Learned 40 Years Later." *Canadian Public Policy* 43, no.1 (2017): 85–104. umanitoba.ca /media/Simpson_Mason_Godwin_2017.pdf.

St. Denis, Jen. "Why Can't We Build Like It's the 1970s?" *Tyee*, April 22, 2022. thetyee.ca/Analysis/2022/04/22/Why-Cant-We-Build -Like-1970s.

Stanford, Jim. "The Three Key Moments in Canada's Neoliberal Transformation." Rabble.ca, April 8, 2014. rabble.ca/columnists /three-key-moments-canadas-neoliberal-transformation.

Statistics Canada. "Distributions of Household Economic Accounts for Income, Consumption, Saving and Wealth of Canadian Households, Third Quarter 2022." January 19, 2023. www150.statcan.gc.ca /n1/daily-quotidien/230119/dq230119b-eng.htm.

Statistics Canada. "Personal Debt." *Perspectives on Labour and Income*, January 2007. www150.statcan.gc.ca/n1/en/pub/75-001-x/commun /4235072-eng.pdf.

Stilborn, Jack, and Robert B. Asselin. *Federal-Provincial Relations*. Political and Social Affairs Division, May 1, 2001. publications .gc.ca/collections/Collection-R/LoPBdP/CIR/9310-e.htm.

Story, Eric. "Coming Home: Veterans, Pensions and the Canadian State After the Great War." *Active History*, January 23, 2018. activehistory.ca/blog/2018/01/23/coming-home-veterans-pensions -and-the-canadian-state-after-the-great-war.

Thatcher, Margaret. "Interview for *Woman's Own*." Interview by Douglas Keay. *Women's Own*, October 31, 1987.

Thiessen, Gordon. "Canada's Economic Future: What Have We Learned from the 1990s?" Speech, Canadian Club of Toronto, June 2, 1999, Toronto. bankofcanada.ca/2001/01/canada-economic-future -what-have-we-learned.

Tomchuk, Travis. "Manitoba's Mincome Experiment." Canadian Museum for Human Rights, August 10, 2022. humanrights.ca /story/manitobas-mincome-experiment.

Toney, G. Jared. "Locating Diaspora: Afro-Caribbean Narratives of Migration and Settlement in Toronto, 1914–1929." *Urban History Review* 38, no. 2 (Spring 2010): 75–87. doi.org/10.7202/039676ar.

Trudeau, Justin. "Working Together to Improve Health Care for Canadians." Prime Minister's Office, February 7, 2023. pm.gc.ca/en/news/news-releases/2023/02/07/working-together -improve-health-care-canadians.

Vailles, Francis. "Une première depuis un quart de siècle?" *La Presse*, November 21, 2017. plus.lapresse.ca/screens/464943fe-749d-4662 -9572-f52f1900f9be|_0.html.

Warnock, John W. "The CCF-NDP in Saskatchewan." In *Challenges and Perils: Social Democracy in Neoliberal Times*, edited by William K. Carroll and R.S. Ratner, 82–104. Black Point, NS: Fernwood, 2005.

Watson, William. "The Budget That Changed Canada." *Financial Post*, February 27, 2020. financialpost.com/opinion /william-watson-the-budget-that-changed-canada.

Weigel, David. "'It's Not a Revenue Problem. It's a Spending Problem.'" *Slate*, April 18, 2011. slate.com/news-and-politics/2011/04/not -a-revenue-problem-a-spending-problem-tracing-the-history-of-a -republican-talking-point.html.

Wilson-Smith, Anthony. "Martin's 1995 Budget." *Maclean's*, March 13, 1995. thecanadianencyclopedia.ca/en/article/martins-1995-budget.

Wright, Barry, Eric Tucker, and Susan Binnie. "Introduction: War Measures and the Repression of Radicalism." In *War Measures and the Repression of Radicalism, 1914–1939*, edited by Barry Wright, Eric Tucker, and Susan Binnie, 3–41. Vol. 4 of *Canadian State Trials*. Toronto: Osgoode Society for Canadian Legal History and University of Toronto Press, 2015.

Wright, Theresa. "Here's How Much Provinces Have in Surplus While Demanding More Federal Health Cash." *Global News*, February 16, 2023. globalnews.ca/news/9488839/health-funding -provinces-surpluses-budget-gains-numbers.

Index

density, 51, 61, 63, 121, 163–64
membership, 37–38, 198
United Empire Loyalists, 22
universal healthcare, 57–58
universal programs, 83–86, 167
Upper Canada, 22, 24, 32
U.S. Federal Reserve, 157

veterans, 36–37, 45, 57
Veterans Charter, 45
voluntary sector, 96–97, 118–19, 154, 168–72, 173
voting rights, 35–36

War Charities Act, 35
War Measures Act, 44
Wascana Centre, 29–30
welfare state
about, 11–12, 24, 27, 62–67

corporate sector, 74–75, 77, 81–82
death of, 137, 181
Marsh, 54–55, 59–60
social responsibility, 83
white majority, 46–47
western Canada, 29, 32, 34–35, 130
white supremacy, 23, 46–47, 56–57, 67, 190–91
Whitton, Charlotte. *See* Marsh Report
Wilson, Michael, 84
See also neoliberalism
Wilson-Smith, Anthony, 108, 109, 110–12, 116
Winnipeg General Strike, 36
Woodsworth, James S., 38, 41, 175
Workmen's Compensation Act (Ontario), 34
World Bank, 101

About the Author

Photo by Jennifer Rowsom

Nora Loreto is a writer, journalist, and podcast producer. She is the editor of the Canadian Association of Labour Media and the co-host of the popular political podcast *Sandy and Nora Talk Politics*, with Sandy Hudson.

An active trade unionist, Nora is the president of the Canadian Freelance Union and trains union members all over Canada in communications, organizing, and mobilization strategies. She is involved in many anti-racist and environmental struggles.

Nora is the author of four non-fiction books and writes for magazine and online publications in Canada and the United States. Her last book, *Spin Doctors: How Media and Politicians Misdiagnosed the Covid-19 Pandemic* (Fernwood 2021), was short-listed for the 2022 Mavis Gallant Prize for Non-Fiction.

She regularly appeared on the CBC News Network before the 2023 round of cuts were announced.

Nora lives with her family in Quebec City.